D1615767

WHEN THE STATE
NO LONGER KILLS

SUNY SERIES IN HUMAN RIGHTS

Zehra F. Kabasakal Arat, editor

WHEN THE STATE
NO LONGER KILLS

*International Human Rights Norms
and Abolition of Capital Punishment*

SANGMIN BAE

STATE UNIVERSITY OF NEW YORK PRESS

Published by
STATE UNIVERSITY OF NEW YORK PRESS, ALBANY

© 2007 State University of New York

For information, contact State University of New York Press, Albany, NY
www.sunypress.edu

Production, Laurie Searl
Marketing, Anne M. Valentine

Library of Congress Cataloging-in-Publication Data

Bae, Sangmin, 1971–
    When the state no longer kills : international human rights norms and abolition of
capital punishment / Sangmin Bae.
        p. cm. — (Suny series in human rights)
    Includes bibliographical references and index.
    ISBN 978-0-7914-7207-1 (hardcover : alk. paper)
    1. Capital punishment. 2. Human rights. I. Title.

HV8694.B34 2007
364.66—dc22   2006037443

10 9 8 7 6 5 4 3 2 1

To my parents,

who taught me how to live with passion

CONTENTS

FIGURES AND TABLES

FOREWORD

The interdisciplinary field of human rights is rather new but rapidly expanding. The SUNY Press series on human rights attempts to advance scholarship on the political and social processes of human rights and disseminate research findings to a large audience in an accessible style. It intends to address vital issues related to the full spectrum of human rights recognized by the International Bill of Rights, as well as different conceptualizations that expand or contract the scope of human rights. Including volumes that examine cultural, economic, political, and international factors that contribute to the violation or improvement of human rights or analyze the consequences of human rights violations, the series aspires to promote human rights, offer policy guidelines that would help improving human rights practices, and contribute to the theory building efforts in social sciences.

Sangmin Bae's *When the State No Longer Kills*, which focuses on the abolishment of the death penalty, is the second book to be published in the SUNY Press human rights series. The death penalty tends to be viewed as a deterrent of crime or device of justice for the worst forms of crime, rather than a form of state violence. As such, it has escaped criticisms directed at some other means of violence or human rights violations (e.g., torture) and enjoyed considerable public support around the world. In fact, even the international human rights community started to frame the issue as a human rights concern rather recently. *When the State No Longer Kills* tries to explain what leads a state to abolish capital punishment or impose a moratorium, by offering in-depth analyses of four countries: Ukraine, South Africa, South Korea, and the United States.

Examining the change and stability of state policies in these countries at the intersection of domestic and international politics, Bae attracts our attention both to the politics of human rights and the relative weaknesses of the major International Relations theories. Her description and analysis of different paths followed by the four countries points to the significance of political elite in adopting international norms—if they are more susceptible to domestic or international pressures and how they define their country's cultural identity.

Zehra F. Kabasakal Arat
Series Editor
March 2007

xi

PREFACE

Why do people, political actors, or states behave as they do? This question has long fascinated me, and led me to study political science. When I entered graduate school in 1993, the rational-choice approach seemed to provide an answer to my question about the human motives of political decisions. The obvious virtues of this approach, including ontological parsimony and methodological rigor, got me interested in the possibilities of this theory in explaining political behavior. Some years later, however, I started to realize that most human motives are too complex to explain by just a few words such as *interest, utility,* or *strategy*. For instance, exactly how do issues in human rights relate to the strategic calculation of cost and benefit? It was coincidental that my academic interests shifted into "nonrational" choice theories in the late 1990s, when the study of international relations saw a rapid growth of literature on international norms. As I learned more about norm theory, I was more persuaded that standards of proper behavior were often a critical source of ideas for state policy change or human behavior in general. And soon after that I came to believe that whether or not norms matter was no longer a question. Instead, I suspect, we need to inquire more specifically into where norms come from, how they spread, how they shape and are shaped by domestic politics, who adopts them and why, how they change over time, why states are more likely to adopt some norms and not others, and so forth.

When I was about to start writing my conclusion, I read a largely forgotten story about Chiune Sugihara, Japanese Consul in Kaunas, Lithuania during World War II, who, exceeding his authority, issued more than two thousand visas to Jewish refugees and helped them leave the country. When asked why he risked not only his career but his own life and that of his family to do so, he humbly replied: "Do what's right because it's right." Sugihara's simple answer stuck in my mind when I wondered why states would adopt international norms, such as the abolition of capital punishment, at the risk of fierce domestic opposition.

Norms play a role in state behavior, but their influence varies greatly. The international norm that prohibits the death penalty, the topic of this book, is influential in most parts of the world, but not everywhere. For most people, the death penalty is considered to be a completely legitimate part of the criminal justice system, and, partly owing to this reason, it has been widely supported by a vast majority of the public in most countries. Yet, despite public support for the death penalty, a remarkable number of countries in different parts of the world have banned capital punishment in all its forms, regardless of the nature of the crime or the criminal. Abolition of the death penalty in compliance with the norm, irrespective of its match with prevailing domestic understanding, has become a central political phenomenon worldwide. This book is my effort to contribute to the debate on international norms by asking *when* norms matter and *how*. More specifically, *when* does the state comply with the norm of banning capital punishment in the face of strong public resistance? Hence the title of this book, *When the State No Longer Kills*.

Many people have contributed in many ways to this book, and I acknowledge them with great pleasure. I wish to express my heartfelt thanks to Ann Marie Clark, my advisor at Purdue for her guidance, tutelage, and tremendous support. Through many years, she helped me to shape, develop, and refine my understanding of international human rights norms. Without her intellectual energy and commitment, this book would not have been the same. Martyn de Bruyn helped me talk through my earliest thoughts about this research, and carefully read every word I wrote at least once - and much of it more than once. I am very grateful to Leigh Raymond, who read my introduction and helped to build a stronger conceptual base. His own innovative work on equity norms provided important insight on issues concerning human interaction. Jay McCann offered me not only cogent comments on the chapters but also timely advice on professional development. My deep gratitude also goes to David Leaman, my colleague and good friend. His comments on the concluding chapter could not have been more reasonable, persuasive, or precise.

I owe special thanks to Jeff Checkel of ARENA for his invaluable comments and suggestions regarding my discussion of the Ukraine case. He was also extremely helpful in giving advice and providing contacts for my research in Strasbourg in the summer of 2002. Christian Boulanger of the Free University of Berlin read different versions of my Korean chapter and provided me with detailed criticism and suggestions. Johan Friested of the Council of Europe kindly took time for an interview with me, and later read my Ukraine chapter and provided helpful comments. Oh Chang-ik and Kim Chulhyo, human rights activists in South Korea, took time from their busy schedules to help me better understand the realities of the death penalty system in Korea.

I extend my thanks to those who reviewed this book in its various manuscript stages and offered insightful feedback: Kevin Anderson, Bob Bartlett, Berenice Carroll, Rosie Clawson, Aaron Hoffman, Stephanie Lawson, Will McLauchlan, Spike Peterson, Jon Strand, Angel Viera-Tirado, and Laurel Weldon. My colleagues at Northeastern Illinois University provide me with the greatest institutional comfort and peer support. I sincerely thank Ellen Cannon, Jeff Hill, David Leaman, Russell Benjamin, Elaine Rodriquez, Sophia Mihic, Greg Neddenriep, Tim Murphy, Laurie Fuller, Erica Meiners, Chielozona Eze, and Nancy Matthews. I would also like to thank Michael Rinella and Laurie Searl at the State University of New York Press for their great assistance throughout the process of writing and publication, and the press's reviewers for their encouraging and helpful comments. I am indebted to Nick Murray, who did a most thoughtful and professional job of editing my manuscript. Jeanette Lieb, my research assistant, reviewed the entire manuscript to check for last-minute glitches. If any errors remain despite all the generous help I have received from the above-mentioned people, they are mine alone.

This book benefited from support by the Purdue Research Foundation dissertation fellowship, the Frank Lee Wilson fieldwork grant, the NEIU COR Grant, and additional travel grants sponsored by the American Political Science Association and the International Studies Association. I am also grateful to the editors for their permission to republish my previous work here. An earlier version of chapter 3 appeared as "The Right to Life vs. the State's Ultimate Sanction: Abolition of Capital Punishment in Post-Apartheid South Africa" in *The International Journal of Human Rights* 9, no. 1 (March 2005): 49–68. Some parts of chapter 4 appeared in *The Cultural Lives of Capital Punishment: Comparative Perspectives*, edited by Austin Sarat and Christian Boulanger, © 2005 by the Board of Trustees of the Leland Stanford Jr. University, and reprinted by permission of Stanford University Press.

I am exceptionally fortunate to have a wonderful family. Martyn de Bruyn has continuously reminded me that intellectual curiosity and ethical commitment should be integral parts of our lives. He is always my toughest critic and my strongest supporter, and I am truly grateful for his friendship and companionship. Although they live far away on the East and West coasts of the continent, and even farther away in Seoul, all my sisters and their families are my closest friends. They have enabled me, with their good humor and moral support, to keep going when my enthusiasm waned. René and Marga de Bruyn have sent me much-appreciated encouragement over the years. My parents, Jongtaek Bae and Keumok Choi, always sacrificed so that I could follow my dreams. For this book and much besides, their unconditional, unfaltering love and support, and their eloquent silences have kept me going.

Sangmin Bae

CHAPTER ONE

INTRODUCTION: PROHIBITION OF THE
DEATH PENALTY AS A HUMAN RIGHTS NORM

Even if a civil society were to dissolve itself by common agreement of all its members—for example, if the people inhabiting an island decided to separate and disperse themselves around the world—the last murderer remaining in prison must first be executed. . . . If they fail to do so, they may be regarded as accomplices in this public violation of legal justice.

—Immanuel Kant, *The Metaphysical Elements of Justice*

"The chief and worst pain may not be in the bodily suffering but in one's knowing for certain that in an hour, and then in ten minutes, and then in half a minute, and then now, at the very moment, the soul will leave the body and that one will cease to be a man, and that that's bound to happen; the worst part of it is that it is certain. To kill for murder is a punishment incomparably worse than the crime itself. Murder by legal sentence is immeasurably more terrible than murder by brigands. . . . Take a soldier and put him in front of a cannon in battle and fire at him and he will still hope; but read the same soldier his death sentence for certain, and he will go out of his mind or burst into tears. Who can tell whether human nature is able to bear this madness? . . . No, you can't treat a man like that!"

—Fyodor Dostoyevsky, *The Idiot*

INTERNATIONAL STANDARDS PROHIBITING
CAPITAL PUNISHMENT

Punishing people with death has a history as old as society itself, and was not considered a human rights violation until the last decades of the twentieth century. Policy regarding the death penalty has been commonly understood to be the prerogative of national governments. In Europe, where executions

1

are completely banned at present, more than two hundred crimes were once punishable by death, including such minor offenses as stealing, cutting down a tree, and robbing a rabbit warren.[1] The state's "right to kill" within the accepted domestic legal system gained increasingly broad public support over time.[2] Especially with regard to heinous crimes, people assumed that the state should demonstrate a fair and determined authority by imposing the ultimate punishment. Even Immanuel Kant, who strongly believed in a person's intrinsic worth and dignity, argued that no one should be spared from the death penalty who, as a rational being, chose not to submit to a common rule of law.[3]

Not until World War II did the death penalty become a major issue on the human rights agenda. The bloody horror of the war and the Holocaust triggered a global revulsion against death and its imposition as a legitimate penalty. With the increasing interest in human rights safeguards during the postwar period, the recognition of the "right to life" as a normative objective gained momentum.[4] The focus shifted from the state's right to kill to a citizen's right not to be executed by the state. Over the years, international bodies have increasingly made statements and adopted policies favoring the abolition of capital punishment on human rights grounds. National court decisions are beginning to support such statements and policies by ruling out the death penalty as a violation of human rights.

The Universal Declaration of Human Rights, which was unanimously adopted by the United Nations General Assembly on December 10, 1948, and which even today provides the most authoritative statement of international human rights norms, declared that "[e]veryone has the right to life, liberty and security of the person" (Article 3), and "[n]o one shall be subjected to torture or to cruel, inhuman or degrading treatment or punishment" (Article 5). Thirty years after the introduction of the Universal Declaration, the United Nations General Assembly adopted a resolution to "progressively [restrict] the number of offenses for which the death penalty may be imposed with a view to the desirability of abolishing capital punishment."[5] Following this, in 1984, the General Assembly of the United Nations endorsed a resolution adopted by the Economic and Social Council that listed nine safeguards guaranteeing protection of the rights of those facing the death penalty, on the understanding that "they would not be invoked to delay or prevent the abolition of the death penalty."[6]

At present, four international treaties call for the abolition of capital punishment: the scope of one is worldwide; the other three are regional.

The Second Optional Protocol to the International Covenant on Civil and Political Rights

The idea of prohibiting the death penalty, which is only vaguely articulated in the Universal Declaration of Human Rights, was strengthened in 1966 when the United Nations incorporated it in the International Covenant on Civil and Political Rights (ICCPR). It was proclaimed even more explicitly in the Second Optional Protocol to the International Covenant Aiming at the Abolition of the Death Penalty, which the UN General Assembly adopted on December 15, 1989. The protocol declared that "[n]o one within the jurisdiction of a State Party to the present Protocol shall be executed" (Article 1.1) and that "[e]ach State Party shall take all necessary measures to abolish the death penalty within its jurisdiction" (Article 1.2). The only reservations permitted under the protocol are those that would provide "for the application of the death penalty in time of war pursuant to a conviction for a most serious crime of a military nature committed during wartime" (Article 2.1). As of January 2006, fifty-six states have ratified the protocol. Eight other states have signed it, indicating their intention to become parties to it at a later date.

Arguing that an appeal to universal human rights potentially limited its sovereign power to impose capital punishment within its territory, the United States voted against the adoption of the Second Optional Protocol. And when it ratified the ICCPR in June 1992, the United States entered reservations both with respect to the prohibition on executing convicted criminals under the age of eighteen and to Article 7, which proscribes cruel and unusual treatment or punishment. The United States declared that it would only be bound by this article to the extent that "cruel, inhuman or degrading treatment or punishment" means the cruel and unusual treatment or punishment prohibited by the Fifth, Eighth, or Fourteenth Amendments to the Constitution of the United States.[7]

Protocol No. 6. to the European Convention for the Protection of Human Rights and Fundamental Freedoms

The European Convention for the Protection of Human Rights and Fundamental Freedoms, hereafter referred to as the European Convention on Human Rights (ECHR), was the first international instrument to embrace the abolition of the death penalty as a policy objective. Protocol No. 6 to the European Convention on Human Rights was opened for signature and ratification in 1983. Since then, states applying for membership to the Council of Europe have been expected to ratify it prior to admission.[8] As of January 2006, the protocol had been ratified by forty-five European states and signed by one other. The protocol outlaws death sentences generally, but narrowly allows countries to retain capital punishment "in time of war or imminent threat of war."

Protocol No. 13 to the European Convention on Human Rights

Over time, in Europe at least, the norm against capital punishment became stronger, more specific, and more closely tied to efforts at monitoring and enforcement. In February 2002, the Committee of Ministers of the Council of Europe took the final step on the road to abolition by signing Protocol No. 13 to the ECHR. Whereas Protocol No. 6 specifies the abolition of the death penalty only in peacetime and allows states to retain the death penalty in wartime as an exception, Protocol No. 13 provides for the *total* abolition of the death penalty in all circumstances, permitting no exceptions. The number of signatories and state parties continues to grow. As of January 2006, Protocol No. 13 had been ratified by thirty-three states and signed by ten others.

The Protocol to the American Convention on Human Rights to Abolish the Death Penalty

In June 1990, the General Assembly of the Organization of American States adopted the Protocol to the American Convention on Human Rights to Abolish the Death Penalty. Article 1 calls upon states to abstain from its use, although it does not obligate them to erase it from the statute books. Like the Second Optional Protocol to the ECHR, it permits reservations with regard to "extremely serious" wartime crimes. This protocol has been ratified by eight states and signed by one other in the Americas. The United States and some English-speaking Caribbean countries, such as Barbados, Jamaica, and Trinidad and Tobago, are still unwilling to ratify.

In the past three decades a substantial number of countries have joined the international movement to abolish the death penalty by excluding it from domestic legislation either for all offenses or for peacetime offences, and by respecting the international treaties forbidding the death penalty. As recently as 1970, only twelve countries had completely abolished the death penalty, and eleven others had abolished it for ordinary crimes in peacetime. The pace of abolition accelerated in the second half of the twentieth century, especially between 1980 and 2000. Since 1985, about seventy countries have abolished the death penalty, and only four countries that had abolished it have reintroduced it. The number of countries that have ended capital punishment in law or practice (124) now exceeds the number that retain it (72), and most of the latter have moratoriums on execution.[9] Moreover, most countries that continue to carry out executions today do so only for murder, although many retain the death penalty in law for other crimes. The rate of executions in most such countries has declined to a point where it represents only a tiny percentage of the number of reported murders.

The death penalty has been deemed inappropriate to the values that international justice is meant to represent. No provision of the death penalty appeared in the statutes of the tribunals set up by the UN Security Council to adjudicate crimes committed in the former Yugoslavia and in Rwanda, nor in the statutes of the International Criminal Court (ICC), which came into force on July 1, 2002, for prosecuting war crimes, genocide, and crimes against humanity. Instead, the maximum penalty is life imprisonment or, for some crimes, a maximum of thirty years imprisonment.[10] Despite the appalling nature of some of these crimes, the death penalty is no longer considered to be an option. Punishments such as the hanging of numerous individuals after the Nuremberg and Tokyo war crimes trials would not take place today. The UN Commission on Human Rights adopted a resolution in April 1998 calling on all countries that retained the death penalty to consider suspending executions with a view to completely abolishing the death penalty. Instruments such as the international conventions, protocols, and treaties enable us to affirm that the attempt to abolish the death penalty has gained a "kind of universal moral consensus."[11] The death penalty is no longer regarded as a domestic, internal, criminal justice issue. It is no longer acceptable to define the death penalty in "relativistic" religious or cultural terms or as a matter purely for national sovereignty.[12] The norm that prohibits this "cruel, inhuman and degrading" penalty has become largely international. It has become a dominant feature among the issues of international human rights as a legitimate focus of global attention.

Yet not all governments are equally concerned about the international human rights norm. In the United States, the number of executions has been significantly increasing since the early 1980s, at a time when most European democratic countries and a growing number of countries in other parts of the globe have joined in the abolitionist campaign. Since the death penalty was reinstated in 1976, the United States has carried out 1,070 executions, and nine hundred-fifty of them have occurred since 1990 (as of April 2007). The death penalty is also widely practiced in Asia and northern Africa. These empirical observations suggest that while international norms are often a critical source of ideas for change in state policy, their impact varies greatly.

Why is the international norm banning the death penalty more influential in some countries? Why do some countries comply with this international norm while others do not? The purpose of this book is to answer these questions. Regarding the question of why the international norm has more influence in some countries than in others, I intend to address how, when, and through what political processes states comply with the international norm. By identifying the political and sociological factors that account for its varying influence, I attempt to specify the causal mechanism that produces compliance with the norm. This research offers an explanation of the domestic empowerment of norms and how their impact varies cross-nationally.

INTERNATIONAL NORMS IN INTERNATIONAL RELATIONS RESEARCH

International norms are commonly defined as "collective expectations about proper behavior for a given identity."[13] According to Janice Thomson, norms emerge as "outcomes of individual beliefs which subsequently can exert influence over behavior independent of the beliefs of individual actors." Yet they grow as "the character of structures once they are embedded in social institutions."[14] My review of the previous literature on international norms focuses on two major elements: (1) whether it attempts to provide a productive dialogue between different theoretical approaches; (2) whether it correctly emphasizes the importance of domestic politics in norm enforcement. For the past decade, a central locus of contention in the field of international relations has been the rationalist-constructivist debate. A series of research projects engaging the rational choice approach have stressed the way norms constrain the behavior of states or argued that norms matter only when they serve state interests. In contrast, constructivist research, focusing on the learning process and socialization mechanism of interest formation, contends that norms do not merely constrain behavior; rather, they help shape agents' identities and interests. The purpose of reviewing these features is not to produce a synthesis from these theoretical approaches or to replace them in any way. Rather, it is an attempt to highlight their limitations and to suggest alternative paths of norm compliance that traditional approaches miss. In other words, it is a way of building bridges between two theoretical views and finding productive ways to combine some of their elements. Avoiding a restrictive methodology of simple dichotomies, I seek richer explanations on the assumption that neither of these explanatory frameworks by itself can adequately explain norm compliance.

In spite of the recent upsurge in scholarly attention to international norms, few attempts have been made to understand the domestic political context of norm institutionalization.[15] The systemic role of domestic variables in norm compliance has not received enough attention. To fill this gap, I examine how the effects of international human rights norms are mediated or conditioned by different domestic political configurations. Without denying the autonomous effects of norms at the level of the international system, I attempt to clarify the domestic structural determinants of norm compliance, which entails a state level of analysis.

International Norms and State Behaviors: Major International Relations Theories

Why do states obey international norms and rules? An obvious answer is that states benefit from doing so. Free trade agreements are made to enlarge markets and to ensure imports of needed goods. Arms control treaties are made to lessen the risk of war and to reduce military costs. States are likely to comply with international norms when they serve their mutual interests and help solve problems of coordination and cooperation. A more complex question, then, is why states comply with international norms when doing so does not appear to serve their interests. Why do states adhere to international norms when such behavior is actually quite costly?

Realists, who theorize a world of international anarchy and state power, do not expect international norms to have much of an impact unless they are enforced by powerful states or secure national interests. Considering the distribution of power among states under anarchy as the chief determinant of state behavior, realists regard norms merely as a reflection of that power relationship. International arrangements that rely upon common principles or norms "are only too easily upset when either the balance of bargaining power or the perception of national interest (or both together) changes among those states who negotiate them."[16] Because the outcomes of international interactions largely reflect the interests and relative strength of the contending parties, norms are reducible, in this view, to optimizing behavior by sovereign, egoistic, and strategic actors that calculate costs and benefits in the pursuit of basic goals. Norms are the products of interests, and a state's obedience to a norm is nothing but an epiphenomenon. International norms are merely post hoc rationalizations of self-interest.[17]

The realist notion of states and anarchy has been a useful analytical tool for explaining unfavorable international agendas in the modern era such as war. One strength of this realist perspective is its ability to describe the difficulty of state cooperation when there is no central government above governments. In this condition, states have few choices aside from following national interests. Yet realism has serious limitations. How do states come to define their interests, and how can interests be redefined through certain political processes? And who decides what the national interest is? Realists tell us little about these questions. In the realist world, interests are simply "out there" waiting to be discovered; thus, there is no chance that states' identities and interests can be defined by prevailing ideas or norms. In favor of material forces such as military and economic might, realists have neglected how states pursue strategies to improve their normative standing. In short, the realist perspective fails to explain why states voluntarily comply with international precepts and standards.

Neoliberal institutionalists, who have a relatively optimistic view of the likelihood of sustained international cooperation, consider norms as more enduring and influential variables than do the realists.[18] Stephen Krasner defines norms, which he sees as one component of regimes along with "principles, rules and decision-making procedures," as "standards of behavior defined in terms of rights and obligations."[19] The norms that help to constitute regimes "serve to constrain immediate, short-term power maximization."[20] Regimes or institutions based on norms "prescribe acceptable forms of state behavior, and proscribe unacceptable kinds of behavior."[21]

Neoliberal institutionalists, however, grant only a limited role to norms, assuming that interests are still the key to state behavior. In their view, norms influence behavior only when they help states advance their interests by resolving coordination problems with other states. Even if a state's compliance with a norm seems to be in conflict with its short-term interest, it is *beneficial* from a long-term perspective. As Robert Keohane says, "[T]he norm requires action that does not reflect specific calculations of self-interest: the actor making a short-run sacrifice does not know that future benefits will flow from comparable restraint by others, and can hardly be regarded as making precise calculations of expected utility . . . but . . . *we should nevertheless assume that regime-supporting behavior will be beneficial to us even though we have no convincing evidence to that effect.*"[22] According to Keohane, therefore, institutions die when members no longer "have incentive to maintain them."[23] The sustained pattern of states responding to norms and rules depends on whether such norms provide each state with satisfactory benefits. States that benefit less from a particular rule will eventually break that rule. Here, norms are intervening variables between material incentives and state behavior.

Even though neoliberal institutionalists have underscored, far more than realists have, the importance and autonomy of norms in world politics, their ongoing reliance on cost-benefit analysis does not explain why states obey international norms even when such norms provide them with no clear benefits. International norms are still seen as instruments whereby states eventually seek to attain their interests in wealth, military might, or some other material capability. States adhere to international norms when doing so brings material benefits or the threat of sanctions. In short, all explanations of neoliberal institutionalists still return to interest-based motives.

In reaction to this rationalist view, constructivists suggest that many international norms do not serve clear functional purposes. It is apparent that states comply with international norms because of power differentials or because they help resolve coordination problems. Yet constructivists argue that modern norms are not consistently enforced by powerful states and do not necessarily resolve coordination problems nor advance the common interests of states. Quite a few scholars, whether they are considered constructivists or not, have maintained that states exist in a normative environment; in other words, normative beliefs serve as important guides to state behavior. Their research agendas vary but include human rights, national security, environmental policy, immigration, economic policy, nationalism, decolonization, regional integration, and terrorism.[24] Investigating how interests are constructed discursively in and through political dynamics, instead of inquiring into the assumed interests of political agents, they suggest that "nonfunctional" norms matter and have powerful effects.

While rationalists see norms as a reflection of the fixed preferences of states, the constructivist approach considers that norms play a role in determining those preferences. Interests are not immediately transparent to states. Norms shape and reshape the goals of states, and build their perceptions of state interests: "Social institutions (norms) are the product of actor interactions, while these actors' identities and interests in turn are defined by such social institutions."[25] Preferences are not just exogenously given. Rationalists are wrong, from a constructivist perspective, when they neglect the role of shared understandings and expectations in "constituting actors with certain identities and interests, and material capabilities with certain meanings."[26] States hold ideas that are often independent of objective material interests and environmental conditions. And states interact in an environment that is fundamentally social and ideational as well as material. As Nicholas Onuf notes, "[C]onstructivism holds that people make society, and society makes people. It is a continuous, two-way process."[27] To put it another way, international norms are major *ex ante* sources of state action separate from interest, not post hoc creations of calculated self-interest. This is a key difference between neoliberal institutionalists and constructivists. For neoliberal institutionalists, norms do not function independently; their impact varies in accordance with the condition of material structures. Rather than independent variables, norms are, instead, "intervening variables that modify the relationship between material conditions and behavior."[28] Constructivists, in contrast, see norms as crucial causal variables—not mere reflections of the distribution of power and other material capabilities—that determine state policy outcomes.

States adopt norms through a process of social interaction and learning.[29] In other words, social context influences actors' preference and choice: "[C]hoices are rigorously constrained by the webs of understanding of the practices, identities, and interests of other actors that prevail in particular historical context."[30] For those who are inspired by sociology, and the Weberian insight in particular, there is an uneasy prediction about the complexity of political behavior: "[I]f there are at all universal regularities in human behavior, then they are shaped not only by interests alone but also by ideology and habit."[31] Interests are no longer considered as objectively given, but neither are they merely subjective. The division between objectivity and subjectivity has been problematized, so that what appears to be necessary and given is shown to be the result of political creation and historical sedimentation. As a consequence, the ideas of "socialization" and the "learning process" are major components of this new research inquiring into political formation.[32]

Interests and preferences, in this view, emerge from social construction in that states must *learn* what they want; in contrast rationalist theories assert that states *know* what they want.[33] Problematizing some of the central assumptions has led to a renewed investigation of the politico-historical processes that produce these identities or interests and structure the political landscape. Such inquiry has opened new areas of investigation previously considered uninteresting or unimportant.

In the realm of international relations, the role of norms is particularly important because there is no formal institutionalized process for the formulation of international laws, much less any central enforcement authority. Since rules and norms are based on predictable and replicable patterns of action such as custom and habit, they would be better than other interest-oriented rules in terms of stability and sustainability. According to the logic of utility-maximization, states are always inclined to retreat from international rules whenever the costs of those rules seem to exceed the benefits. By contrast, if state adherence to rules and norms relies mainly on ideas and shared knowledge and is thus embedded in societies, heedless retreat from the rules will be more difficult.

Domestic Sources of Norm Compliance

With the growing academic interest in international norms, many empirical works have highlighted domestic variables as the primary determinants of state compliance with international norms. Adopting the position held by many comparativists, they argue that domestic political factors and structures mediate the impact of international norms on policy choice. Andrew Cortell and James Davis maintain that international norms have important effects on state behavior via domestic political processes, especially when they are incorporated into national law and the administrative regulations of domestic agencies.[34] Similarly, Jeffrey Checkel suggests that the effects of international norms are conditioned by domestic structures, that is, by the congruence of the norms with domestic political culture and political settings.[35] Jan Egeland analyzes how "small and big nations are differently disposed to undertaking coherent human rights–oriented foreign policies."[36] In his comparison of the foreign policies of the United States and Norway regarding human rights, Egeland argues that the domestic political setting and culture make Norway quick and bold and entrepreneurial in international work, which allows this country to play an important role in conflict areas and humanitarian work. According to Andrew Moravcsik, an independent civil society and robust domestic legal institutions can take advantage of international human rights norms to pressure governments from within.[37] International norms, besides being imposed from outside, can affect a nation's foreign policy because governmental and nongovernmental actors involved in policymaking may promote them out of moral and legal considerations, reputational concerns, or just a desire to emulate others.

Given the importance of domestic variables, we want to understand exactly how these variables matter in determining state compliance with international norms, and which domestic variables contribute most to such compliance. According to Thomas Risse-Kappen, it is crucial to understand how the state is associated with civil society. For him, the ability of transnational actors to promote principled ideas and to influence state policy is largely dependent on domestic structure understood in terms of state-societal relations. He sees the role of domestic structure as mediating two stages through which international norms reach the domestic arena: (1) getting on the agenda for social and political discussion (norm access); and (2) getting support at the level of decision making (norm institutionalization, norm legalization). The significance of identifying different stages lies in the fact that international norms are more likely to get easy access to the political system in a society-dominant domestic structure; however, it is rather difficult, in these pluralist societies, to implement norms and thus bring about policy changes. In contrast, in a state-controlled society, norms are less likely to gain access to the political agenda in the first stage, but once they do so, they are more likely to be effectively implemented by strong political leadership.[38] In a similar fashion, Jeffrey Checkel also gives special attention to domestic political structure in order to explain how international norms affect domestic political change. He argues that certain regime types—namely, "statist" regimes—are largely impenetrable to grassroots advocacy, so that change in such regimes only occurs through elite learning.[39]

While I do not disagree that the systemic role of domestic variables is significant, I argue that there are two major shortcomings in the current literature on norms. First, they have so far concentrated on single countries or regions, rather than how and why the impacts of norms vary cross-nationally. Such narrowly focused research does not help us to explain similar dynamics in other countries. It leaves our understanding of the causal mechanisms of norm diffusion incomplete. Instead, we need a methodology of the cross-national comparison, which ought to help reduce the problem of overdetermination and allow us to acquire reproducible evidence on norms. The comparative case study offered here includes cases in which a given international norm enjoyed various degrees of state compliance across national contexts. Additionally, such an approach may help to overcome a general problem of large-n methods, which can tell us whether hypotheses hold but cannot explain why they hold: "[A] large-n test of a hypothesis provides little or no new insight into the causal process that comprises the hypothesis' explanation, nor does it generate data that could be used to infer or test explanations of that process."[40]

Second, the literature shows a tendency to rely on cases in which norms "mattered" and have actually affected state policies. In other words, scholars tend to highlight only successful cases of norm compliance. As Paul Kowert and Jeffrey Legro note, "Efforts to identify and measure norms . . . suffer from a bias toward 'the norm that worked.' "[41] Similarly, Checkel maintains that "there has been a bias to focus on successful cases of [norm] diffusion; thus, in terms of research design, there is often a failure to consider the 'dog who didn't bark.' "[42] This bias overlooks two questions: (1) Why do some international norms penetrate the domestic political discourse more easily than others (For example, free-trade rather than human rights norms)? (2) Why does an international norm resonate in some countries but not in others? (For example, Europe complies with the norm against capital punishment, but the United States does not.)[43] A necessary first step in answering these questions is to pay attention to those norms that apparently do *not* seem to affect domestic policy change, or certain cases that have *not* changed despite the wide-spreading norm. Examining "negative cases" does not directly explain cause and effect, but it does allow us to identify the conditions that obstruct domestic salience of international norms.

METHODOLOGICAL AND ANALYTICAL ISSUES

Case Selection: Why These Four Countries?

Different types of governments differ in the way they punish criminal offenders. A number of theoretical perspectives suggest that as states modernize, civilize, and democratize, social control shifts inward and people become more tolerant of social deviance.[44] In his analysis of the evolution of the death penalty and civilization, Jeffrey Reiman argues that the "abolition of the death penalty is part of the civilizing mission of modern states."[45] Drawing upon Durkheim's laws of penal evolution, he notes that civilization results in less use of violence in society as people develop more civilized ways of resolving disputes and problems. The reduction in use of violence to solve problems at the national level contributes to a nation's decision to abolish the death penalty. As Robert Badinter points out, there is an "indissoluble link between dictatorship and death penalty."[46] In authoritarian or totalitarian regimes, the death penalty is far more likely to be enforced than in liberal democracies. China, Iran, and Saudi Arabia still make assiduous use of the death penalty not only for criminal but also for political or moral offenses, whereas the Netherlands, Sweden, Denmark, and Switzerland banned the death penalty decades ago for all crimes and in all circumstances. Since the death penalty is "the ultimate expression of the absolute power that the rulers wield over their subjects," most dictatorships frequently use the death penalty.[47] In describing the perception and use of the death penalty in terms of their relation to types of political rule in various states, Bertil Dunér and Hanna Geurtsen note that 70 percent of countries categorized as "free" according to the standards defined by Freedom House have signed one of the three protocols abolishing capital punishment, whereas only 30 percent of countries labeled "partly free or not free" have done so: "It seems likely that this statistical connection is in the first place a manifestation of the interests of the governing elites of authoritarian states to suppress opposition. In other words, the death penalty is one of many instruments for regime preservation."[48] Given that the number of non-abolitionist democracies is steadily decreasing, abolition has been strongly linked to democratic regimes.[49]

To avoid "researching the obvious," I did not choose repressive authoritarian regimes that abuse the death penalty as retentionist cases, nor did I choose established democracies as abolitionist cases. Instead of focusing on cases merely explained by a "civilization/democracy hypothesis," I have chosen theoretically and empirically "significant" cases that seem to have a much stronger potential to reveal different pathways of norm compliance.

I examine four countries: Ukraine, South Africa, South Korea, and the United States. The first three either abolished the death penalty relatively recently or have a moratorium on executions. These countries ban the death penalty for different political reasons and through different political processes, which capture theoretically significant pathways of norm compliance. At the same time, the three countries' policy changes regarding the death penalty are outlier cases in each region. Ukraine, South Africa, and South Korea attempted to comply with the international norm when many other Asian and African countries and former Eastern Bloc countries were still hesitant to do so. Explicitly devoted to analyzing the conditions and practices of those countries that make such outcomes possible, this research calls attention to how different outcomes are heavily conditioned by domestic sociopolitical factors.

Also, I investigate possible factors that determine U.S. policy toward the death penalty.[50] Studying its peculiarities, estranged from the uniform trend among other Western industrial nations, is worthwhile because of the general merit of research on extreme outlier cases: "We select cases where the values on the dependent variable are high and its known causes are absent."[51] To address this situation is the first step in understanding why this society in general continues to embrace the death penalty, which has been abandoned by every other developed nation in the West, as well as in exploring the broader issue of "U.S. exceptionalism" in matters pertaining to human rights in general. Table 1.1 presents the four cases examined in this book.

Table 1.1. Cases: Different Stages of Norm Compliance

Abolitionists	Under Moratorium	Retentionist
South Africa (1995) Ukraine (2000)	South Korea (no executions since 1998)	United States (38 of 50 states retain the death penalty)

Specification of the Variables

As Victor Kvashis notes, "In any country the death penalty is not only an institution of criminal law but also an instrument of criminal policy, a social-cultural phenomenon. Attitudes toward this institution are an indicator of the sentiments dominant in a particular society. Such an attitude is formed on the basis of a complex interaction of historical, political, cultural, legal, and many other social factors."[52] An understanding of death penalty policy and abolition processes in a particular country, therefore, requires a review of relevant historical, sociopolitical, historical, psychological, and criminal situations.

The dependent variable in this study is norm compliance, that is, a political phenomenon in which domestic policymaking and practice incorporate the international norms concerning the death penalty. Studies of norms exhibit three different levels of analysis: norm emergence, norm development, and norm internalization.[53] All three are worthwhile subjects of analysis.[54] The focus of this research, however, is limited to the last phase of norm implementation, relying on the assumption that domestic conditions are major factors affecting states' compliance with international rules and norms. By observing cases that reached different stages of norm compliance, I attempt to identify the factors that determine the variance in the dependent variable.

The explanatory variables that influence a government's response to the international human rights norm are grouped into five main categories: (1) Domestic Agents (public opinion, elite leadership, and grassroots activities); (2) International or Regional Forces; (3) Radical Political Transformation; (4) "Cultural Match" (crime rates and social inequality); and (5) Domestic Institutional Structures. Among these five categories, the first two are actor-centered (agent-centered), whereas the last three are context-centered (see table 1.2). We can also divide the variables into two groups on the basis of domestic or international factors: (1) domestic context and agents, that is, differences in internal normative and institutional arrangements, major political events such as regime change, prevailing public beliefs, and the role of political leadership; and (2) international context and agents, that is, the extent to which state behaviors are influenced by international or regional human rights regimes and transnational networks. In any case, norm compliance may be a function of one or more of these variables.

Before we can explore empirically how these variables interrelate, we must first identify and analyze each individually. In the following sections, I develop and operationalize the variables and factors that are likely to influence government response to the international human rights norm.

Table 1.2. Variables Categorized by Two Axes

	Actor-centered	Context-centered
Domestic	Domestic agents (public opionion, elite leadership, grassroots activities)	Radical political transformation Cultural match (crime rates, social inequality) Domestic institutional structures (centralized vs. decentralized)
International	International or regional human rights regimes	

Domestic Agents

PUBLIC OPINION

International norms are likely to have more impact if they promote ideas, beliefs, and values that fit well with preexisting, domestic social understanding. Where international human rights norms resonate with domestic cultural understandings and beliefs, states are more likely to respond to human rights pressures. In the case of capital punishment, general public opinion has been considered as an important domestic factor because of the belief that strong public support contributes to the continued use of the death penalty.[55] Death penalty supporters commonly cite public opinion to buttress their argument. Given its importance, I explore how different social groups hold different attitudes toward the death penalty, and what such opinions and attitudes are based on.[56] Escaping the simplistic "for or against" opinion polls on the death penalty, I examine public attitudes with more elaboration and qualification. A simple approach to public opinions obscures the underlying determinants of death penalty support, including race or income. Clearly, careful consideration and evaluation of the underlying causes of attitudes to the death penalty should be in order.

In most countries, however, the death penalty has consistently been supported by a majority of people anyway since systematic polling began. This raises the question: If public attitudes on the death penalty follow similar patterns across countries, what accounts for differences between various countries in death penalty policy? Why do different countries have different policy outcomes despite similar public opinions on the death penalty?

ELITE LEADERSHIP

The role of political leaders and their evolving beliefs must be taken into account in explaining how some countries have abolished the death penalty despite majority public support for its continued use. Successful abolition of the death penalty has required elite leadership to persuade a reluctant public to accept abolitionist norms. Research on norm compliance usually portrays state elites as the ones who initially hesitate to empower international human rights norms in the domestic arena.[57] It takes perhaps five to ten years of societal pressure before political elites are finally ready to comply with them. In this regard, it is interesting to note that the process in the case of the death penalty norm runs contrary to the implicit dichotomy between the "good" activists, civil society and nongovernmental organizations, and the "bad" state and elite decision makers. According to Checkel, this dichotomy-based research, by focusing only on the coercive function of grassroots activists, can neglect the dynamics of the elites' learning process: "[P]olitical/ state agents do not simply or always calculate how to advance given interests;

in many cases, they seek to discover those interests in the first place, and do so prior to significant social mobilization."[58] It is apparent that "elite voluntarism" is sometimes more important than social pressure from below in obtaining state compliance with international normative prescriptions.

GRASSROOTS ACTIVITIES

One of the most important pathways of norm diffusion involves the mobilization of societal pressure from below. International relations scholars have argued that socialization can occur as a result of the actions of nonstate actors and may involve the use of "soft" power resources, such as moral leverage and technical knowledge ("epistemic communities"). Margaret Keck and Kathryn Sikkink identify transnational advocacy networks as an important influence for states that come to adopt international norms. These transnational groups succeed not only "by holding governments . . . accountable to previous commitments and the principles they have endorsed," but also by framing their ideas in ways that "resonate or fit with the larger belief systems" of the target states.[59] As Ann Marie Clark suggests, societal pressure is the predicted mechanism for bringing international norms to the domestic arena.[60] Nonstate actors routinely use both norms and power to pressure governments to improve their human rights records. They attempt to influence government decision makers to favor policy changes on relevant issues.

International and Regional Forces

Transnational human rights organizations have rallied around the norm when pressuring governments to ratify international human rights treaties. Nongovernmental organizations and their transnational advocacy networks play a role in persuading and pressuring political elites to embrace internationally promoted norms and principles.[61] Along with the societal pressure dynamics of nongovernmental organizations, we should emphasize the pressure on political elites by intergovernmental institutions.[62] The independent activities of international institutions are "teachers of norms."[63]

More than ten years have passed since the UN General Assembly adopted its first protocol calling for the abolition of the death penalty. Cruel treatment and punishment are now prohibited by virtually all contemporary international human rights instruments. That those international laws evidence a trend in favor of abolishing the death penalty seems to be beyond dispute. In the modern conscience, the death penalty is no longer an internal matter of justice, but a matter of general, universal concern. International bodies, including the European Union and the United Nations, have endorsed and promoted the global trend toward abolition of the death penalty. An active network of international nonstate and intergovernmental actors has sought to mobilize and coerce decision makers to embrace the human rights norm against the death penalty. The Parliamentary Assembly of the Council of Europe, which has become one of the most effective and robust international human rights regimes in operation today, recommended, in 1994, the addition of a further protocol to the European Convention on Human Rights that would provide for the complete abolition of the death penalty, with no possibility of reservations being entered for its retention in any special circumstances.

Radical Political Transformation

Research from several theoretical perspectives attempts to discover empirical associations between the occurrence of important historical events (such as wars, revolutions, or major crises) and policy change. Many of these key events are hypothesized to trigger elite learning.[64] As John Keeler points out, political crises "create a sociopolitical context for governance uniquely conducive to the passage of reforms."[65] They "open the window for reform," and decision makers are more willing to listen to new ideas espoused by transnational actors or regional governments.[66] It is a truism that "politics opens up, becomes more fluid, under conditions of crisis and uncertainty."[67] In terms of operationalization, I associate this variable with a radical political transformation. The political transition captures and broadens the imagination of policymakers, leading them to question commitments to existing practices. When a regime changes drastically from authoritarianism to democracy, the new government usually adopts different kinds of human rights discourse in order to distinguish itself from the former authoritarian rule that marginalized human rights norms and actors. For example, after experiencing the long era of apartheid, the first decisions taken by the new Constitutional Court of South Africa modified the criminal justice system to make it more friendly to human rights for every member of society.

"Cultural Match"

Domestic political conditions of norm compliance have been recently highlighted in terms of the "cultural match" between domestic practices and international norms,[68] also described as "domestic salience,"[69] or "normative fit."[70] With regard to punitive policies, Warren Young and Mark Brown suggested that variations in such policies across nations are deeply rooted in cultural values about punishment, which in turn reflect the historical experiences of nations.[71] Theda Skocpol warns against the misuse or abuse of cultural factors, however, arguing that previous studies on culture or national values are "too holistic and essentialist" to offer explanatory leverage.[72] To avoid this error, we must delve into specific aspects of culture that may account for the variance in the level of compliance with the international norm.

There seems to be a certain correlation between religion and the death penalty. Latin America, predominantly Catholic, is largely free of capital punishment: only Cuba and Guatemala still apply the death penalty.[73] It is interesting to note, however, that the Philippines, where 95 percent of the population is Catholic, is also one of very few regions that have reinstated the death penalty after abolishing it. In addition, a substantial number of Muslim countries have abolished the death penalty in recent years, although some Islamic scholars maintain that Islamic Law "demands" the death penalty. Among countries with large Muslim majorities, Azerbaijan, Bosnia-Herzegovina, and Turkmenistan have abolished the death penalty, and Tajikistan and Uzbekistan have substantially reduced its scope. These examples suggest that religion is not a determining factor in explaining the variance in cross-national death penalty policy. Hence, my measure of "culture match" contains only nonreligious elements, such as crime rates and social inequality.

CRIME RATES

Crime rates are relevant to national variations in use of the death penalty because higher crime rates are more likely to provoke a stronger demand for capital punishment. In fact, the main justification for the death penalty offered by its supporters is deterrence. Scores of researchers have examined the possibility that the death penalty has a greater deterrent effect on homicide rates than long-term imprisonment. While some econometric studies in the mid-1970s claimed to find deterrent effects,[74] these studies were soon found to suffer from critical flaws.[75] Virtually all of the deterrence studies done in the past thirty years conclude that no scientifically proven correlation exists between the use of capital punishment and crime reduction. The claim that the death penalty should be used to curb rising crime rates seems to be a response to the demands of the public, most of whom are opposed to abolition.[76]

SOCIAL INEQUALITY

The degree of social inequality or social exclusion must also be considered as one of the societal characteristics associated with abolition or retention of the death penalty. Several studies have highlighted the relationship between the use of the death penalty and a nation's failure to assimilate minorities into the mainstream of national life. William Bowers and his colleagues argued that the characteristic of "incomplete incorporation" was the single most important factor predicting which nations retained the death penalty in their total sample of the "highly developed" countries (n = 36).[77] James Marquart and his colleagues maintained that a "cultural tradition of exclusion," deriving from slavery and its legacy of racial discrimination, accounted for the disproportionate number of executions in the United States.[78] Tony Poveda argued that "the tradition of social exclusion" is one of the key factors explaining why some countries continue to justify the execution of criminal offenders.[79]

In different terms, but in a similar vein, other studies have noted the high frequency of the death penalty in polarized societies. The death penalty is more likely to be applied to the "others" in polarized societies as an instrument enforcing the social hierarchy.[80] In this view, a society's punitive policies are part of, and reflect, a society's general tolerance of inequality, so that such policies should be associated with the degree of relative inequality in nations. The measure of different sentiments about the death penalty among different groups in a society, which are strongly shaped by in-group favoritism and out-group prejudice, offers a compelling alternative explanation of why the death penalty prevails under certain contexts of social relations.[81] In the United States, those who favor the death penalty tend to be disproportionately white, male, Republican, middle-class, and Southern.[82]

Domestic Institutional Structures

If conventional cultural accounts based on a homogenous "political culture" are too holistic in explaining a state's attitude and receptiveness toward international norms, another strategy is to incorporate an institutional approach. A variety of scholars have argued that the influence of international norms depends on domestic institutional structures, suggesting that differences in the key political institutions of states explain variations in norm adoption. According to Harald Müeller, pathways by which international rules become relevant domestically depend on the interests and actions of state and societal actors during a given policy debate.[83] In his study on U.S. ambivalence with regard to the application of global human rights norms, Andrew Moravcsik argues that the exceptionally decentralized and divided nature of political institutions is of particular importance in limiting U.S. support for domestic enforcement of norms.[84]

Especially in cases of low congruence between the international norm in question and widespread domestic public beliefs, as is the case with the death penalty, the features of decision-making structures matter even more as they mediate the leverage of political leadership in enforcing unpopular international norms at home. In a centralized state, political elites preserve a greater autonomy vis-à-vis public demands, and thus crucial policy decisions can be taken in the absence of mass public consensus. Decentralized federal political institutions, by contrast, are open to pressures of local decision makers and public opinion, making it less likely that a government will pursue any policies in the face of public opposition. In such a society, the rationalists' instrumental logic is more often effective in capturing the domestic effect of systemic social structures than it is in other countries where

Table 1.3. Summary of Variables

Explanatory Variables	Intervening Variables	Dependent Variable
Domestic agents (public opinion, elite leadership, grassroots activities)	Domestic institutional structures (centralized vs. decentralized)	Norm compliance: domestic policy change regarding capital punishment
	Radical political transformation	
Cultural match (crime rates, social inequality)		
International or regional human rights regimes		

decision makers have greater autonomy and insulation from society. Distinctive structures of political institutions, especially the degree of their centralization, have a profound effect on political behavior and often play a key role in producing policy variation across nations.

Methodologically, this book offers a comparative and historical case study of norm compliance. For the "successful cases" of nations that have abolished the death penalty—Ukraine and South Africa, and, to some extent, South Korea—I compare the conditions under which the international human rights norm is institutionalized. Regarding the case of the United States, I make some comparisons between the U.S. and European liberal democracies and identify some cases that make this country's pattern unique.

Concerning research materials and evidence, I synthesized qualitative content analysis of primary sources with additional analysis of secondary sources selected from published studies. I used three types of primary source data in this research. First, Ukrainian, South African, Korean, and U.S. press reports, and the reports of human rights groups, including intergovernmental organizations, were useful in chronicling state behavior regarding death penalty policies and the corresponding human rights pressure on each country. I used the public documents and pronouncements of each government and of intergovernmental organizations, which included published and draft versions of legislation as well as public interviews and speeches of high-level officials. I carefully reviewed and analyzed the complete set of detailed records written by the Council of Europe, for which I visited public libraries and archives in Strasbourg, France.

Second, I conducted interviews with top legal advisors, high-level government officials, members of human rights nongovernmental organizations, and low-level intergovernmental organization officials. The interviews ranged in time from one hour to more than three hours each, and sometimes occurred in two different sessions.

Finally, for recent survey data concerning the death penalty, I consulted the Data Archive of Social Indicators provided by the Interuniversity Consortium for Political and Social Research (ICPSR) as well as the Gallup database. Statistics on the death penalty issue provided by the Bureau of Justice Statistics and the NAACP Legal Defense and Education Fund were thoroughly probed for the case of the United States. Crime rates are assessed by both data of the UN Crime and Justice Profile and the Federal Bureau of Investigation.

The book is organized as follows. Chapters 2 through 5 take up a specific country to explore under what circumstances it comes to comply, or not, with the international norm of banning the death penalty. More specifically, Chapters 2 and 3 examine the cases of two countries, Ukraine and South Africa, where the international norm concerning the prohibition of the death penalty has been embraced and legitimized in the domestic arena. Chapter 4 explores the practice of capital punishment in South Korea, focusing on whether, or to what extent, the evolving human rights norm is associated with democratic institutional and behavioral change. Chapter 5 offers an explanation for the U.S. aversion to acceptance and enforcement of the norm, and its consequences. The last chapter begins with a summary of each case. Making comparisons between the "successful" cases and the "unsuccessful" case, as well as within the "successful" cases of domestic implementation of the international norm, the chapter goes on to specify a causal mechanism that leads to state compliance or noncompliance with the norm, and finally assesses broad theoretical debates.

CHAPTER TWO

UKRAINE

In the unified Europe of the future the solemn abolition of the death penalty ought to be the first article of the European Code we all hope for. There will be no lasting peace either in the heart of individuals or in social customs until death is outlawed.

—Albert Camus, "Reflections on the Guillotine"

For the Council of Europe of today, there is no right way to apply the death penalty, because the death penalty itself is wrong. Our ambition is to further contribute to speeding up the unstoppable movement towards universal abolition.

—Walter Schwimmer, Secretary General of the Council of Europe

When an execution was carried out in Ukraine in March 1997, it was hardly expected to be the last one in that country. It became the last, though, not only for Ukraine but also for all of Europe to date.[1] How and under what conditions did Ukraine, formerly one of the world's leaders in executions, rule out the death penalty? The purpose of this chapter is to evaluate the abolitionist campaign that has been successfully conducted on the European continent. The chapter highlights the crucial role of the Council of Europe (CE) in the movement to ban executions in its forty-six western and eastern member countries. Since the last execution in one of the council's member states took place in Ukraine in 1997, this chapter asks how the Council of Europe managed to enforce the norm against capital punishment in Ukraine, especially during a period of political transition, and when the rate of violent crime was drastically increasing. The process culminating in Ukraine's decision to end the death penalty contains valuable lessons for abolitionists and human rights advocates, as this country's experience demonstrates that even a once notorious executioner is likely to acknowledge the right to life when conditions are favorable.

I examine first the role and influence of the Council of Europe in its attempt to build a death-penalty-free zone in Europe. Next I describe the process through which Ukraine finally outlawed the death penalty, after a long period of resistance to the Council of Europe's demands. Finally, I discuss the political, social, and economic conditions of post-Soviet Ukraine that contributed to or limited the prospects for the abolition of the death penalty. The conclusion assesses the chapter's theoretical implications.

THE COUNCIL OF EUROPE AND THE DEATH-PENALTY-FREE ZONE

The European Movement

Following the death and destruction of people and communities during World War II, the governments of ten nations (Belgium, Denmark, France, Ireland, Italy, Luxembourg, The Netherlands, Norway, Sweden, and the United Kingdom) met in London in May 1949 in order to build a regional organization that would help to "unite Europe around the shared principles of the rule of law, respect for human rights and pluralist democracy."[2] Thirteen others joined soon after (Austria, Cyprus, Finland, Germany, Greece, Iceland, Liechtenstein, Malta, Portugal, San Marino, Spain, Switzerland, and Turkey), and other Eastern and Central European countries have been admitted since 1990 (Andorra, Albania, Bulgaria, Croatia, the Czech Republic, Estonia, Hungary, Latvia, Lithuania, Macedonia, Moldova, Poland, Romania, Russia, Slovakia, Slovenia, and Ukraine). With a membership of forty-six nations—geographically the most extensive European political organization—the Council of Europe has been considered to be the oldest, most effective, and most robust international human rights organization in operation today.

As a major part of the program to achieve a greater unity among its members throughout Europe, the Council of Europe devised about 165 international agreements, treaties, and conventions. The European Convention for the Protection of Human Rights and Fundamental Freedoms (commonly known as the European Convention on Human Rights, or ECHR) of 1950 exemplifies what the Council of Europe ultimately pursues: "[T]he aim of the Council of Europe is the achievement of greater unity between its Members and . . . one of the methods by which the aim is to be pursued is the maintenance and further realization of Human Rights and Fundamental Freedoms."[3] Since the collapse of communism in 1989, one of the council's missions has been to help the countries of eastern and central Europe to democratize their constitutions, legal codes, and political systems. The Council of Europe developed extensive programs of cooperation and assistance that were made available to all new member states. In return, according to Articles III and IV of the Statute of the Council of Europe, member states must agree to promote human rights and fundamental freedoms within their jurisdictions, and to cooperate in realizing the council's aims.

Most important, the Council of Europe required prospective and existing member states to commit to abolishing the death penalty. Even though some countries no longer imposed the death sentence in practice, the death penalty was still on the statute books in all the founder states when the Council of Europe was established. Walter Schwimmer, the Secretary General of the Council of Europe, stated, "[I]t is a well-known fact that in Europe, a continent which had to survive the brutality of two world wars and several totalitarian regimes and dictatorships [in the] last century, the abolition of the death penalty did not come easy."[4]

A motion for a resolution on the abolition of the death penalty was presented in the Parliamentary Assembly of the Council of Europe (PACE) in 1973, but it was not accompanied by any enforcement mechanisms. It was in April 1980 that the Council of Europe adopted Protocol No. 6 to the ECHR concerning the abolition of the death penalty, which was opened for signature by the member states in April 1983, and entered into force in March 1985.[5] The Council of Europe thus became the first body in the world to sign an international agreement obliging the signatories to abolish the death penalty. In other words, Protocol No. 6 was the first agreement under international law containing a legal obligation to abolish capital punishment. The Council of Europe has since persuaded each member to exclude the death penalty from domestic law, aiming to make Europe the first region in the world to permanently outlaw the death penalty. The council evaluated the introduction of Protocol No. 6 as follows: "With Protocol No. 6, Europe completely changed tack from tolerating to prohibiting statutory killing. . . . Rejection of the death penalty was thus made one of the cornerstones of European identity and one of the continent's universal values."[6]

Another important decision came in the wake of the First Summit of Heads of State and Government held in Vienna in 1993, which affirmed that applicant states should undertake to sign and ratify the ECHR. As it extended membership to the former Soviet bloc states and observed the frequent use of capital punishment in those regions, the PACE took a stronger and more specific stance regarding this issue: all member states must sign and ratify Protocol No. 6 to the ECHR promptly. Any country that wished to become a member of the Council of Europe was required to introduce an immediate moratorium on executions and sign Protocol No. 6 within one year, and to ratify it within three years from the time of accession. The Council of Europe demonstrated the simple but strong reasoning as to why capital punishment should no longer be acceptable: "[The death] penalty has no place in a civilized democracy. Abolition of the death penalty is the mark of a civilized society and a civilized Europe."[7]

By setting up a number of detailed procedures and affirming the principle of confidentiality and nondiscrimination, the Council of Europe monitored states' full compliance with several major points that all member states had unanimously accepted, including freedom of expression and information, the implementation and protection of democratic institutions, and adherence to the ideals of human rights in the functioning of the judicial system, local democracy, the rejection of capital punishment, and the operation of police and security forces. Among these points, the issue of capital punishment appeared in countries' monitoring reports most frequently. For detailed guidance in monitoring capital punishment, the ministers' deputies of the Council of Europe accepted the outline of basic issues presented in Table 2.1 in November 1998.

Table 2.1. Council of Europe's Monitoring Procedure on the Death Penalty

I. Legal Issues	1. Legal basis (status of the legal norm which has abolished the death penalty [constitution, law, . . .], state of preparations / time frame for such abolition) 2. Legal guarantees against reintroduction (ratification of Protocol No. 6 to the ECHR, state of preparations / time frame for such ratification, constitutional guarantees, etc.) 3. Nature and solidity of any moratorium on executions (legal basis thereof, applicable procedures for amnesty / pardon / commutation of sentence, etc.) 4. Crimes for which death penalty has so far remained on statute books (including, for both first-instance courts and superior levels of jurisdiction, the mandatory or discretionary nature of such punishment for the crimes in question) and legal limitations on imposition / execution (minors, [pregnant] women, . . .) 5. Situation with respect to crimes committed in time of war or imminent threat of war 6. Public availability of information on executions (data, place, etc.) 7. Legal effects of the existence of death penalty in another country (e.g., refusal of extradition on account of risk of death sentence)
II. Factual Data	1. Number of death sentences pronounced in last three years (including commutations and death sentences overturned on appeal) 2. Total number of persons under sentence (including names of persons under sentence of death and places of detention) 3. Date of last execution 4. Access to the body after execution 5. Detention conditions of persons sentenced to death (specific detention regimes, visiting rights, access to lawyers, security measures, access to activities, health care, material conditions of detention, . . .)
III. Policy Issues and Attitudes	1. Measures / campaigns / programs (awareness-raising, training, education) vis-à-vis public opinion and relevant professional groups (law enforcement personnel, the judiciary, etc.), public opinion polls 2. Capital punishment and sentencing policy in general (availability of and recourse to alternative types of punishment) 3. Views / public statements of government and political parties concerning capital punishment and its abolition

Source: Council of Europe, "Capital Punishment: Outline of Basic Issues," unpublished Report. No. S42A-C, Council of Europe Archives, Strasbourg, France, 1999: 7.

From the perspective of member countries, the complete abolition of the death penalty became a vital obligation to the council. Among the countries that abolished the death penalty in the early 1990s were Ireland, Hungary, Romania, the Czech Republic, Slovakia, Switzerland, and Greece. Bulgaria introduced a moratorium on the death penalty in 1993, and Moldova and Italy announced its complete abolition in 1994. Spain joined the abolitionist movement in 1995, and Estonia, which had not carried out an execution since 1991, completely outlawed capital punishment in early 1997. Lithuania and Poland abolished it in 1999 and 2000 respectively for all crimes, and Latvia and Albania abolished it in 1999 and 2000, respectively, except for crimes under military law or crimes committed in exceptional circumstances.

As of January 2006, forty-five member countries have ratified Protocol No. 6 leaving the Russian Federation as the only one not to have done so. Russia signed the protocol in 1997 and has had a moratorium on all executions since 1996. Despite strong social pressures to restore the death penalty, President Vladimir Putin remains committed to eventual de jure abolition, and since 1999 all death sentences have been commuted to life imprisonment.[8] As the forty-fifth member state in the Council of Europe, Serbia/ Montenegro signed the protocol on its accession in April 2003, and ratified it in March 2004. Turkey, despite a de facto moratorium applied since 1984, kept the death penalty much longer than any other European countries. In August 2003, however, this country also joined the European abolitionist movement by removing the death penalty from its criminal code. As a logical follow-up to a series of important legal changes, Turkey ratified Protocol No. 6 in December 2003.[9]

In early 2000, the PACE recommended that a further protocol to the ECHR should be established to provide for the complete abolition of the death penalty, with no possibility of reservations. The council's Committee of Ministers adopted Protocol No. 13 in February 2002 and opened it for signature by all member states in May 2002. Unlike Protocol No. 6, which allows the death penalty under exceptional circumstances, Protocol No. 13 bans it in all circumstances, including in times of war or imminent danger of war. It is apparent that the European continent has become a de facto death-penalty-free area, as all the council's member states have either abolished capital punishment or instituted a moratorium on executions. Although popular support for the death penalty may continue in many European countries, the present regional legal regime makes it impossible for member states to reintroduce it without violating the European Convention and its protocols.

Beyond the European Continent

In current European politics, the death penalty is considered fundamentally to be an issue of international human rights that should not be governed by national prerogatives. The policy of ending all executions is "one that Europeans seek to apply to all nations with any claim to civilization."[10] This goal of European modern morality has come to be pursued on a global scale. In addition, the Council of Europe now wishes to extend prohibition of the death penalty to Japan and to the United States. These two countries have been granted observer status by the council's Committee of Ministers, but both have retained and carried out capital punishment.[11] From the council's perspective, the United States and Japan are in violation of their obligations under Statutory Resolution (93) 26 on observer status; that is, a state wishing to become a Council of Europe observer state must be willing to accept the principles of democracy, the rule of law, and the enjoyment by all persons within its jurisdiction of human rights and fundamental freedoms. Because the Council of Europe is asking all countries that aspire to observer status to abolish the death penalty, it has made the same demands of countries already enjoying this status.[12]

In June 2001, the PACE urged Japan and the United States to institute a moratorium on executions as an initial step on the path to full abolition of the death penalty, and to improve conditions on death row immediately, which includes "the ending of all secrecy surrounding executions, of all unnecessary limitations on rights and freedoms, and a broadening of access to post-conviction and post-appeal judicial review." The Council of Europe resolution was strong enough to add that the countries' observer status could be withdrawn unless they made significant progress.[13]

In an effort to initiate a dialogue with the observer countries, the Committee on Legal Affairs and Human Rights of the PACE invited pro-abolition parliamentarians from Japan and the United States on several occasions and supported their endeavors to institute moratoria on executions and to abolish the death penalty.[14] The PACE also organized a series of seminars on the abolition of the death penalty in Japan and the United States. The Tokyo conference, in May 2002, included not only high representatives of the Japanese authorities and lawmakers, but also representatives from Belgium, Estonia, South Korea, and Ukraine. They discussed a variety of themes relating the death penalty, including the death row situation in Japan and the prospects for abolition. Aware that a sizable group in the Japanese parliament had been campaigning against the death penalty, Renate Wohlwend, chair of the Committee on Legal Affairs and Human Rights, said in an interview with Radio Free Europe/Radio Liberty (RFE/RL): "[T]he fact that a measure to abolish the death penalty is now wending its way through South Korea's legislative process seems to be arousing Japan's competitive instincts."[15]

Several of the conferences organized by the Council of Europe in observer states took place in the United States. In the two-part conferences held in Springfield, Illinois—one of thirteen U.S. states to have instituted a moratorium on executions—and Washington, D.C. in April 2003, former death row prisoners exchanged views and compared experiences with U.S. federal and state senators and representatives, as well as abolitionist campaigners. The U.S. conferences focused especially on protection from wrongful convictions, which was the leading argument for the moratorium on the death penalty introduced in several U.S. states. Emphasizing that the divergence of views on the death penalty could have significant consequences for relations between allies, Renate Wohlwend stated in the opening session of the Springfield conference that "if any Council of Europe member state arrested Osama bin Laden, for example, it would not be able to extradite him to the United States unless it was given assurance that the death penalty would not be sought."[16]

Recalling a frequent question received by the Council of Europe delegation during its missions, Wohlwend said, "Some Americans and also Japanese people [asked], '[W]hy do you want to put your eye only on us? There are [many] more executions and very tough living conditions [for] people in Asia, in the Far East, in the Muslim countries, [and in] Africa.' " She answered, "The Council of Europe opposes capital punishment everywhere but believes it has more influence in countries such as the United States and Japan, which have observer status or other connections with the Council. . . . It is not so easy for us to go [to the Middle East and North Africa], as they have no cooperation with the Council of Europe."[17] The Council of Europe fights for the total abolition of the death penalty, not only within Europe but globally.

POLITICAL TURBULENCE AND RISING CRIME RATES

Ukraine has been a member of the Council of Europe since November 1995. Post-Soviet Ukraine's first president, Leonid Kravchuk, and his successor Leonid Kuchma often proclaimed their desire to integrate Ukraine politically into Europe. Like most candidate countries for membership, Ukraine hoped to use the Council of Europe as a bridge to greater integration with Western countries, and eventually to join the European Union (EU). In his 1997 address in the session of the PACE, President Kuchma described Ukraine's foreign policy objectives, and reaffirmed that full membership in the EU was of vital importance to the national interest.[18] In the same period, Kuchma repeatedly told the Assembly of the Western European Union (WEU) that Ukraine's strategic objective was integration into European and Euro-Atlantic structures:

> I would . . . like to note that our foreign policy terminology should reflect the principled political line of the state. Along with the strategic choice of adhering to the processes of European integration, Ukraine's firm and consistent line is the line of maximum broadening and deepening of bilateral and multilateral forms of cooperation both within and outside the framework of the Commonwealth of Independent States (CIS) while safeguarding the principles of mutual benefit and respect for each other's interests and abiding by the generally recognized norms of international law.[19]

Despite the obvious value of gaining membership of the Council of Europe, it was not easy for Ukraine to fulfill all obligations required by the council. This newly founded nation was understandably hesitant when contemplating an early loss of sovereignty, which they believed would accompany a close association with the Council of Europe. The Ukrainian government was especially unsympathetic to death penalty reform. The classical logic of economic costs, that life imprisonment is more expensive than the death penalty, was one reason. Another important reason for Ukraine's desire to keep the death penalty was that the country had gone through a drastic transition.

After several years of independence, the political condition of Ukraine is described as follows: "You have a government that is weak . . . a Parliament which thinks it is an executive and parliamentary committees which think they should be doing the work of cabinet ministers."[20] It was true that Ukraine continued to provide a hospitable environment for organized violent crime. The lid that the government had kept on society, repressing all societal grievances in Soviet times, was blown off, and all social problems spilled over. The rapid political and social transition allowed criminals to exploit a general weakening in the state structure. The growth of crime in Ukraine was a response to social disorganization, increased social differentiation, and social strain. According to the Den newspaper in 1998, "Every three years, starting from 1992, the death rate of people murdered at the hands of killers in Ukraine is as high as Soviet army casualties during the war in Afghanistan. Every day—twelve killings."[21] As Table 2.2 indicates, crime rates drastically increased during the period of political transition.

As Elliot Currie describes, high levels of violent crime in Ukraine were perhaps generated in part by the radical change to a Darwinian "market

Table 2.2. Criminality in Ukraine, 1972 and 1988–98

Year	Registered Crimes	Intentional Murder	% Growth From Preceding Year	Crime Coefficient (per 100,000)
1972	135,646	1,577	—	283
1988	242,974	2,016	2.2	473
1989	322,340	2,589	32.7	623
1990	369,809	2,823	14.7	713
1991	405,516	2,902	9.7	780
1992	480,478	3,679	18.5	922
1993	539,299	4,008	12.2	1,032
1994	571,891	4,571	6.0	1,096
1995	641,860	4,783	12.2	1,241
1996	617,262	4,896	−4.0	1,208
1997	589,208	4,529	−4.8	1,164
1998	575,982	4,563	−2.3	1,137

Sources: Todd S. Foglesong and Peter H. Solomon Jr., Crime, Criminal Justice, and Criminology in Post-Soviet Ukraine (Washington, DC: National Institute of Justice, 2001), 20–24.

society."[22] The society became enamored of the values of material accumulation, yet very few had access to legal ways of obtaining wealth. Universal benefits of the Soviet planned economy, which included job guarantees, regulated wages, vacations, job training, child care, and often housing, were reduced or eliminated.[23] Hyperinflation accompanied the first three years of independence, and between 1991 and 1998, Ukraine's real gross domestic product (GDP) declined by 63 percent (compared with slightly more than 40 percent in Russia).[24] No sector or industry escaped a deep and broad depression. In terms of overall competitiveness, the World Economic Forum ranked Ukraine as the fifty-second of fifty-three countries in 1997; fifty-third of fifty-three countries in 1998; fifty-eighth of fifty-nine countries in 1999; and fifty-seventh of fifty-nine countries in 2000.[25] Additionally, unemployment has become pervasive in the transition economy. In March 1993, the State Center of Employment revealed that nearly 14.6 percent of the people were on long-term leave. During the period in which the process of abolishing capital punishment was ongoing, registered unemployment, let alone "hidden unemployment," grew quickly from 162,000 in 1996 and 351,000 in 1997 to 1,052,000 in 1998.[26]

The fear of an unprotected society in an uncertain political and economic environment made being "tough on crime" the most important principle of state policies. The Ukrainian government thought that the state's strong legal apparatus was necessary and desirable in order to make the transition successful. Retaining a strong criminal policy seemed especially important until some level of stability could be achieved. In 1996, both President Kuchma and the parliament demonstrated that the country was not ready for immediate abolition of the death penalty: "The country's crime rate does not allow for canceling the death penalty," stated the chairman of the parliament during a meeting with an official delegation from the Council of Europe in November 1996.[27]

Along with rising crime rates, another impediment to death penalty reform was the very nature of Ukraine's political transformation. The death penalty was abolished sooner among the losing powers of the World War II—Italy, Germany, and Austria—than among the major victorious powers, such as England and France, which kept the death penalty for decades after the war's end. Experiencing drastic regime changes as the war ended, the defeated nations were able to precipitate legal reforms that might have taken much longer to accomplish under stable governments. By comparison, Ukraine's transition was incremental. Although 1991 was considered to be the dawn of a new era in Ukrainian history economically and institutionally, the legacy of the Soviet Union was powerful and enduring. The former Soviet administrative and political elites retained great power and influence at the center of government in newly independent Ukraine. Because the regime transition occurred peacefully, the entire governmental system was not destroyed and, more important, Soviet-era social and political attitudes and beliefs persisted. As D'Anieri and his colleagues point out, Ukraine's institutional continuity fostered stability in the short term, but in the long term it led to a powerful inertia obstructing reform: "Because the collapse of the Soviet Union was accomplished peacefully, there was no chance to completely erase the past and the ancient régime or to start with a clean slate."[28] Even if chaos and violence were avoided in the peaceful process of the transition, Soviet institutions and values have in many respects continued to govern post-Soviet Ukraine.

UKRAINE'S RESISTANCE TO THE COUNCIL OF EUROPE

The Council of Europe called for an immediate moratorium on executions from the day of accession. Ukraine was also required to ratify Protocol No. 6 by November 1998, that is, within three years of its entry. Ukraine signed the Protocol in May 1997, but did not ratify it until the council's deadline. The number of executions actually increased. According to a report prepared by the assembly's monitoring committee, 212 people were executed between November 9, 1995, the date Ukraine joined the council, and March 11, 1997, the date the state signed the protocol.[29] During 1996 alone, Ukraine conducted 167 executions, which, worldwide, was second only to the number in China.[30] Executions were carried out without informing even the families of the prisoners, and the bodies were buried in unmarked graves. Secret executions also continuously took place at a rate of more than a dozen each year.[31]

Noting Ukraine's failure to fulfill its obligations, the Council of Europe officials remarked: "Asking Russia and Ukraine to abolish the death sentence tomorrow would be like asking them to get rid of their governments tomorrow." "I feel I cannot trust the Ukrainian authorities any more," admonished Renate Wohlwend, who was then the Council's Legal Affairs Committee Rapporteur.[32] Among the member countries of the Council of Europe, Ukraine's persistence in conducting executions continued for more than a year after accession made it a rare case.

PUBLIC OPINION ON THE DEATH PENALTY CONTROVERSY

As soon as Ukraine joined the Council of Europe in 1995, the death penalty became the subject of intensive political discussion there. Public opinion steadfastly favored the death penalty. Worn down by the chaos of everyday life, weary of waiting for positive results from reforms, and still a long way from an understanding of democratic values, most of the population believed that any violation of the law should be dealt with harshly. With fear and insecurity strong in a society in transition, a prevalent public view was that capital punishment would restrict crime rates. The political and economic transformation, accompanied by a rise in crime, gave rise to popular demand for a strong deterrent. People were skeptical about the government's ability "to build strong enough prisons that will guarantee that sadists and rapists will never break free from them."[33] According to a survey conducted by the Institute of Sociology of the National Academy of Sciences of Ukraine in 1994, 67 percent of the Ukrainian population wanted the death penalty maintained or expanded, while 12 percent wanted to make gradual progress toward abolition. Only 5 percent of the people supported the immediate abolition of the death penalty. This opinion persisted for several years; 69 percent were in favor of the death penalty and 16 percent against in 1995; 63 percent were in favor and 18 percent against in 1996; and 62 percent were in favor and 15 percent against in 1997. In addition, most of those supporting the death penalty believed that it should be retained even if Ukraine lost the support of European countries.[34] Among the general public, Ukraine's obligations and commitments to the Council of Europe were not persuasive reasons for abolishing the death penalty. Pro-death penalty opinion is not unique among the Ukrainian public, however; public sentiment on criminal policy has been conservative everywhere, and a majority of the public, regardless of political and social backgrounds, always favors the death penalty.

Ukrainian civil society as a whole is weak and young. The Ukrainian nongovernmental organizations are extraordinarily inactive compared to their Western, Asian, or even Russian counterparts: "[L]ack of experience and poor networking with like-minded organizations have resulted in many false starts and weakened their ability to mobilize public pressure."[35] When Ukraine emerged from the Soviet Union in 1991, civil society was too weak to play any significant role in a democratic political system. Furthermore, ongoing deadlock between the legislative and the executive branches, which seriously hampered reform in Ukraine, made it more difficult for civil society to develop, because a robust civil society at a time of socioeconomic crisis was not welcome to the Ukrainian authorities. As D'Anieri, Kravchuk, and Kuzio note, "Dmytro Vydryn, a former presidential adviser to Kuchma, believes that a fully developed civil society is very inconvenient for the authorities, as it would prevent abuse of powers, authoritarianism, and large-scale corruption."[36] Ironically, two contradictory logics coexisted: Ukraine was initiating a transformation from totalitarian communism and external dominance to an independent democratic system; at the same time, however, it circumscribed the development of civil society to facilitate the efficient and "convenient" transition to democracy. Civil society therefore remained weak in Ukraine. Few Ukrainian citizens belonged to civic organizations of any type, and the major Western nongovernmental organizations operating in the country focused only on fair elections and free media.[37] The question of the death penalty was not part of a public debate. Civil organizations were nowhere close to including the subject of capital punishment in their agendas for action. Domestic pressure for death penalty reform simply did not exist.

THE PROCESS OF ENFORCING THE
COUNCIL OF EUROPE NORM

The Parliamentary Assembly of the Council of Europe issued a series of warnings, resolutions, and threats against Ukraine for disregarding its obligation. In 1997 the PACE issued Resolution 1112, which demanded Ukrainian compliance, warning that it would "take all necessary steps to ensure compliance" and even "consider the non-ratification of the credentials of the Ukrainian parliamentary delegation." In December 1998, the council again warned the Ukrainian delegation that the country might not be represented in the PACE in January 1999 because of its failure to comply with the moratorium. The Council of Europe maintained that the Ukrainian authorities, including the parliament, were responsible to a great extent for the country's failure to respect and fulfill its obligations and commitments, in particular those that were to be met within a year of accession, such as establishing legal policies for the protection of human rights, a new criminal code and code of criminal procedure, and a new civil code and code of civil procedure.[38]

Strong warnings were made repeatedly in January 1999. In accordance with Rule 6 of its Rules of Procedure, the PACE decided that the credentials of the Ukrainian parliamentary delegation would be annulled unless Ukraine made significant changes. It also called for the suspension of Ukrainian representation in the Committee of Ministers.[39] Furthermore, the Council of Europe reported Ukraine's "misbehavior" to the major international and regional economic organizations in an initiative akin to an economic sanction against this country: "The Assembly decides to transmit this resolution [Resolution 1179 on the honoring of obligations and commitments by Ukraine] to the European Parliament, the European Commission, the OSCE, the European Bank for Reconstruction and Development, the World Bank, the International Monetary Fund, the Congress of Local and Regional Authorities of Europe and the Social Development Fund."[40]

In light of Ukraine's ongoing failure to meet its obligations, the Committee of Ministers of the Council of Europe took a different approach from the PACE. Whereas the PACE did not hesitate to issue public warnings and criticisms, the Committee of Ministers took a less aggressive approach, maintaining a continuous dialogue at all levels and collecting information on Ukraine from government bodies, nongovernmental organizations, academics, the parliament, the judiciary, the presidential administration, and the Constitutional Court.[41] The Committee of Ministers held regular, confidential monitoring sessions in Strasbourg, in which delegations from all member states participated. "It was certainly not an easy task to have a discussion on this subject because the majority population in many countries concerned, including Ukraine, was against the abolition of the death penalty. In fact, it was very difficult for our organization as a whole to persuade the government to go against public opinion," stated Johan Friestedt of the Monitoring Department of the Council of Europe.[42]

All participants in these monitoring sessions might have shared Ukraine's dilemma, since most of them had had to abolish the death penalty some years earlier, also against the will of the public. By sharing their experiences in dealing with this subject and emphasizing the fact that abolition would not increase crime rates, the Council of Europe and representatives of member countries had an opportunity to persuade Ukrainian elites to reform their death penalty policy. The Committee of Ministers repeated: "[W]e are here not to criticize you, but to identify with you where the problems come from and how we can help you overcome your difficulties."[43]

Late in 1998 Ukrainian president Kuchma called on the Ukrainian parliament to pass a law removing the death penalty. In September the parliament passed the first reading of the new criminal code abolishing capital punishment. Immediately following the council's fact-finding visit to Kiev in early 1999, when the PACE claimed that no substantial progress had yet been achieved, the president of the parliament issued instructions to the relevant parliamentary committees regarding steps to be taken to honor certain obligations and commitments by Ukraine, including banning the death penalty.[44]

On December 29, 1999, the Ukrainian Constitutional Court ruled that the death penalty was unconstitutional. Based on the constitutional appeal of fifty-one People's Deputies of Ukraine, the Ukrainian Constitutional Court proclaimed that Article 24 of the Criminal Code of Ukraine, the death penalty provision, violated the principle of respect for human life, which is envisaged by Article 3 (the right to life) and Article 28 (the right to respect of dignity) of the Ukraine Constitution; its ruling stated that "application of death penalty as an exceptional kind of punishment should be regarded as lawless deprivation of a human being of its right to life."[45] It went on to say that the death penalty violated "the principle of the right to life, which is enshrined in the country's constitution, and contravene[s] the constitutional provision that no one should be subjected to torture or to cruel or inhuman treatment or punishment." The Constitutional Court added that "[t]he right to life belongs to a person from birth and is protected by the state."[46]

After the Constitutional Court's decision, complete abolition proceeded quickly. On February 22, 2000, an overwhelming majority of members of the Ukrainian parliament decided to eliminate the death penalty from the criminal code, the Criminal Procedure Code and the Corrections Code, and to replace it with other mechanisms—everything from life imprisonment and hard labor to experimental, New Age psychiatric treatments. Two months later, the parliament ratified Protocol No. 6 to the ECHR. At the same time it formulated a new criminal code abolishing the death penalty in both peacetime and wartime, setting life imprisonment as the nation's maximum punishment. The new criminal code also specified that people under eighteen and over sixty-five and women pregnant when they committed a crime or during sentencing would not be subject to life terms. The new code also introduced more "civilized" penalties including "public work" as a new form of punishment for less serious crimes: up to 240 hours of public work for adults and up to 120 hours for minors.[47] President Kuchma signed the new criminal code in May 2001. The death penalty was officially abolished, effective immediately, aligning Ukraine with most European countries.

CONDITIONS FOR DEATH PENALTY REFORM

An important question is how the decision on death penalty abolition was made in this new transitional state, especially when the government and public were alarmed by remarkably growing crime. What motivated this country finally to adopt the council norm? Despite national interest in European integration, Ukrainian society was not prepared psychologically, culturally, and institutionally to accept penal reform, yet it had to comply with normative and compulsory guidelines provided by a European human rights regime. The Ukrainian experience raises the following issues: the role of external leadership, internal leadership, and the insulated institutional setting.

External Leadership

For the Council of Europe, the death penalty is an "unacceptably inhuman and degrading punishment." The council, through both moral persuasion and political pressure, compelled Ukraine to adopt the regionally promoted human rights standard. While issuing various official recommendations and resolutions, the council also worked on closed-door dialogue with Ukraine. Aside from explicit public threats to suspend their membership, a number of private meetings between council officials and the Ukrainian elites were held to persuade them to comply through dialogue and interaction. Through compassion and support rather than ridicule and blame, the meeting sessions helped Ukraine join the abolitionist cause. As Checkel points out, promoting national compliance with international procedures and norms is not just a matter of getting the incentives and threats right. The very process of social interaction within the international organization can promote state compliance by means of "policy dialogues, jawboning, learning, persuasion and the like."[48]

However, no one would deny that the incentive to acquire membership was crucial in Ukraine's compliance with the Council of Europe's human rights standard. In Europe, the council has become recognized as the "gateway" organization for integration in the European Union. Members regard the organization as a path to greater integration with Western countries and eventually aim to join the European Union. Membership in the council is seen as a prerequisite to membership in the European Union, which is a declared ambition of Ukraine. Therefore, membership in the council is clearly important to the interests of this newly independent country: "Without the Council of Europe, the drafting of the new criminal code might have taken years. . . . The European parliament set a condition: If Ukraine didn't give some serious thought to human rights, it could forget about even being a member of the Council of Europe. Kiev responded to this approach: A new version of the code was drafted in just a few months . . ."[49]

Johan Friestedt, an administrator working in Strasbourg on the monitoring performed by the Committee of Ministers, said, "I am not sure how effective it would have been if only one method was used, that is to say, either public threats or diplomatic pressure."[50] Through the complementary efforts of the PACE, with its multiple official warnings and resolutions, and the behind-the-scenes meetings with the Committee of Ministers, the Council of Europe successfully urged the authorities in Kiev to adhere to the standards they accepted when they joined the Council of Europe.

Focusing on the social communication between international institutions and state actors, Checkel writes: "[P]ersuasion is more likely to be effective in promoting compliance when the persuader is an authoritative member of the in-group to which the persuadee belongs or wants to belong."[51] The desire to belong was a crucial incentive. By remaining in good standing with the Council of Europe and building a good reputation in the eyes of its "colleagues," Ukraine was eventually able to seek membership in the European Union. Ukraine knew that, like other Central and Eastern European countries, it would not survive without access to Western Europe's markets, which basically entailed membership in the European community.

The Ukrainian Constitutional Court demonstrated that the decision to abolish capital punishment was based not only on the general rule of human rights, but also on the country's relations with the Council of Europe. According to the court's ruling opinion, removing the death penalty from the criminal code was a major commitment by Ukraine with regard to its membership in the Council of Europe: "Ukraine's joining the Statute of the Council of Europe has confirmed Ukraine's dedication to the 'ideals and principles which are the common property of the European nations.' "[52] A new version of the criminal code was drafted in just a few months after this decision.

Internal Leadership

In seeking to understand the abolition of the death penalty, what emerges most clearly is the critical importance of strong, consistent leadership on the part of the president and other key state authorities. Leadership by the political elites is important, since abolition went against the majority opinion of the people. In any abolitionist countries, elite leadership has been required from the beginning to persuade a reluctant public to accept the abolitionist cause, and yet governmental actions for death penalty reform neither expect nor require public support. It is therefore a central irony that if abolitionist countries were more democratic, they would be much less likely to abolish the death penalty.

Some countries cited the international human rights law and norm when abolishing the death penalty. For instance, in excluding the death penalty from the legal system in 1995, the ruling of the Constitutional Court of South Africa stated that retaining the death penalty was against international human rights standards. With regard to public opinion favoring the death penalty, the court made it clear that a distinction between the wishes of the majority and the role of the state in protecting the rights of the minority should be drawn, especially concerning matters of life and death.[53]

In contrast, Ukraine's case was less voluntary, less norm-based, in that the decision to abolish the death penalty came as a response to the coercive persuasion of the Council of Europe, and not as a normative change. Faced with the proper incentives, namely, accession to the Council of Europe, Ukrainian decision makers engaged in cost-benefit calculations that finally led them to align domestic policy and behavior with conditions set by the Council of Europe. This was a strictly instrumental decision on the part of the Ukrainian leadership.

Insulated Institutional Setting

The Council of Europe coerced Ukraine, and the Ukrainian elite could implement the decision to forego the death penalty without the approval of society. The autonomous and insulated nature of the Ukrainian state institution made it easier for administrative officials to bargain with international and domestic agents in the process of eliminating the death penalty. Ukraine is the largest and the most prominent of the successor states to the Union of Soviet Socialist Republics (USSR) after Russia. Like its Soviet predecessor, Ukraine remains a unitary state with an extremely centralized executive authority. Within the hierarchical structure of three tiers of government—national, regional, and local—regional (*oblast*) and local (*raion*) governments are subordinated to higher-level governments in virtually every respect, even though some elementary features of federalism are present.[54] The "semipresidential" or "presidential-parliamentary" system that was in place from 1991 to 1996 was eliminated. Instead of the "mixed presidential" system, which appeared to be prone to problems of ambiguity and confusion over the separation of powers, and thus appeared to be too weak and fragmented for effective governance, the "semistrong presidential" system was constituted. The president received very broad powers, including extensive control over the government, veto power over legislation, and the authority to appoint the prime minister, certain individual ministers, and the heads of local state administrations, upon the recommendation of the Cabinet of Ministers.

A further extension of the presidential prerogative was proposed by President Leonid Kuchma after his reelection in October 1999. Calling for a referendum on constitutional changes, Kuchma claimed that the then-current constitution gave insufficient power to the president and thus stymied policy initiatives. Proposed changes to the constitution included giving the president the right to dissolve parliament, lifting the immunity of lawmakers, and creating a leaner, bicameral legislature.[55] In a national referendum in April 2000, Ukrainians voted overwhelmingly in favor of strengthening the power of the president at the expense of the parliament, which subsequently led to major political disputes over the distribution of power between the two main branches of government.[56]

Ukraine's centralized state structures, described as "extremely executive-oriented and top-down in nature,"[57] allowed state leadership to take political actions rather easily, even without public support. Such centralization was helpful because policy reform regarding the death penalty was made in the face of growing public opposition. Where political leaders are more susceptible to political controversies and public opinion, as they are in the United States, any political initiatives on penal reform are much more likely to be screened by public sentiment. In most abolitionist countries, public opinion was not a principal factor in the abolitionist cause, partly because the choice between abolition or retention was a legal decision requiring judicial review in the courts, and partly because of constitutional protection for the rights of minorities and others who cannot protect their rights adequately through the democratic process. In Ukraine, the continuing centralization of state structures enabled the president to decree a moratorium on executions without "hearty public support."

CONCLUDING REMARKS

In light of Ukraine's interest in European integration, a debate has focused on how to balance the former authoritarian stance against more liberal methods of deterring crime. Ukraine abolished the death penalty during a dramatic surge of violent crime, indicating that crime rates do not necessarily explain or predict the retention of capital punishment. The hypothesis regarding social inequality seemed compelling, but Ukraine's rejection of the death penalty when economic and social inequalities were rapidly increasing suggests that this thesis does not solely explain why a state either abolishes or retains the death penalty. Nongovernmental organizations and human rights pressure groups, weakly organized and mainly ignored by the government, have had little influence, if any, in empowering the norm against the death penalty in politics and society. The key to understanding death penalty reform in Ukraine lies in the combination of the adamant role of the Council of Europe in attempting to build a death-penalty-free zone in Europe and Ukraine's strategic will to be integrated with the regional community. The Ukrainian institutional setting, autonomous and insulated from society, made it easier for political elites to bargain with international and domestic agents in abolishing capital punishment. Ukrainian discourse and laws on the death penalty had to change in ways consistent with new international understandings promoted by the Council of Europe.

The learning and socialization process plays a substantial role in promoting human rights norms. In Ukraine's case, an ongoing series of monitoring sessions and peer-group persuasion helped the Ukrainian leaders acquire and improve a new understanding of the death penalty system. Perhaps most important, however, the learning/socialization process became more effective because of the material incentives involved. Had either of the two crucial elements—the continuing threats of expulsion from the Council of Europe and the efficiency of persuasion process—been missing, Ukraine would have taken much longer to abolish the death penalty. Although we should recognize the importance of learning and socialization in analyzing state behavior, especially with regard to a state's compliance with norms, we must also acknowledge that material incentives have a profound effect on political behavior. Checkel argued that "elite learning occurs when individuals are taught, *in the absence of obvious material incentives*, new values and interests from norms."[58] But elite learning that is greatly amplified by the process of dialogue or persuasion is more likely to occur when pressure and material incentives *do* exist. Thus, while not denying the importance of the socialization/learning analysis, I argue that the Ukrainian case strongly suggests that material incentives for collaboration provide a most plausible answer to the question of why states are willing to comply with an imposed norm.

At present the debate on the abolition of the death penalty continues unabated in Ukrainian society. Not only the general public, but also some top governmental officials, including Deputy Prosecutor-General Oleksiy Bahanets and State Secretary Oleksandr Hapon, of the Interior Ministry, maintain that criminals have become conspicuously more aggressive since the ban on capital punishment was announced.[59] Instead of sympathizing with widespread sentiment in favor of reinstating the death penalty, in March 2003 the Ukrainian parliament ignored it and ratified Protocol No. 13 to the ECHR, which absolutely bans the death penalty in both peacetime and wartime. Contrary to the idea that national debate on the death penalty is conducted in purely *domestic* terms, Ukraine provides a striking example in which the *international* dimension proved equally significant. Like those who promote the slogan against drunk driving, "Friends do not let friends drive drunk," the Council of Europe does not let friends execute their citizens.[60] Some of the Ukrainian evidence is specific to that country, yet the issues of peer-group pressure, diplomatic persuasion, the learning process, and the motivation to be in harmony with a wider international community were important there, as they are in many other countries that retain the death penalty.

CHAPTER THREE

SOUTH AFRICA

The proclamation of the right and the respect for it [life] demanded from the state must surely entitle one, at the very least, not to be put to death by the state deliberately, systematically and as an act of policy that denies in principle that value of the victim's life.

—Justice Didcott of the Constitutional Court of South Africa

In a landmark decision on June 6, 1995, Arthur Chaskalson, president of the Constitutional Court of South Africa, declared, "Everyone, including the most abominable of human beings, has a right to life, and capital punishment is therefore unconstitutional." The eleven justices of the new Constitutional Court unanimously decided to remove the death penalty from the criminal code and commuted the death sentences of some 450 people to life imprisonment. The opinion of the Constitutional Court, one of the first in the world to abolish the death penalty on the basis of its substantive inconsistency with "the right to life" and other fundamental human rights, signaled a new development in the international movement to end the use of capital punishment. Archbishop Desmond Tutu, the head of the Anglican Church and leading campaigner against apartheid, welcomed this decision, stating: "It's making us a civilized society. It shows we actually do mean business when we say we have reverence for life."[1] Amnesty International remarked: "This historic court ruling puts Africa and South Africa in the forefront of the international movement to abolish the death penalty."[2] Given that the capital, Pretoria (now known as Tshwane), was once called "the hanging capital of the world," the Constitutional Court's ruling took its own constituency and the world by surprise.[3] By choosing the death penalty as the first issue to be ruled on by the post-apartheid Constitutional Court, the justices underscored the importance of that issue in shaping the New South Africa's arrangement of rules, values, and identities.

Yet the ruling did not sit well with all South Africans, prompting outrage among the vast majority of people who felt that the upsurge in crime and violence had devalued these very rights to "life and dignity." Deputy President Frederik de Klerk of the Afrikaner National Party (NP), the predominantly white minority political party that shared power with President Nelson Mandela's African National Congress (ANC), stated that he would use all possible means to reinstate the death penalty. At present, more than ten years after the last execution in South Africa, controversies continue unabated with regard to whether the abolition of the death penalty was good for the well-being of New South Africa.[4] The impact of capital punishment goes beyond its political and legal aspects, having a pervasive effect on the constitution of culture.[5]

The purpose of this chapter is to investigate how South Africa struck down the decades-old practice of executions, examining the basis for its decision and noting who played the key roles. In so doing, I seek to explore how South Africa sought to embed an international human rights norm in the national consciousness. The chapter begins with a discussion of how the death penalty was abused during the apartheid years, emphasizing the fact that state authorities at that time viewed the death penalty not just as a weapon against common crime but also as a political tool for enforcing the system of racial separation. Next, I summarize and evaluate the anti–death penalty movement before the end of apartheid and its political consequences. Following that, I explain how a moratorium on executions was achieved in such a seemingly unfavorable climate of political turbulence and in the face of skyrocketing crime rates. I then examine the process of the formal abolition of capital punishment via judicial review, focusing on the key legal case, *State v. Makwanyane and Mchunu*. The chapter concludes by considering the roles of key actors in death penalty reform.

CAPITAL PUNISHMENT UNDER APARTHEID

The African instruments of execution are, for the most part, the noose and the firing squad, although beheading has been used in Mauritania and the Congo Republic, while the Sudan—where the crucified corpses of criminals are sometimes put on display after they have been hanged—still permits the biblical practices of stoning offenders to death. Hanging was the method of execution employed in South Africa. Dr. Christian Barnard, a famous heart surgeon, described this method of killing as "slow, dirty, horrible, brutal, uncivilized and unspeakably barbaric." He described the process of electrocution, which may take up to twenty minutes before "the end," as follows:

> The man's spinal cord will rupture at the point where it enters the
> skull, electro-chemical discharges will send his limbs flailing in a

grotesque dance, eyes and tongue will start from the facial apertures under the assault of the role and his bowels and bladder may simultaneously void themselves to soil the legs and drip onto the floor.[6]

For forty-six years of apartheid and nearly 350 years of systematic discrimination against nonwhites, South Africa's system of capital punishment had violated norms of customary international law in many ways. More than 4,200 people have been executed since South Africa's political independence from the United Kingdom and the creation of the Union of South Africa in 1910. At the height of the anti-apartheid struggle between 1978 and 1988, when about half of all those executions were carried out, norms of procedural fairness were routinely breached in capital cases.[7] Death sentences and executions were arbitrary and unequal, and the circumstances surrounding executions and the conditions on death row in South Africa certainly violated international norms against cruel and inhuman treatment.

As the death penalty became a sociopolitical tool of repression, the number of capital crimes rose. The high number of capital crimes in turn became a major reason for the sharp rise in executions in South Africa. In 1958, for example, the laws were amended to extend the range of offenses, so that kidnapping, child stealing, treason, rape, robbery with aggravating circumstances, and even housebreaking with aggravating circumstances— offenses that had never before drawn the death penalty—became capital crimes.[8] For the crime of murder, it became mandatory for judges to impose the death penalty. The Criminal Procedure Act of 1977 (CPA) provided that unless the offender was under the age of eighteen, or extenuating circumstances attended the commission of the crime, the court had no option but to impose the death sentence for murder. In practice, it was rare for fresh evidence regarding extenuating circumstances to be introduced, mainly because of the poor quality of legal representation.[9] Judges thus seldom had any choice but to impose the death sentence.

Anti-apartheid political strife was another direct cause of the considerable number of executions for several decades. In the wake of outlawing the ANC and the Pan-Africanist Congress (PAC) after the Sharpeville Massacre in March 1960, and after the abandonment of nonviolence by the liberation movement, the apartheid government started to define both violent and nonviolent political acts as capital crimes.[10] The broadly defined crime of "sabotage" was added to the list of capital crimes in 1962, followed in 1963 by "undergoing training or obtaining information that could further an object of communism" and "advocating . . . economic or social change in South Africa by violent means through the aid of a foreign government and institution."[11] Both the "ordinary" criminal justice system and the draconian state security machine, which became known as the Drastic Process, carried out this sizable wave of political executions. Among those executed in the mid-1960s were about sixty members of the PAC military force. As Barend van Niekerk revealed, South Africa in those years accounted for almost half of the world's known executions.[12]

Politically motivated death sentences were repeatedly imposed until the late 1980s, as in the cases of the Sharpeville Six and the Upington 26. When a township official was killed by a number of people during a political protest in Sharpeville in 1984, the Sharpeville Six, although they had taken no action related to the victim's death, were nevertheless convicted of murder under the "common purpose" doctrine, which means that they were allegedly associated with the acts of a politically motivated crowd despite no direct involvement in the killing. In other words, the Sharpeville Six were determined to have had a "common purpose" with the actual killers.[13] Although the international attention that the case received finally led the government to grant a reprieve to the six defendants in November 1989, five executions for a different case took place that same week.[14] Similar circumstances prevailed in the Upington 26 case, in which a policeman was killed after police teargassed a peaceful assembly in 1989. While one of four persons was believed responsible, twenty-five people were convicted for the murder under the common purpose doctrine, and fourteen of them were sentenced to death.[15]

Numerous leading figures of the ANC, the PAC, and other groups of the liberation movement were sentenced to death and actually executed until the apartheid government fell in the late 1980s.[16] According to an Amnesty International survey conducted between 1985 and mid-1988, more people were executed in South Africa during this time than in any other country in the world save Iran.[17] The underlying motivation of the apartheid government in capital cases was clear. As Nathan Holt points out,

> Capital punishment in South Africa has been viewed as a tool specifically for controlling and punishing opponents of *apartheid*. These motivations are particularly evident in the state's treatment of accused members of banned liberation movements. In 1983, for instance, the execution of three convicted ANC combatants was timed to coincide with the seventh anniversary of uprisings in the black township of Soweto.[18]

The evidence implies that capital punishment in South Africa was the product of neither procedural justice nor racial neutrality. Even without considering political offenses, ample evidence exists that racial discrimination played a significant role in the administration of the death penalty in apartheid South Africa. As early as 1947, for instance, an official law reform commission stated that "capital punishment could not be abolished in view of the 'barbarism' of eighty per cent of the population."[19]

Whites account for about 10 percent of the South African population. In the early apartheid years, between 1910 and 1975, twenty-seven times as many blacks as whites were executed.[20] According to Graeme Simpson and Lloyd Vogelman, for the period between June 1982 and June 1983, of the eighty-one blacks convicted of murdering whites, thirty-eight were hanged. By comparison, of the fifty-two whites convicted of killing whites, only one was hanged, while none of the twenty-one whites convicted of murdering blacks was hanged.[21] In 1990, 270 of the three hundred people sentenced to death were blacks. A study of rape sentencing between 1947 and 1969 found no whites executed for the rape of black women, despite 288 such convictions. During the same period, 120 black men were executed for raping white women, out of 844 convicted for such crimes.[22] The Minister of Justice, C. R. Swart, stated in 1969 that during his tenure no black man had received a reprieve for rape of a white woman.[23] Michael Radelet and Margaret Vandiver confirm the hypothesis that the likelihood of the death penalty being imposed was disproportionately higher when the offender was black and the victim was white than for any other racial combination of victim and offender.[24]

In the sample of prisoners on death row profiled in the Black Sash Research Report in 1989, 90 percent were black. The majority of prisoners in the sample were raised by single parents or by other relatives, and 85 percent of all death row prisoners grew up in families that struggled financially. The vast majority suffered disrupted schooling patterns, and most received no further education or skills training after leaving school. It is difficult to deny that the prevalence of executions in South Africa was part and parcel of the systemic social destructiveness of apartheid.

From the early apartheid years to the late 1980s, the number of executions per year continued to rise almost every year. In the face of increasing momentum for de facto or de jure abolition of the death penalty in other parts of the world, hangings became so much a part of the South African way of life during the whole period of apartheid that statistically a prisoner was hanged almost every other day.[25] Force and terror maintained a system of brutality, and executions became more common than under colonial rule.

THE ABOLITIONIST MOVEMENT AND THE ROLE OF EXTERNAL DONORS

Ellison Kahn notes that abolitionist sentiment in South Africa dates back to at least 1861 when an editorial in *The Friends of the Free Press* asserted, "We are convinced that capital punishment does no good, inasmuch as we believe that the dread of it never deterred a man from committing murder."[26] Opposition to the death penalty was hardly tolerated, however, under the apartheid regime. Professor Barend van Niekerk of Natal University, one of the cofounders (along with Ellison Kahn) of the Society for the Abolition of the Death Penalty in South Africa (SADPSA), was prosecuted in 1970 for "contempt of court" after his two publications in *The*

South African Law Journal. His crime was that he had asked questions and published answers relating to racial prejudice and discrimination in the imposition of the death penalty (*State v. van Niekerk*). A considerable number of his respondents believed that blacks stood a better chance of receiving the death penalty than whites, and a substantial proportion of that number thought that the differentiation was "conscious and deliberate." Even though van Niekerk was acquitted for lack of *mens rea*, academics and reformers were forewarned that publishing such research would not be tolerated. One commentator stated that "[t]here can be little doubt that in the [twenty years after the van Niekerk trial] the warning that the judgment contains has seriously inhibited research into racial disparities in capital sentencing."[27] The abolitionist cause became a forgotten issue in South Africa for almost the next two decades. Not only did van Niekerk's trial discourage any further debates on the subject of capital punishment, but also SADPSA, the first abolitionist organization, became moribund in 1981 with the sudden death of van Niekerk at the age of forty-two.

It is true that there was a marked drop in the number of executions in the years immediately following the van Niekerk case. Concerning this, some argued that the publicity surrounding van Niekerk's prosecution "gave the greatest impetus ever to the abolitionist cause."[28] Yet the rate of executions began to rise again in 1975, and then the government even began to suppress information about executions. As Janos Mihalik points out, the temporary drop in executions may not have been the result of public protest: "The only reasonable conclusion about this marked drop in executions is that public opinion has very little effect on the number of offenders (if any) who are to be executed in a country. . . . The number of executions depends on the judiciary and can be influenced by the executive, which appoints the judiciary and as a last resort may commute sentences if and when the rate of executions seems to it to be too high."[29]

Pressure from outside Africa to promote human rights and the rule of law continued to grow. From the Sharpeville Massacre in 1960 and the Soweto uprising in 1976 to a series of more recent events involving racial repression, including the Uitenhage massacre in 1985, the South African government kept provoking international protests that resulted in economic and moral sanctions. In response to human rights pressure and the shifting attitudes among white South Africans, the government became increasingly concerned with the legitimacy and long-term stability of its apartheid regime. A few reprieves in the 1980s, as in the cases of the Sharpeville Six and Paul Setlaba, were made in the face of strong international human rights pressure.[30]

At the domestic level, the abolitionist cause and calls for an investigation of the death penalty, dormant after van Niekerk's trial, reemerged in the late 1980s. As at least 172 people were executed in 1987—South Africa's highest annual figure ever—domestic protest against capital punishment exploded. The South African Youth Congress, a new anti-apartheid organization, launched a campaign in 1987 focusing on saving the lives of thirty-two political prisoners on death row.[31] A variety of professional organizations joined the abolitionist movement and pressured the government. In 1989 alone, Lawyers for Human Rights, the Death Penalty Monitoring Project, the Institute for Race Relations, the Association of Law Societies, the Society of University Teachers of Law, the General Council of the Bar, and even the Medical Association of South Africa issued statements pleading for an end to capital punishment. Most of these bodies had urged the government to investigate "disturbing aspects of capital punishment" and to place a moratorium on executions.[32] The Families of People on Death Row maintained a high level of campaigning on behalf of all prisoners on death row.[33] The prestigious human rights organization Black Sash published a large number of articles on capital punishment that stimulated public awareness. Most prominently, SADPSA was relaunched in 1988, under the national directorship of Professor Dennis Davis, after the long stagnation following the van Niekerk prosecution. With SADPSA playing a leading role, the aforementioned groups worked jointly in a loose alliance in favor of abolition. They mostly encouraged and produced "advocacy scholarship," conducted practical legal aid, and organized picketing. From a strategic point of view, they believed that persuading two persons was crucial to win the battle for abolition: President de Klerk and the Minister of Justice Kobie Coetsee. They were targeted by telephone, mail, and fax, and received numerous comments and articles produced by abolitionist groups. Members of SADPSA appeared on a number of radio and television programs related to the death penalty and its controversies, and published their comments and research articles in various newspapers and journals.[34]

Around this time, the issue of the death penalty was revived in parliament. In 1988, the Opposition Spokesman for Justice in parliament asked for an investigation into capital punishment, pointing out that even the last director general of the Department of Justice had called for such an inquiry. Although rebuffed, opponents of capital punishment renewed their request for an inquiry during the 1989 session of the Black Houses of Parliament. This was the first time in the history of South Africa that colored parliamentarians had spoken on the death penalty in parliament.[35] In that session, members of the Labor Party, represented in the "colored" House of Representatives, called for a commission of inquiry and, ultimately, the abolition of capital punishment. Arguing that a high incidence of executions is a mark of uncivilized and primitive justice, members of the department of the Democratic Party, represented in the "white" House of Assembly, joined their call for the appointment of a commission of inquiry. A Nationalist parliamentarian took an ambivalent stance stating only that "various views and proposals regarding the death penalty can be exchanged in a positive way."[36] The minister of justice repeated that the death penalty system should remain, even though certain proposals such as the abolition of the mandatory death sentence and the granting of an automatic right of appeal could be accepted after more discussion.[37] There was no grand consensus in the 1988 and 1989 parliamentary debates on the death penalty, yet these controversies in parliament stimulated public awareness, and the abolitionist cause gained momentum. This renewed interest coupled with mass demonstrations against executions placed tremendous pressure on the government to reform its policy on capital punishment.

THE MORATORIUM ON EXECUTIONS

Toward the end of the 1980s the apartheid system could no longer withstand the onslaught of escalating social conflict and the costs of international economic sanctions and diplomatic isolation. The crisis of the apartheid state deepened with the successful "ungovernability" campaign of the United Democratic Front. In the general election of September 1989, the ruling National Party lost support to both left-wing and right-wing opponents and faced a serious threat to its forty-year dominance of white politics. Negotiations with black leaders within an apartheid framework had come to a dead end. More crucially, there was little chance of the ideological and diplomatic sanctions being lifted.[38] The majority of whites continued to desire acceptance by the Western world. If apartheid satisfied their material desires, it increasingly left unrequited the yearning of people for recognition of their own worth and value. Whites in South Africa knew that democratic reform had become the price of admission to the Western world.[39] President de Klerk became convinced that continued coercion was not the solution: only a new political strategy could ensure stability and survival. These conditions partly, or perhaps entirely, explain how de Klerk came to his decision on whether to maintain the apartheid regime.

The almost unbroken upward trend in the annual number of executions during the 1980s, which reached at least one hundred a year, changed in 1989: "only" fifty-three people were executed, and it was the last year of executions in South Africa. The dramatic reduction in executions in 1989 was to a large extent due to presidential reprieves, which numbered sixty-six that year.[40] In his speech to parliament on February 2, 1990, President de Klerk announced that in response to "the intensive discussion [of the death penalty] in the recent months," the law regarding the death penalty would be revised to limit its imposition to extreme cases, to allow the establishment of a special committee to investigate the death penalty, and to allow an automatic right of appeal for those sentenced to death. President de Klerk added that "all executions have been suspended and no executions will take place until parliament has taken a final decision on the new proposal."[41]

With this announcement, the execution of 443 death row prisoners was suspended indefinitely, even though death sentences continued to be passed until 1995 for murder with aggravating circumstances. In the same speech, de Klerk announced that the ANC, PAC, and other opposition groups that had been struggling for freedom were no longer banned. At the same time, he announced the impending release of ANC leader Nelson Mandela. Nine days later, Mandela was finally released from prison, initiating the tortuous process of negotiating the framework for a common future.

A Criminal Law Amendment Bill (B93-30) published in consequence of the president's announcement embodied fundamental reforms to the death penalty system. The new legislation reduced the list of capital crimes to murder, treason in wartime, robbery or attempted robbery with aggravating circumstances, kidnapping, child stealing, and rape. Housebreaking was no longer a capital crime. The imposition of the death penalty became discretionary in all cases where the death penalty was competent; that is, the bill envisaged that the death penalty would be imposed only after a judicial determination of all aggravating and mitigating factors. In addition, the mandatory death sentence for murder where no extenuation is found to be present, and the onus of proof, which required the accused to prove extenuating circumstances, fell away. The new statute also required a mandatory review by the Appellate Division of the Supreme Court for any death sentence, which had not previously been the case. Five-and-one-half months after de Klerk's announcement, on July 27, 1990, the Criminal Law Amendment Act, which included the Death Penalty Act, was published in the government gazette. This new act introduced executive and judicial reconsideration whenever the death sentence was imposed.

Yet the government's views and the abolitionist sentiment still seemed irreconcilable. While the issue of the death penalty was being negotiated, the government attempted to end the moratorium and announced the imminent execution of seventeen condemned prisoners. President de Klerk, who played an important role in reforming South Africa's death penalty policy in the spring of 1990, attempted to push for its restoration exactly three years later. He addressed the opening of parliament in 1993:

> At present a moratorium on carrying out death sentences is in force, with a view to negotiating a bill of fundamental rights. The wave of heinous crimes and murder, the prevailing disrespect for human life and the delays in negotiation make it extremely difficult for the government to allow this moratorium to continue indefinitely. The government is determined . . . to do everything in its power to strengthen the hands of our courts by providing adequate sentencing options, in order to express properly society's aversion to these crimes and to ensure effective application of sentences.[42]

This announcement met with strong criticism; even pro–capital punishment parties argued that it would be better to wait for a new dispensation
to decide the question. President de Klerk succumbed to the pressure and
soon announced that the moratorium would remain in effect.[43] The issue was
sent to the Technical Committee on Fundamental Rights, the drafting committee for the multiparty Bill of Rights. The first suggested draft allowed the
death penalty statute to remain, but provided that no sentence should be
carried out until the adoption of the permanent Bill of Rights by the elected
constitution-making body.[44]

Even after fully democratic elections were held for the first time on
April 27, 1994, which formally brought the apartheid era to an end and
brought a legitimate national government to power, the controversy over the
death penalty continued. The rule that any party winning at least eighty
seats in Parliament was to designate an executive deputy president allowed
Nelson Mandela to share power with de Klerk of the NP. The results of the
elections are shown in table 3.1

The power-sharing government was split on the issue of capital punishment. The predominantly black ANC opposed the death penalty, charg-
ing that it was selectively applied to blacks. Since the late 1980s, leaders of
the ANC had continued to call for a halt to politically motivated death
sentences as an essential condition for negotiations with the white minority
government.[45] Before he came to power, ANC leader Mandela had already
stated that "the death penalty could not be divorced from the policy of
apartheid because statistics indicated more blacks had been executed."[46] On
the other hand, de Klerk's party claimed that, given the remarkable increase
in crime rate, the death penalty should continue to be enforced. Contrary to
Mandela's belief that the death penalty was "a barbaric form of punishment,"
which had not succeeded in reducing crime anywhere in the world, de Klerk
argued that the death penalty could deter crime and violence more effectively than other punishments. This difference in perspectives on the death
penalty between the major parties meant that there was no certainty of a
reprieve under the new administration.

Table 3.1. South Africa's Power-Sharing Government

	Popular vote	Parliamentary distribution
African National Congress (ANC)	62.6%	252 seats
National Party (NP)	20.4%	82 seats
Inkatha Freedom Party (IFP)	10.5%	43 seats

Source: South African Independent Electoral Commission (IEC), "Elections '94." Available
http://www.elections.org.za/.

POLITICAL TRANSFORMATION AND CRIMINAL SOCIETY:
"CRIME IS OUT OF CONTROL!"

Throughout the apartheid years, violence was strategically used to maintain and fortify the privileged position of whites. A radicalized authoritarian order required the use of violent coercion by security forces that served the state rather than the law—as witnessed in the murder and torture of political detainees and the infamous massacres. As Mark Shaw put it, crime and politics in South Africa have been closely intertwined: "[I]n the era of racial domination, apartheid offences were classified as crimes; conversely, those people engaged in 'the struggle,' particularly from the mid-1980s onwards, justified forms of violence as legitimate weapons against the system."[47] Crime in South Africa, at the same time, reflects social and economic inequality. According to Corinna Schuler, the major cause of crime has to do with the gap between the haves and the have-nots: "We have to solve some social problems before we can solve the crime problem."[48]

Political liberalization after apartheid did not bring about better conditions for curbing the crime rate, however. Social theory views crime as one of the common symptoms of the loss or dissolution of a broad social order, as exemplified by the former Soviet countries. South Africa had been awash in crime even though the new and nonracist forms of government struggled toward full democracy and greater equality. While the growth of crime in South Africa began in the early 1980s, it peaked in the early and mid-1990s. Although political violence—except in parts of KwaZulu-Natal—had ended, all types of ordinary crimes characterized the transition era. The violence during the transition period claimed far more lives than did the fight against apartheid itself; more than sixteen thousand lives were lost between 1990 and 1994.[49] Anthony Ginsberg described the crime situation in South Africa as follows:

> A serious crime is committed every 27 seconds in South Africa, a murder every half an hour, a housebreaking every two minutes, and an assault every three minutes. At present only 77 people are arrested for every 1,000 crimes committed. A mere 22% of reported crimes are ever prosecuted. Our prisons cannot even cope with those who are convicted. With more than 4 in every 1,000 citizens in jail, South Africa qualifies as one of the nations with the highest proportion of people in jail.[50]

Social and political controls were loosened and spaces opened that allowed all types of criminal activities to increase. As change proceeded, society and its instruments of social control were reshaped, and new opportunities, bolstered by the legacies of the past, opened up for the development of crime.

According to Schuler, reported rapes have increased by 23 percent and violent assaults by 13 percent in the post-apartheid era.[51] Murder has reached the rate of fifty killings per 100,000 people, which is seven times higher than the murder rate in the United States and ten times higher than the worldwide average. Johannesburg alone recorded the highest murder and rape rates per capita in the world.[52] In September 1996, President Mandela admitted for the first time that crime in South Africa was "spiraling out of control."[53]

Some of those who believed that the official justice system had failed to deter or punish offenders took the law into their own hands. Extragovernmental mechanisms of law and order grew as citizens lost confidence in the power of the state and the police to guarantee a safe environment. Forms of self-protection varied: the wealthier members of society contracted with the private security sector, while less fortunate communities organized groups of vigilantes. Vigilante activities, in particular, occurred sporadically elsewhere in the country. Vigilante groups, composed of both blacks and whites, young and old, conservatives and communists, are widely known for harsh punishment, including whipping, clubbing, and at times the killing of alleged criminals; they are therefore a controversial source of security.[54] For instance, John Magolego's group, Mapogo-a-Mathamaga, grew from a band of one hundred frustrated businessmen in 1996 to an organization with ninety branch offices and some forty thousand members in 1999.[55] One Mapogo member summarized the vigilante movement's philosophy as "an eye for an eye. If you kill somebody in a hijacking, you will be tracked down and killed. Punishment is inflicted in public. The world must know what happens to those who turn to crime."[56]

Although violent crime was a major source of fear among all sectors of the community, public opinion on the issue of the death penalty varied significantly, mainly according to race and income level. Statistics show that people with higher incomes favored a broad application of the death penalty much more frequently than those with lower incomes.[57] Higher-income groups are much more likely to feel vulnerable and therefore respond to violent crime in a more authoritarian fashion. Similarly, one would expect racial groups that have historically been more privileged under apartheid to show a similar response pattern. To be sure, the country's white population is far more in favor of the death penalty than blacks, although a majority of blacks have also favored capital punishment. While whites complained of a spreading sense of impunity, many blacks reacted by noting that they had been disproportionately made victims of the death penalty in the past through wrongful arrests and convictions. With death sentences much more likely to be applied to blacks than to whites under apartheid, the issue of the death penalty has become as emotionally powerful for many blacks as crime has become for many whites. One survey found that, among those against the death penalty, quite a few respondents (45 percent), both blacks and whites, agreed that the death penalty should be abolished because blacks were more likely to be sentenced to death than whites.[58]

THE CONSTITUTIONAL COURT'S RULING ON THE DEATH PENALTY

On August 31, 1990, six people attempted to rob a bank security vehicle in Johannesburg.[59] During the robbery, two occupants of the bank vehicle were killed, and a third was seriously wounded. The robbers also killed two police officers in an accompanying vehicle. Because three of the suspects were later killed by the police, and another managed to escape from police custody, Themba Makwanyane and Mavusa Mchunu were the only two defendants at the subsequent murder trial. On April 14, 1992, the trial court found the two defendants guilty of four counts of murder, one count of attempted murder, and one count of attempted robbery. Two weeks later, they were sentenced to death. As provided for under the new legislation, the Appellate Division automatically reviewed the death sentences, and concluded that the death penalty was indeed "the only proper sentence." However, the Appellate Division referred the case to the Constitutional Court for a determination of whether the death penalty was consistent with the constitution.

At the time of the *Makwanyane* referral, the Constitutional Court only existed on paper: its justices had not yet been selected. President Mandela, who had the power to select and appoint the president of the Constitutional Court, soon chose Arthur Chaskalson, one of his former lawyers and a veteran of the struggle against apartheid, as the president of the Constitutional Court.[60] Prior to this appointment, Chaskalson was the director of the Legal Resources Centre, one of South Africa's most distinguished nongovernmental organizations. Mandela then appointed four sitting justices as members of the Constitutional Court: Justice Richard Goldstone, former chair of the Commission of Inquiry regarding Public Violence and Intimidation, and the prosecutor at the Hague International Criminal Tribunal dealing with war crimes in the former Yugoslavia; Justice Ismael Mahommed, a highly respected judge, who continued to be chief justice of Namibia and president of the Lesotho Court of Appeals; Justice Lourens Ackermann, an authority on international human rights law; and Justice Tole Madala, one of the first black justices of the Supreme Court of South Africa. In 1994, President Mandela chose the final six justices, who were all well known for their strong stance on civil and human rights.[61] Each of the eleven justices—racially diverse and reflecting the population's heritage—had played some role in the long struggle against apartheid.

After the three-day hearing of the *Makwanyane* case, the Constitutional Court unanimously held the death penalty to be unconstitutional. The decision could not be appealed, and thus any attempt to change the

constitution, restoring the death penalty, would be struck down. In a strong
show of support for the ruling, each of the court's eleven justices issued a
written opinion backing the decision on *State v. Makwanyane and Mchunu,*
which was based on a belief that the right to life and dignity is the most basic
of all human rights and the source of all other personal rights in the Bill of
Rights. "With effect from the date of this order . . . the State and all its
organs are forbidden to execute any person already sentenced to death,"
Constitutional Court President Arthur Chaskalson declared.[62] Justice
Chaskalson added, "Retribution cannot be accorded the same weight under
our Constitution as the right to life and dignity. It has not been shown that
the death sentence would be materially more effective to deter or prevent
murder than the alternative sentence of life imprisonment would be."[63] Justice Mahommed suggested that the death penalty affects not only the dignity
of the person about to be executed, but also the dignity of the society as a
whole: "Very arguably the dignity of all of us, in a caring civilization, must
be compromised, by the act of repeating, systemically and deliberately, albeit
for a different objective, what we find to be so repugnant in the conduct of
the offender as a whole."[64]

The justices shared their view that there was no proof the death penalty was an effective deterrent. Opposing the traditional public belief that
the death penalty is a unique deterrent force and that society is safer with
the death penalty than without it, Justice Didcott argued that the statistics
tendered in evidence actually demonstrated that the moratorium had no
effect whatsoever on the murder rate.[65] Noting that the high incidence of
violent crime could not simply be attributed to the failure to carry out the
death sentences, President Chaskalson wrote that the crime wave in modern-
day South Africa was explained by a number of factors, including political
violence, homelessness, unemployment, poverty, and the frustration conse-
quent upon such conditions.[66] Chaskalson stated that the most effective
deterrent is the knowledge that the offender will probably be caught, convicted, and punished, not the very existence of the death penalty.

Most of all, the new Court noted that the death penalty system in
South Africa was seriously flawed, susceptible to error, and unreasonably
wide-reaching. As President Chaskalson stated, "It cannot be gainsaid that
poverty, race, and chance play roles in the outcome of capital cases."[67] "Poverty and race" mean that some are more likely than others to be condemned
to die. Chaskalson emphasized the inadequacy of South Africa's legal aid
system, under which indigent defendants were often represented by inexperienced and poorly paid counsel. "Accused persons who have the money to
do so," explained President Chaskalson, "are able to retain experienced attorneys and counsel, who are paid to undertake the necessary investigations
and research, and as a result they are less likely to be sentenced to death than
persons similarly placed who are unable to pay for such services."[68] Although
such arbitrariness is inherent in all criminal proceedings, the fatal conse-

quences of death penalty cases give this problem paramount importance, for any injustice becomes irrevocable. "Death is different": the death sentence cannot be undone.[69]

Those who wished to remove the death penalty, including the ANC leaders, considered the death penalty a manifestation of the apartheid system. The political regime responsible for extensive use of the death penalty, they argued, had severely curtailed civil and political rights by discriminatory and repressive legislation. The system bred crime through oppressive socioeconomic conditions and denied black defendants due process and adequate legal representation while arbitrarily condemning them to death. With this in mind, the Constitutional Court stated that racial differences in its application were the main reason for abolishing the death penalty. South Africa's ruling on the death penalty was based on, inter alia, the requirement of equal justice.

The majority of South African whites were opposed to the ruling of the Constitutional Court, mainly invoking high crime rates. Former president de Klerk announced that his National Party would campaign to have capital punishment reinstated. Danie Schutte, justice spokesman for the former ruling National Party, stated that the decision "gives out the wrong signal in a country where the crime rate is the highest in the world for a country not at war." "The rights of murderers and rapists are being held in higher regard than those of their victims," claimed another conservative white group. The day after the ruling, one caller on radio talk show remarked: "Under the ANC, the message is that people can commit any crime and get away with it."[70]

A series of negative responses prompted a question as to whether it was necessary to consult the people by means of a referendum before a decision was made regarding the constitutionality of the death penalty. On this question, the Constitutional Court's stance was decisive: public opinion should not be a principal factor that determines the death penalty decision. President Chaskalson admitted that "the majority of South Africans agree that the death sentence should be imposed in extreme cases of murder."[71] Yet he stated that "the question before us . . . is not what the majority of South Africans believe a proper sentence for murder should be. It is whether the Constitution allows the sentence . . . the issue of the constitutionality of capital punishment cannot be referred to a referendum, in which a majority view would prevail over the wishes of any minority."[72] He asserted that the choice between abolition and retention was a legal decision requiring judicial review in the courts. Stating that the constitution protects the rights of minorities and others who cannot protect their rights adequately through the democratic process, including the "social outcasts and the marginalized people of our society," Chaskalson revealed a view of democracy as a system based on a particular set of values that protects the rights of individuals and minorities against the will of the majority.[73]

There is a large gray area between popular democracy and constitutionalism in every society. In the lengthy individual reasons supporting the unanimous conclusion, all eleven justices of the South African Constitutional Court reflected their sensitivity to the tension between their roles in the newly established democratic dispensation and their concern for popular democratic ideology. The members of the court appeared to believe that their duty was to interpret the constitution based on its historical and legal context, not to gauge public sentiment. All the justices addressed this issue, and all concluded that the autonomy of the justices of the court with regard to the will of the majority or public opinion is fundamental to the court's successful operation.

Repealing the death penalty also importantly meant cooperating in an international human rights project. The justices of the South African court were, inter alia, eager to look up international and foreign law precedents in order to compare and contrast their experiences with those of others. Stating that "[t]he movement away from the death penalty gained momentum during the second half of the present century. . . . In some countries it is now prohibited in all circumstances, in some it is prohibited save in times of war, and in most countries that have retained it as a penalty for crime, its use has been restricted to extreme cases," the justices saw themselves as internationalists who can gain from—and in turn reinforce—the entrenchment of such international norms and the emergence of a comparative constitutional law.[74] They also quoted quite a few judicial decisions from the United States. As an observer wrote, "The opinion of the court's president, Arthur Chaskalson, and ten concurring opinions owe much to the writings of American liberal justices, but they also have much to teach the United States."[75]

POST–DEATH PENALTY ABOLITION YEARS: THE DEBATE CONTINUES

Despite (and perhaps also because of) the ruling of the Constitutional Court in *Makwanyane*, the debate about the death penalty continues. Its primary concern is whether the ruling is beneficial in any sense for the New South Africa and, if not, whether a return to the death penalty is necessary. Not surprisingly, reactions are deeply split along racial lines. "[The Court's decision] reflects a sober and humane consideration of the issue, and it is in line with contemporary civilized norms," stated Mandela's African National Congress; "never, never and never again must citizens of our country be subjected to the barbaric practice of capital punishment." On the other hand, whites criticize what many of them say is a gradual slide away from law and order. The main organized bodies that support the restoration of the death penalty include the National Party, the Freedom Front, Inkatha Freedom Party, the Dutch Reformed Church, and the South African Agricultural Union.[76]

The experience of Western Europe suggests that once the abolitionist policy becomes embedded in the national consciousness, public support for capital punishment gradually diminishes, and pressure to reinstate it weakens. After a country has become abolitionist in practice, the death penalty as the subject of widespread debate tends to be forgotten among the public.[77] In South Africa, however, despite the fifteen-year ban on the death penalty, a strong pro-restoration campaign backed by the major opposition party has persisted and remains one of the most vociferous social movements in the post-apartheid era. A national poll in 1999 showed that 91 percent of whites and 68 percent of blacks supported reinstating the death penalty.[78] Even some ANC members support it.

The government has so far successfully resisted considering such a move. Responding in 1998 to public demands for the return to the death penalty as a deterrent to violent crime, Nelson Mandela remarked: "It is not because the death sentence has been scrapped that crime has reached such unacceptable levels. Even if the death sentence is brought back, crime itself will remain as it is."[79] Mandela's interview with the *Independent* is worth quoting at some length.

> Reporter: When you came out of prison, South Africa, like the United States, was high up on the international league of legal executioners. When you came into power one of the first things you did was to abolish the death penalty. But in light of the high crime rate in South Africa there are people, even within your own organization, who mutter about restoring the death penalty in order to combat crime more effectively. What is your position on this issue?
>
> Mandela: I am totally against the death sentence, because it is a reflection of the animal instinct still in human beings. There is no evidence that the death penalty anywhere has brought down the level of crime. What brings down the level of crime is the knowledge, on the part of criminals, that if I commit an offence I will end up in jail. In other words, an efficient police system with the capacity to deter crime, that is what is required. . . . So the death penalty is not the answer. This is also linked to the history of our country. Because the death sentence has been used as an excuse to slaughter human beings in this country because it applied most to blacks and did not affect whites to any large scale, . . . I don't think we will gain anything by bringing the death sentence back. At the back of the minds of the white minority—although there are some blacks who support it—is the idea that the death sentence is going to be used against blacks, not really against whites. Because that is the tradition of the country, even if it is one that we have put behind us now.[80]

Although only a relatively small proportion of the public are willing to put aside their own preferences and accept the decision of the court, observers predict that it will not be easy to reintroduce the death penalty in near future.[81] Mandela's successor, Thabo Mbeki, who has repeatedly declared his opposition to reconsidering the ban, has to make it work and satisfy the expectations of a better life for the victims of the apartheid era in what he terms the African Renaissance.

WHO AND WHAT PLAYED THE MAJOR ROLES?

The long apartheid period has left its imprint on the overall system of social relations, including the law-government relationship, which was characterized by complete subordination of the legal system to the government. The criminal justice system primarily served the government's political objectives. Tied ultimately to the maintenance of racial apartheid, the severe penal code and extensive use of the death penalty at the time were seen as necessary instruments to protect the white minority and to preserve white dominance. The sheer number of those sentenced to death and the apparent arbitrariness of sentencing clearly described the judicial condition of South Africa.

When the apartheid regime had been dismantled, the key sociopolitical issues for the post-apartheid era were federalism versus unitarism; cabinet posts for every 5 percent of the vote versus majority rule; property guarantees versus the right to carry out land reform; freedom of speech versus prohibition of racial hate speech; and question of whether parliament should remain in Cape Town or move to Pretoria or Bloemfontein.[82] The question of the right to life versus the death penalty remained an issue that has plagued post-apartheid governments.

The unprecedented eruption of violent crime in post-apartheid society may well be the key reason for the relentless controversy over the death penalty. The perception of a fearful public that prison is not a sufficient punishment and the demands for heavier penalties for criminals have certainly impeded the abolitionist cause. Despite the complex and violence-stricken social situation, however, the new Constitutional Court outlawed capital punishment. Its reasoning in reaching that constitutional decision and the basis for the decision itself contain a valuable lesson for international human rights advocates concerned with the right to life. This section briefly describes the key actors in death penalty reform.

First, the roles of the two main actors, President de Klerk and Chief Justice Corbett deserve emphasis. It was de Klerk who ordered an investigation of the "whole issue of capital punishment," which resulted in the moratorium in February 1990. Justice Corbett's speech to the Johannesburg Bar in 1989 has often been quoted as evidence of his personal credo: "I believe firmly in the importance of . . . human rights. . . . In the gray areas of uncertainty, . . . I believe that our common law and our legal tradition require that the importance of human rights should be kept well to the fore."[83] Corbett referred to the question of capital punishment shortly after assuming office. Even though de Klerk's stance on capital punishment changed under the power-sharing government in the early 1990s, his initial attitude to death penalty reform and the ultimate decision on a moratorium on executions built a sociopolitical environment where "the unconstitutionality of the death penalty" could mature within five years.

Second, civic organizations played an important role in breaking the long silence on capital punishment. Since the late 1980s, a considerable number of South African civic groups have dedicated themselves to the abolitionist cause, mounting various campaigns and producing detailed accounts of the status of capital punishment in the country. Their relentless abolitionist campaigns and publications have made the public aware of the situation surrounding the death penalty system in South Africa. It is perhaps not coincidental that in the year 1989, when the abolitionist campaign was most vigorous, the number of commutations by the president exceeded the number of executions for the first time since the early 1930s. As Mihalik aptly put it, "It would be naïve to believe that the high number of commutations in 1988 and . . . 1989 was based on considerations of mercy and justice." It was in part the result of the civic groups' faithful and unyielding campaign against executions.[84]

Third, the Constitutional Court, as a key political actor in the democratization process, took the lead in getting acquiescence to an unpopular decision. Breaking from the traditional idea that courts are impotent and often subordinated to the government, the South African Constitutional Court demonstrated its strong initiative and persuasive power. Of course, a few conditions contributed to the court's success. According to Christian Boulanger, these include, first, a particular institutional setting that allows for a strong judiciary. Courts must have the power of judicial review, that is, "the power to declare law made by the legislature or executive orders to contradict the Constitution, or judicial precedent." Second, a court's powers of persuasion also depend upon the position the justices adopt. Their personal experience and political and legal philosophy are therefore important in predicting their success in playing a "countermajoritarian" role. Third, the presence of a strong social pressure group is necessary in promoting the abolitionist cause among the population. Finally, courts need strong support among the political elite in the executive and legislative branches.[85]

In a time of political transformation, the South African Constitutional Court was fortunate that these conditions were present and allowed it to serve as a protector of a civilized legal system against a determined majority. Reflecting the divergent voices of the South African society and committing to a vision of judicial activism in order to satisfy democratic and human rights aspirations, the Constitutional Court became an effective partner in the social transformation envisioned by the constitution. As William Schabas notes, "the [South African] Court could do no better than to position itself as the judicial component of Nelson Mandela's social revolution."[86] Anticipating the inevitable public disaffection, the court moved quickly to establish its voice among the country's new political structures and to engender public support for its role. The task required the jurists to have courage and conviction.[87]

Last but not least, the crucial role of the ANC leadership cannot be overstated. Indeed, the apartheid experience, especially the prison experience of the ANC leadership, caused them to reconstruct their view of the death penalty, which they now consider as a relic of a barbarous past that has no place in a civilized legal system. They believe capital punishment should be assessed in light of "the evolving standards of decency that mark the progress of a maturing society."[88] That view goes beyond a sophisticated calculation of how changing the death penalty policy and system would affect national interests. The value of human personality reached deeper, and it reconstituted leaders' identities and preferences around the issue of capital punishment. The beliefs and ideas of the political leadership were strong enough to make them operational in policy analysis regarding the death penalty, as Franklin Zimring aptly points out:

> The abolition of the death penalty in South Africa . . . was not a complacent gesture by a nation where violent crime was under control. It was a high-stakes statement of principle at a time when violent crime was one of the major threats to nation building after apartheid. Such exemplary abolitions helped the anti–death penalty voices take a monopoly hold on the moral high ground in the 1990s.[89]

CONCLUSION: THE POLITICS OF PRINCIPLE

Ultimately, legal abolition of capital punishment in South Africa depended upon the civic, judicial, governmental, and moral commitment to respect the sanctity of human life. Those involved with the movement to end state-sanctioned killings acknowledged that the death penalty violated the norm upholding such fundamental rights as the right to life, the right to equality, the right to dignity and the protection against cruel, inhuman, or degrading treatment or punishment. As there is a certain relationship between the degree of human misery and constitutional progress, Justice Albie Sachs, a longtime anti-apartheid advocate, has suggested that the experience of such widespread abuses of human rights may be necessary to make a polity realize the fundamental importance of constitutionally protecting human life and dignity from state-sanctioned killings. In his concurring opinion in the Makwanyane case, Sachs wrote that "Germany after Nazism, Italy after fascism, and Portugal, Peru, Nicaragua, Brazil, Argentina, the Philippines and Spain all abolished capital punishment for peacetime offenses after emerging from periods of severe repression. They did so mostly through constitutional provisions."[90]

Many other countries in Africa still retain the death penalty for certain crimes and resort to it with varying frequency. Like the rest of the globe,

African countries have persisted in arguing that capital punishment is a deterrent against crime and that their people support it.[91] In the African context, in particular, it is easy for those who favor the death penalty to argue that the complexity of life should take precedence over "imported universal slogans." For them, African cultural features and economic realities, such as entrenched religio-ethical attitudes toward crime, along with widespread infectious diseases, high infant mortality and maternal morbidity rates, are far more significant in determining how a human life is valued. Responding to this argument, abolitionists point to the endemic violence that has plagued large sectors of the continent, in precisely those countries where executions are freely carried out. From this point of view, the very fact that the state kills its own citizens contributes to the low value Africans appear to place on human dignity and physical integrity. Whichever view is correct, South Africa's action has encouraged the debate over the continued practice of the death penalty in Africa. In the past decade, Gambia, Mozambique, and Namibia removed capital punishment from their statute books. Following those countries, Angola, Guinea-Bissau, Djibouti, Mauritius, and Côte d'Ivoire joined the trend toward full abolition.[92] This is certainly remarkable, given that not a single African country fully abolished the death penalty until the early 1990s, although some used it sparingly or not at all. In this climate, it is very likely that the debate on whether to reintroduce the death penalty in South Africa may decide the fate of death row prisoners in other African countries not only because of this country's leading role in industry and commerce but because of the impact that Mandela and the "miracle" of South Africa's liberation have had on the hearts and minds of Africans everywhere.

CHAPTER FOUR

SOUTH KOREA

We now desire to abolish a system that allows one human being to take away the life of another in the name of law and, thus, effectuate a renewed sense of respect for life and human rights in this society.

—Rep. Chyung Dai-chul, initiator of the 2001 abolitionist bill

Although hatred of them [killers] is understandable, it cannot match the feeling of desperation of those wrongly convicted and sentenced to death.

—Rep. Yoo Ihn-tae, initiator of the 2005 abolitionist bill

In stark contrast to the worldwide abolitionist trend, the death penalty remains most entrenched in East Asia. China is the world leader in the frequency and scope of its use. This country alone regularly accounts for more executions than all other countries combined, and applies it to as many as seventy crimes—ranging from counterrevolutionary sabotage to selling a panda skin, and from tax evasion to murder. The intentional spreading of the SARS virus was also added to the list of capital crimes.[1] Although the government guidelines reserve the death sentence for extreme cases only, provincial courts apply it massively and inconsistently and without much regard for due process. The official number of executions is a tightly held state secret each year. Yet Amnesty International has been able to document 2,468 executions in China in 2001, 1,060 in 2002, and 726 in 2003. The apparent downward trend was reversed in 2004, when the number of executions went up as high as 3,400, with the actual figure believed to be even higher.[2] Since the Strike Hard anticrime campaign was launched in 1996, in particular, Chinese authorities have dramatically increased the use of the death penalty.[3]

China's enthusiasm for capital punishment finds an echo in other East Asian countries. After a three-year hiatus from 1990 to 1992, Japan has executed several people every year for the past decade. Executions take place in strict secrecy, usually when the Japanese Diet (Parliament) is in recess, in order to avoid parliamentary debate and publicity. Taiwan has been one of the top ten executioners over the years; thirty-eight criminals were executed in 1997, thirty-two in 1998, twenty-four in 1999, and seventeen in 2000, which amounts to more executions per capita than in the United States.[4] In the Philippines, President Gloria Arroyo lifted an almost four-year moratorium on executions in December 2003. Singapore imposes mandatory death sentences for murder, treason, firearm offenses, and drug trafficking. Despite a relatively low crime rate compared with other Asian nations, at least 420 people have been executed in Singapore since 1991, giving the small city-state by far the highest per capita rate of executions in the world.[5] According to a Singapore representative to the United Nations, the maintenance of capital punishment for the purpose of controlling drug trafficking is "an important precondition for the preservation of human dignity and the promotion and enjoyment of other human rights," and therefore "capital punishment itself is not a human rights issue."[6] The persistence and prevalence of executions in Asia confirm that the death penalty is far from dying out and the road that leads in the direction of complete and universal abolition is still quite long. As Franklin Zimring put it, contrary to Europe, which is a "death-penalty-free zone," the Asian continent is almost an "abolition-free zone."[7]

Yet, the Republic of Korea (South Korea) appears to have been following a different path over the past few years, in terms of both the social attitude surrounding the death penalty and its actual use.[8] The government has not carried out a single execution since December 1997. In legislation, bills on the abolition of the death penalty have been presented to the National Assembly three times, in 1999, 2001, and 2005. Major religious groups, individually and jointly, have mounted anti–death penalty campaigns. The growing abolitionist movement in Korea stands in marked contrast to its authoritarian past, during which the death penalty was regularly imposed on political dissidents as well as common criminals.

This chapter examines a change in the cultural and societal context surrounding capital punishment in Korea, focusing on the way in which the system of capital punishment was symbolically constructed, enforced, and finally challenged. The chapter begins with a brief overview of how capital punishment was enforced as a powerful social institution in the contemporary history of South Korea. For this, I touch briefly on relevant highlights of Korean history, including the dominance of military authoritarian regimes and drastic economic growth. Using this as a backdrop, I move on to trace the evolving trend regarding the death penalty in Korea. Given that democracy implies the promotion and protection of individual freedoms and rights, I explore whether, and to what extent, the evolving social norm regarding the death penalty is associated with democratic institutional and behavioral changes. In light of the persistent imposition of death sentences, although actual executions are suspended, I go on to ask why even a responsive, accountable, civilian government has not committed itself to reformining penal policy. The chapter seeks to describe key obstacles encountered by political leaders in proposing and implementing the human rights norm against capital punishment. The concluding section draws out some of the chapter's wider implications.

DICTATORSHIP, ECONOMIC MIRACLE, AND HUMAN SECURITY (1948–1987)

Korean criminal law traditionally recognized the death penalty as a statutory penalty for most crimes against the national interest and for murder, robbery, and the "theft of national treasures." Since Korea's first republic in 1948, 902 people have been executed by the general courts. This number does not include anonymous executions carried out by the military court. Frequent use of the ultimate sanction and other oppressive penal means was often taken for granted under a series of upheavals that characterized the South Korean modern political landscape—associated with, among other things, Japanese colonial rule, the division of the nation, and the thirty years of military-dominated authoritarian rule.

Although opinions differ regarding the precise weight to be given to the influences of Korea's modern political culture, it is agreed that the long history of patrimonial-bureaucratic government and the subsequent colonial experience were a poor preparation for the emergence of a human rights regime in South Korea. The liberation from Japanese colonial rule in 1945 created a geopolitical vacuum in northeast Asia, and neither of the two superpowers, first the United States and then the Soviet Union, was willing to relinquish political hegemony to the other or to Koreans themselves. In less than five years, the interaction of these forces, internal and external, led to a devastating civil war, in which an estimated one million civilian lives were lost. What the war left to Koreans was not only the loss of beloved families and mistrust and fear of each other but also the formidable military and security apparatus. The strong penal system was used more as a tool for suppressing political dissent than for punishing common offenders. When the Universal Declaration of Human Rights was launched in the international community in 1948, South Korea passed its National Security Law (NSL) in the very same year. This draconian law banned any acts "praising" or "benefiting" the enemy (generally meaning North Korea) and even the vaguest expression of sympathy for communism. Violators of the NSL were subject to harsh punishment, including the death penalty. Given Korea's geopolitical condition, the fear of (alleged) communist subversion provided the authoritarian government with many excuses to deploy its forces against antigovernment protests.

Until 1987, when Korea began a process of democratization, more than half of those executed had been convicted of violating the National Security

Law, the Anti-Communism Law, and/or the Special Law for Safeguarding the Nation.[9] The various security-related legal measures meant that executions occurred largely within the judicial framework. As Frank Gibney remarked, the human rights situation in Korea under the authoritarian governments was a "legalized lawlessness," because "repression was justified by law, wherever possible." The authoritarian presidents knew how to keep up the appearance of a constitutional democracy.[10] Darren Hawkins is correct in saying that "many . . . authoritarian governments have a stronger interest in legitimacy than most analysts realize."[11] South Korea was no exception. The "legitimate" use of the death penalty was, indeed, a major social control mechanism employed against those who refused to collaborate.

For more than thirty-two years (1961–1993), military governments ruled the society. During a great part of his tenure from 1961 to 1979, President Park Chung-hee kept almost all political activities, labor unions, and popular movements of any sort under tight control. All the coercive or persuasive powers of the Korean Central Intelligence Agency (KCIA) and the nationwide network of "anticommunist" or other pro-government and neighborhood organizations were thoroughly mobilized in support of the military governments. A certain sense of reality and understanding of the nature of society can be constituted and maintained through political discourse. Park claimed that an essential obligation of all citizens was to subordinate themselves to the state to ensure its survival. For the survival of the nation, therefore, the most coercive judicial measures should be freely exercised, according to Park. The authoritarian regimes continued to use the rhetoric of national security as a rationale for restrictions on civil rights and liberties and to justify coercive punishment. President Park's statements in the mid-1970s demonstrate the values considered most important in this security-sensitive society: "If we wish to develop our democracy and to enhance the basic human rights of individuals, while also maintaining freedom and peace, we ought, first of all, to protect all such values from the threat of the North Korean communists. . . . If we indiscreetly pursue freedom we will be deprived totally of the freedom of survival by the North Korean communists. We are doing our best to prevent this tragedy from occurring."[12]

In contrast to traditional modernization theory, which assumes a positive correlation between economic development and democracy, the success of modernization and economic growth did not entail any corresponding political liberalization or democracy in South Korea.[13] During a period of drastic national transition from an agrarian to a largely industrialized society, Korea relied heavily on cheap labor and high productivity. Individuals were compelled to sacrifice themselves for the sake of economic prosperity for the whole society. Trade union rights and the right to strike were held in check by harsh labor laws. The independent trade union movement was considered leftist, aiding North Korea, which would ultimately become a major threat to national security and economy. Contrary to the predictions of modernization theory, Korea's industrialization process consistently involved gross violations of human rights, which, in turn, caused social disintegration. Human rights violations were justified in the name of political and social stability, yet they undermined this stability because the denial of basic civil rights provoked political discontent and opposition among the people. This led to a vicious circle of excessive emphasis on stability, human rights violations, and additional political and social instability. President Park claimed that Korea should "resort to undemocratic and *extraordinary* measures in order to improve the living conditions of the masses.... [O]ne cannot deny that people are more frightened of poverty and hunger than totalitarianism...."[14]

Under these sociopolitical conditions, the traditional role of law and the judiciary is to enforce punishments. As David Steinberg points out, a wide variety of punishment options in Korea were seen "as the weapon of an administration against those who were obviously guilty of circumventing societal norms."[15] The death penalty was routine under the authoritarian regimes, as Figure 4.1 illustrates, and it was regularly abused for political purposes. The spikes in the number of executions in 1972 and 1974, for instance, occurred when President Park's measures to suppress resistance were at their peak. In October 1972, Park proclaimed martial law, suspended the constitution, forbade political activity and imposed rigid press censorship. In addition, he introduced the seventh set of constitutional reforms in order to create the *Yushin* ("revitalizing reform") Constitution, which, among other things, permitted the president an unlimited number of six-year terms.

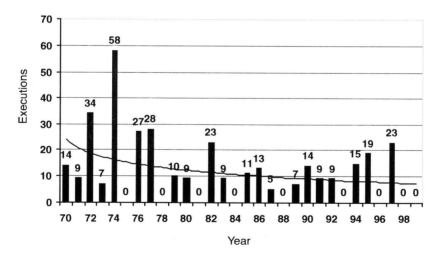

Source: Korea National Statistical Office (KNSO), quoted in In-sup Han, "*Yeoksajuk Youmoolroseoui Sahyung* [The Death Penalty as a Historical Artifact]," *Samok* (Seoul: Catholic Bishops' Conference of Korea), 28.

Figure 4.1. Number of Executions in South Korea, 1970–1997

Death sentences were imposed to demonstrate that offenses against the public order would be dealt with severely, as in the *Inhyugdang* (People's Revolutionary Party) case.[16] In June 1964 Park declared martial law when public protests arose against the government's submissive diplomacy in relation to Japan. At the same time, the KCIA asserted that an established secret revolutionary group known as *Inhyugdang* was conducting "spy activities" and leaking national secrets to North Korea. When investigation revealed that the people in this case had confessed under severe torture, however, fourteen of the twenty-six people indicted were found to be innocent and released, and only one was sentenced to a three-year imprisonment. This became known as a fabricated espionage case and was forgotten for a decade. Yet ten years later, in 1974, when Park's obsession with the presidency drove him to change the constitution in order to remove the term limits on the presidency, the government suddenly brought up this case again. This time, the members of *Inhyugdang* were accused of attempting to overthrow the military regime of Park Chung-hee. Unbearable torture and fictional evidence resulted in eight people being sentenced to death, and less than twenty-four hours after the verdict, all eight were hanged. Since their executions were carried out under martial law, they were not even included in the death penalty statistics (See Figure 4.1: no executions in 1975).

Politically motivated death sentences continued in the 1980s. In May 1980, the most fierce and sustained street demonstrations took place in Kwangju, the capital of South Cholla Province, against unjust and oppressive authorities and full martial law administered by General Chun Doo-whan. At the peak of the demonstration, three hundred thousand people, almost the entire population of the city of Kawanju, joined in demanding democracy and the rule of law. Paratroopers commanded by Chun subjected Kwangju's citizens to a most barbaric carnage. Government estimates suggested that between two hundred and four hundred people died; eyewitnesses and a 1986 Asia Watch report suggested a more likely figure of two thousand.[17] The government accounts of the time portrayed the demonstration as "unlawful rioting by the communists" controlled by "North Korean spies and their collaborators who infiltrated into Kwangju."[18] About one hundred people were charged under martial law in connection with the uprising shortly after the bloody incident, and a quarter of them were summarily sentenced to death. Among those was Kim Dae-jung, who was then a strong opponent of military dictatorship and later became the fifteenth president of Korea. He was convicted of conspiracy in managing the Kwangju uprising.[19] When his death sentence was commuted in January 1981, Kim was forced to leave the country instead. During his stay in the United States as a political exile, Kim was interviewed by the *Journal of International Affairs* and expressed his views on human rights and the right to life: "[M]easures such as release and reinstatement cannot be called improvements in the human rights situation. Only when human rights are gained as a basic right of the people can we say that there is an improvement in human rights. Human rights are not the charity of dictators. Life is not a thing to be given as charity from dicta- tors."[20] Believing that violence begets more violence and that the death penalty contributes to the cycle of violence, he later became the first Korean president under whose administration no one was executed.

DEMOCRATIC TRANSITION AND THE CONTINUING USE OF THE DEATH PENALTY (1987–1997)

The prolonged authoritarian regimes could not endure as the dangerous ten- sion between the state and civil society increased. On June 29, 1987, Roh Tae-woo, presidential candidate of the ruling Democratic Justice Party (DJP), announced his intention to permit political liberalization, which was re- garded as a surrender to an oppositional civil society alliance among student groups, trade unions, and religious organizations. The June 29 announce- ment was not only a cornerstone of political development but also a symbol of civil society's long overdue victory. From that moment on, a succession of political events radically reshaped the political power structure. As state repression substantially declined, citizen's movements were organized around a wide variety of issues, including economic justice, environmental integrity, fair elections, consumers' rights, and gender equality. Such organizations as the Citizen's Coalition for Economic Justice and the Korean Federation for the Environmental Movement were formed and gained increased public at- tention and support in the early years of democratic transition.

Despite a wide variety of reform programs affecting the society, how- ever, capital punishment did not appear on the agenda. Political convicts were still sentenced to death. Among those were two college students, Yang Dong-hwa and Kim Song-man, who were found guilty in 1991 of meeting North Korean officials either in North Korea or in a third country and of receiving instructions for antigovernment student movements.[21] Executions continued for about a decade, and from the moment South Korea formally entered a new stage of democratic transition in 1987 until the last execu- tions in 1997, 101 people were put to death.

The Seventh Republic (1993–1997) of Kim Young-sam, the country's first truly civilian leader since 1961, promised extensive reforms in order to deepen democracy and improve accountability. Significant democratic experi- ments proceeded under Kim's presidency, from outlawing all anonymous finan- cial transactions to reshaping civil-military relations, and from encouraging the activities of civil society groups to recruiting several high-ranking public offi- cials from citizens' movements. Concerning penal reform, however, the new government made no difference; instead, civilian President Kim endorsed execu- tions even more strongly than his predecessor, Roh. During Roh's tenure from 1988 to 1992, there were thirty-nine legal executions, but under Kim's admin- istration, fifty-seven prisoners were killed, including the twenty-three convicts who were executed in a single day (on December 30, 1997), which was the worst mass hanging in one day in the past twenty years.[22]

Among the 101 people executed in Korea between 1987 and 1998, there was no one who had graduated from college: twenty-five had graduated from high school, thirty from junior high school, forty from elementary school, and six had no education.[23] That no college graduates were executed in this period can be partly explained by the fact that no political convict has been executed since 1987. It also demonstrates, however, that those with less education and low socioeconomic status are unable to afford good legal representation and are thus more likely to be sentenced to death. Korea is thus like most retentionist countries, which often impose the death penalty disproportionately on members of disadvantaged social groups in a discriminatory fashion.

THE EMERGENCE OF THE ABOLITIONIST MOVEMENT

The history of anti–death penalty activism in Korea is short. As Amnesty International reported in the late 1980s, Korea had no organized abolitionist movement; only a small number of defense lawyers and judges developed critiques of the death penalty. The activity of the International Human Rights League of Korea, the first organization to publicize its anti–death penalty stance, was confined to conducting several surveys on capital punishment.[24] Even human rights activists did not regard the death penalty as a human rights issue; it was a matter relating to the penal system. Until the late 1980s, the death penalty was not the subject of national debate, nor did anti–death penalty activism exist.

With democratization well on its way, however, demands for the reform of the inhuman penal practice began to grow. Less than a year after the aforementioned Amnesty International publication, which had noted the absence of the abolitionist movement in South Korea, the first Korean anti–death penalty organization was formed in April 1989. It was not a coincidence that the abolitionist movement emerged in the same year that the United Nations General Assembly adopted the Second Optional Protocol to the International Covenant on Civil and Political Rights Aiming at the Abolition of the Death Penalty. Inspired by democratic progress at home and an evolving standard of human rights internationally, the Association for the Abolition of Capital Punishment, or Sapehyup, became operational in Korea. Its members came from the academic and legal communities, and some were from religious groups that had worked with prisoners sentenced to death. A group of defense lawyers in Sapehyup, notably including lawyer Lee Sanghyug, helped people accused of capital crimes. Sapehyup summarized its main purposes as follows: "First, to effectuate the Constitutional Court's judgment that capital punishment is unconstitutional by filing a constitutional appeal with the Court; Second, to prohibit capital punishment by law by filing a legislative petition concerning abolition of capital punishment with the National Assembly."[25]

Sapehyup actually filed three petitions, in 1989, 1990, and 1996, requesting review of the constitutionality of the death penalty.[26] The repeated petitions fostered more deliberation and ample consideration in the court. The 1996 appeal, filed by Chong Sok-bong, who was sentenced to death for murder and pleaded that the death penalty of Criminal Court Clause 250 was an infringement of the human right to life and physical integrity, succeeded in publicizing the question of whether capital punishment was legitimate. Seven of the nine justices asserted that the death penalty violates neither the principle of proportionality nor the constitution, ruling that the current system of the death penalty was constitutionally legal. The majority of justices noted that "[t]he death penalty system is inevitably selected by the nation as a necessary evil." As part of this "necessary evil" argument, they suggested that the death penalty had deterrent and retributive effects.

Unlike the previous cases, however, the 1996 decision included the minority opinion of two justices who believed the death penalty to be inhumane, cruel, and unconstitutional. According to Justice Kim Jin-woo, one of the dissenters on the Constitutional Court, cruel and inhumane punishment that deprives a citizen of life is incompatible with the Constitution of Korea, Article 10 of which states: "All citizens are assured of human worth and dignity and have the right to pursue happiness. It is the duty of the State to confirm and guarantee the fundamental and inviolable human rights of individuals."[27] For Justice Kim, capital punishment is inhumane in the sense that it infringes on the freedom of conscience and dignity of the judges who have to sentence in capital punishment cases and of the people in charge of actual executions. The other dissenter, Justice Cho Seung-hyung, stated that the death penalty violates the proviso of Article 37 of the constitution, which declares: "The freedoms and rights of citizens may be restricted by law only when necessary for national security, the maintenance of law and order, or for public welfare. Even when such restriction is imposed, no essential aspect of the freedom or right shall be violated." According to Justice Cho, the death penalty fails to conform to a central meaning and purpose of punishment, which is to make a criminal understand and repent the crime committed and return to society.[28] The 1996 ruling was significantly different, again, in that the court included a remark on the possibility of change in the future: "Regardless of its constitutionality the debate on the death penalty should be continued. Once a broad national consensus is achieved with the shift of social and cultural attitudes, the death penalty can be and should be eliminated from the Criminal Code."[29]

Given that an independent judiciary is central to democratic governance, it will be interesting to see whether the South Korean Constitutional Court will be willing to take the lead in reshaping the authoritarian penal system that has infringed on human rights, following the example of the

Constitutional Court of South Africa. The South Korean judiciary was never autonomous, and the normative power of the constitution has always been weak.[30] The constitution has so far been amended nine times. All the amendments, with exceptions in 1960 and 1987, were intended to extend the term of office of the incumbent president or to provide ex post facto justifications of a military coup d'etat (1961 and 1980). The courts were subservient to the executive branch, and significant judicial decisions were greatly influenced by the executive's recommendations. This legal tradition has always made judiciary leadership or action to reform the death penalty seem very unlikely.

CHANGING POLITICAL CONDITIONS FOR DEATH PENALTY ABOLITIONISM (1998–PRESENT)

When Kim Dae-jung, a persistent advocate of democracy and human rights and later a recipient of the Nobel Peace Prize, won the 1997 presidential election in South Korea, a number of observers commented that his victory indicated the increasing maturity of Korean democracy.[31] For David Steinberg, the election was a national triumph in a trough of despondency over the sudden economic debacle of those years: "[T]he most free presidential election . . . result[ed] in the first peaceful transfer of power to an opposition political party through the elective process in South Korean history, and [was] an event even quite rare among all Asian nations."[32] It was, at the same time, a result of President Kim's personal desire for democratic consolidation. John Kie-chiang Oh remarked: "In terms of the suffering that one man could endure and survive, Kim is probably rivaled by only one other person alive, Nelson Mandela of South Africa."[33]

Nevertheless, a number of problems in the area of human rights remained unsolved during Kim's tenure from 1998 to 2002. Most important, legislative reform to ensure fundamental human rights, including the right to freedom of expression and association, was still lacking. Owing mainly to the economic structural changes conducted as part of an International Monetary Fund reform package following the economic crisis in 1997, conflicts and tensions among labor unions, corporations, and the government were only growing. Hundreds of trade unionists were arrested and harassed. Despite the release of most political prisoners after several amnesties, a few dozen political prisoners continued to be detained under the vaguely worded provisions of the National Security Law. Approximately 1,600 conscientious objectors to military service—most of them Jehovah's Witnesses—were imprisoned because the option of alternative service is not available.[34]

Notwithstanding the remaining problems, international and domestic human rights groups have commended the general improvement regarding human rights in Korea.[35] The establishment of both the Presidential Truth Commission on Suspicious Deaths and the National Human Rights Commission was seen as an important step in increasing human rights protection and awareness in the country. The truth commission, the presidential advisory body established in 2000, shed light on the mysterious deaths of people allegedly involved in democratization movements in the 1970s and 1980s. The National Human Rights Commission, established in November 2001, has committed itself to improving the human rights conditions of everyone, especially minority groups. President Kim also took a different stance with regard to cultural constraints on human rights. When leaders in many other Asian countries—notably Lee Kuan Yew of Singapore—advocated "Asian values," challenging international human rights norms as a Western ideological imposition, Kim staked out a position defending the universality of human rights.[36]

With regard to the death penalty, no death row inmate has been executed since President Kim Dae-jung came to power in 1998, and thirteen death sentences have been commuted to life imprisonment in three separate special amnesties during his tenure.[37] During his presidential campaign, Kim stated, in an interview with the Seoul Catholic archdiocesan weekly *Pyonghwa Shinmun*, that the death penalty should be gradually phased out.[38] Among his reasons were that it was ineffective in preventing crimes and that state-sanctioned executions contributed to the low value that Koreans appear to place on human life and dignity. Kim's personal background, as a Roman Catholic who had himself spent time on death row under the military government, perhaps strengthened his belief in the abolitionist cause. Yet, during his presidency, no official statement was ever made regarding the death penalty, let alone any actual effort to reform the penal system. Knowing that the vast majority of the public favored capital punishment, the president did not want to risk losing popularity by directly expressing his opposing view. Even if he was recognized as one of the most progressive politicians in Korea and deserved credit for his role in the furtherance of human rights, his individual belief did not prevail over the obstacles to reforming the death penalty system.

THE ABOLITIONIST CAMP: CATHOLIC CHURCH, AMNESTY INTERNATIONAL, AND LEGISLATORS

The activities of *Sapehyup*, the first anti–death penalty organization, did not reach the mainstream public or popular consciousness. For more than ten years, the organization confined its activities to lectures in law schools or among legal circles, and handled the subject on a case-by-case basis, lacking a coherent strategy. It was not until the late 1990s that the death penalty became a subject of public debates and the abolitionist cause started to gain public attention. The anti–death penalty movement gained strength through the leading roles of three actors: the religious community, Amnesty International and its Korean branch, and legislators.

While secular human rights groups have been silent regarding death penalty reform from, the religious community has taken the lead in the abolitionist movement. Korea has no single, dominant religion; Shamanism, Buddhism, Confucianism, and Christianity coexist there, making Korea, "one of the most religiously pluralistic countries in the world."[39] Buddhism, Protestantism, and Catholicism are considered the three major religions, while Confucianism remains a set of overarching ethical codes rather than a religion. One foreign observer notes that the Korean scenery includes a plethora of churches and temples scattered across the nation: "Large Christian Churches may be found in any city or town. At night, one may look into a skyline and see numerous neon crosses lighting the sky in a single vista. . . . Buddhist temples are also abundant. Most neighborhoods have at least one small temple, and ancient temples dating as far back as the ninth century may be found in many prefectural and national parks."[40]

The religious community is traditionally a key opinion leader in Korean society. Christianity, in particular, played a role in putting a great deal of pressure on dictators to respect human rights and to hold democratic elections. The Catholic Church, during a time of fierce repression, was alone in raising its voice on behalf of freedom and democracy. Myongdong Cathedral, the spiritual center of Catholicism, located in downtown Seoul, still serves as a staging area for protests and demonstrations against large corporations or the government. The Catholic community, especially the Korean Bishop's Committee for Justice and Peace, and the Social Correction Apostolate Committee of Seoul, has been using its social influence to raise public awareness on the issue of the death penalty. Most of all, the Catholic leaders have frequently visited politicians and asked them to introduce appropriate legislation for abolition. When a special bill commuting the death penalty to life imprisonment was presented to the National Assembly in 2001, Cardinal Stephen Kim Sou-hwan, the country's top Roman Catholic leader, met with the head of the Korean legislature, National Assembly Speaker Lee Man-sup, to urge support for the bill. According to Cardinal Kim, no one has the right to take another life; the death penalty undermines human dignity and should not be used as a tool of punishment. He added that Korea should be the first Asian country to abolish the death penalty.[41] Though Representative Lee expressed reservations about the bill, saying that lawmakers should spend more time discussing it before deciding on this crucial matter, the meeting attracted wide public attention. It had been rare for top religious leaders and politicians to exchange their opinions on the death penalty. In seeking to gain public support, the Catholic Church organized a national lecture tour and held a petition drive entitled "Cherish Life by Abolishing Capital Punishment." With the start of the "Year of Jubilee" in 2000, the church named that year the "Year of the Abolition of Capital Punishment." Public response to the campaign was encouraging: more than one hundred thousand signatures were collected within a year before other religious groups were asked to join the effort.[42]

Although not as active as the Roman Catholic Church, other religious bodies have joined the abolitionist cause. The Protestant Church established its own anti–death penalty organization, the "Korean Christian Counsel for Capital Punishment Abolition Campaign," with members from both liberal and conservative denominations.[43] The Buddhist community has also established an organization, the "Buddhist Committee for the Anti–Death Penalty Campaign." At the end of 2000, the Catholic, Protestant, Buddhist, Won Buddhist, and Chongdogyo cooperated to launch a nationwide, pan-religious campaign against capital punishment. Their religious faith, as an important source of the abolitionist cause, put them on the frontline of the anti–death penalty movement. Leaders from different religions issued a common statement: "All life is sacred, including the lives of criminals who have committed heinous crimes. The campaign is inevitable as capital punishment undermines human dignity by taking state revenge on someone for . . . past mistakes."[44] As an alternative to what they call brutal executions, they propose life imprisonment without parole should rehabilitation be unsuccessful. Their history as "resistance groups" for many years before Korea's democratization helps as the churches take the initiative in the largely unpopular movement against the death penalty. They have continued their efforts to persuade political and judicial leaders as well as the general public to support the abolitionist cause.

The Korean office of Amnesty International has also played a significant role in placing the death penalty at the heart of the human rights agenda, especially when most human rights organizations were not active in the abolitionist movement. Amnesty International regards the death penalty as a violation of fundamental human rights, including the right to life and the right not to be subjected to cruel, inhuman, or degrading treatment or punishment. Both of these rights are recognized by the Universal Declaration of Human Rights, other international and regional human rights instruments, and national constitutions. Amnesty International has organized an ongoing campaign against capital punishment, and produced detailed accounts of the status of the death penalty both in Korea and in the rest of world. Every year during President Kim Dae-jung's tenure, the Korean office of Amnesty International released the reports on the extent of improvements in human rights conditions, with special attention to the death penalty. When he met with President Kim Dae-jung in Seoul, Secretary-General of Amnesty International Pierre Sané expressed his special concern with Korea's death penalty system, which remained in force, and recommended that Kim take measures to abolish the death penalty and improve the treatment of those on death row.[45] During the presidential election campaign in November 2002, Amnesty International's Korean branch called on leading presidential candidates to support the abolitionist cause, providing detailed guidelines: (1) "expedite passage into legislation of the bill calling for the abolition of the death penalty in the National

Assembly"; (2) "support commutation of the death sentences of those currently under sentence of death and ensure that no further executions are carried out"; (3) "support ratification of the Second Optional Protocol to the International Covenant on Civil and Political Rights, aiming at worldwide abolition of the death penalty."[46]

Last but not least, several legislative initiatives are noteworthy. The first of its kind in Korea, the Special Bill for the Abolition of the Death Penalty was submitted in 1999 to the Fifteenth Session of the National Assembly with the assent of ninety-one of the 299 members. The major premise of the bill is to remove the provision of the death penalty from the Criminal Code and the Special Act, and to make life imprisonment the maximum punishment. Two years later, in 2001, the bill commuting the death penalty to life imprisonment was again presented to the National Assembly. This time the bill carried stronger political weight, since it was submitted with the signatures of 155 lawmakers from both the ruling and opposition parties.[47] These two attempts, however, went nowhere: the bills could not even pass the Legislative and Judiciary Committee of the National Assembly. The committee was mostly composed of former prosecutors who have strongly supported the death penalty, and thus there was initial skepticism about the committee's role in helping to enact such abolitionist legislation. In 2005, the debate over the death penalty was revived in the National Assembly for the third time in six years, when a group of 175 lawmakers again submitted the abolitionist bill. As the same bill has been repeatedly presented, more and more lawmakers have joined the cause and put their names to it. They share the view that it is a contradiction to take the life of a criminal in the name of justice, that doing so is at odds with the idea of human dignity and the right to life guaranteed by the constitution.[48]

It seems likely that, in general, Korea's elite no longer perceive the death penalty as necessary for the state's protection of national security from outside aggression; they now appear to feel that it violates the most fundamental tenets of human rights. According to Representative Chyung Dai-chul, who took the lead in drafting the 2001 bill: "Capital punishment should be brought to an end as soon as possible on the grounds that it stands against the spirit of the Constitution that stipulates human dignity and respect for life."[49] At a joint seminar on Asia's death penalty in Tokyo in May 2002, organized by the Parliamentary Assembly of the Council of Europe (PACE) and the Japanese Diet Members' League for the Abolition of the Death Penalty, Chyung Dai-chul stated that state executions in South Korea should be abolished mainly because it was a global trend, a hundred nations around the world having so far pursued abolition in their legal systems.[50] To abolish capital punishment, he implied, was to join an international human rights project. The death penalty is a topic that transcends national debate; it entails a significant international dimension.

The abolitionist movement has stimulated public debates on the death penalty, which until recently had been almost entirely absent in Korea. Furthermore, as the debate has continued, the public attitude toward the death penalty seems to have become more lenient. According to a 2001 poll conducted by the Korean newspaper *Chosun Ilbo* and the mobile research institute *Mbizon*, 36 percent of 838 respondents over age twenty opposed the death penalty, compared with 34 percent in 1999 and 20 percent in 1994.[51] Other polls have yielded similar findings. The Korea Survey Research Organization poll in 2002 found that 54 percent favored the death penalty and 45 percent were against it. When the same questions were asked in 1992, 67 percent were in favor of the death penalty, while only 20 percent opposed it.[52] Gallup Korea's survey confirmed that opponents of capital punishment have significantly increased over the years: 20 percent opposed it in 1994, 31 percent in 2001, and 40 percent in 2003. In 1994, 70 percent of Koreans reportedly supported the death penalty; this had dropped to 55 percent by 2001, and to 52 percent by 2003.[53] There is no doubt that a majority in Korean society still support capital punishment, yet a growing number favor its abolition. The abolitionist efforts of the past decade to make the death penalty a social and political issue have played a role in influencing public opinion. Given that one of the salient traits of sociopolitical culture in Korea has been an orientation toward authoritarian values and penal systems, this change seems significant.[54]

WHY NOT ABOLITION RIGHT NOW?

Following the 1995 revision of Korea's Penal Code, the scope of crimes subject to the death penalty was much restricted. However, eighty-seven offenses defined in seventeen laws are still punishable by the death penalty, including forty-two capital offenses in the Military Penal Code. The death penalty is also included in the National Security Law, implying that, in addition to ordinary criminals, any political convict can, at least in theory, be executed. The death sentence is still regularly imposed, and nearly sixty people remain on death row without a guarantee of commutation as of June 2005. The sixteenth South Korean president, Roh Moo-hyun, a former human rights lawyer and dissident known to be even more prone to reform than his predecessor, Kim Dae-jung, has yet to make any statement on the abolition of the death penalty or on penal reform in general. What obstacles stand in the way of abolishing the death penalty? At least five issues are relevant in explaining why Korea has not committed itself to abolishing the death penalty in a timely manner: (1) political will regarding cultural vales; (2) lack of regional enforcement; (3) the authoritarian legacy; (4) the paradox of democracy; and (5) weak roles of human rights groups.

Political Will Regarding Cultural Values

Confucianism is one of the central cultural traditions in East Asia. In spite of widespread debate on the compatibility of Confucianism and democracy, it is fair to say that Confucian values, which place a high value on harmony, consensus, order, and respect for hierarchy, take preference over the central tenets of pluralist democracy such as individual freedom of expression, self-determination, disagreement, and competition.[55] In Korea, conformity, compliance with authority, and acceptance of a hierarchical social order have long characterized the patterns of political socialization as they have in neighboring countries. Indeed, a strong emphasis on hierarchical social order helped shape Korea's criminal justice system. The state, like the head of a household, had supreme authority and control over the rest of its members. Noncompliance drew a variety of sanctions, ranging from verbal warnings, ostracism, and expulsion from communities, to corporal punishment, including the death penalty. Ethical codes and punishment provided a regulatory and normative hierarchical framework that citizens respected. Punishment was a weapon of the administration against those who were guilty of circumventing societal norms.[56] Penal institutions were major elements in a generalized and concerted disciplinary strategy based on the ideological tenets of order and hierarchy. Erich Fromm's reflection on the father's image in relation to state-imposed killing is very relevant to this paternalistic society:

> The central factor in the father's power is the power to castrate, to cause serious bodily injury. It is no accident that the kaiser or the president is legally empowered to pardon those sentenced to death, that he therefore is allowed to make the final judgment about life or death. He is the symbolic embodiment of paternal authority, and he proves himself as such through his right to decide about life and death.[57]

Political leaders continued to propagate the state's dominant cultural ideology in a variety of ways, from the way they excused themselves from developing social policies for the elderly to the way they persisted in harsh punishment for wrongdoers. For example, politicians promoted a cardinal virtue of the Confucian ethical and relational system, which requires the son's obligation to and responsibility for his parents, in order to minimize the social welfare package they provided for the elderly. The state's rhetoric was: "Government social service programs to assist the elderly would substitute for family care and, thus, undermine the Confucian culture."[58] The state's attitude might well entail social sanctions against those who neglected their "obligations" and family responsibilities. Unlike the way imperial Britain resolved a number of economic crises in the 1890s (i.e., expanding the range of penal sanctions while introducing a mass of social welfare legislation), penalties and welfare programs did not work as complementary strategies in Korea. In order to justify or maintain the underdeveloped social welfare programs for the elderly, Korean political leaders emphasized the traditional Confucian family system. Yet Confucian virtues can be interpreted in a different way, which would argue for strong government intervention on behalf citizens' well-being: "This [Confucian] teaching is a political philosophy that emphasizes the role of government and stresses the ruling elite's moral obligation to strive to bring about peace under heaven (*pingtianxia*)."[59]

Cultures are neither monolithic nor static; however, there are people "who benefit from making it monolithic and keeping it static."[60] Under the impacts of technological development, economic change, and social transformation, no culture remains the same. At the least, the traditional Confucian value of hierarchy has been challenged in Korea. If we can identify any cultural aspect that impedes the abolitionist movement, we must acknowledge that it is subservient to a political will that seeks to prolong the culture of order and discipline and justifies doing so by appealing to geopolitical conditions in this security-sensitive country. Thus, the impediment is not culture in itself, but the political manipulation of cultural values. In other words, the source of Asia's differences in terms of the use of the death penalty is not a deterministic, preexisting culture, but rather acts of will.

Lack of Regional Enforcement

Although their effectiveness varies, regional human rights organizations or instruments do exist and have some influence on most continents. The African Human Rights Convention, the European Convention on Human Rights, and the Inter-American Convention on Human Rights were all formed to promote human rights in their regions. Asia is the only continent with no regional human rights enforcement agency. Like other Asian countries, Korea has been immune from the direct influence of international human rights injunctions against capital punishment on its own continent, and has never experienced peer pressure to advance the abolitionist cause. This is quite different from the situation in Europe, where the abolitionist movement has been strongly contagious. Decisions on the abolition of the death penalty are often influenced, for whatever reason, by the actions taken in neighboring countries. Many European governments have followed suit when other countries in their region abolished the death penalty.

The Strasbourg-based European Parliament did make a number of formal resolutions urging the abolition of capital punishment in Japan, South Korea, and Taiwan.[61] With regard to "Asian values" on the issue of capital punishment, a member of the Labour Party of the European Parliament remarked in the 2002 session: "There is no Asian way to the rights of man. There is a universal way to the rights of man and democracy, and to win over the camp of the [anti-abolition] countries, of countries as important as Japan,

South Korea and Taiwan, is essential to uphold the universal nature of the rights of man."[62]

The Authoritarian Legacy

While the two aforementioned factors contribute to explaining the persistent practice of the death penalty in East Asia in general, the key to Korea's specific context might relate to the very nature of its political transformation. The number of democracies that still impose the death penalty is being progressively reduced worldwide, and there seems to be a high correlation between democratic progress and the abolitionist trend. With only a few exceptions, the abolitionist movement has thrived in countries where democracy has advanced. And the more radical the political transition, that is, the less continuity the former state institutions have, the easier it is for the state to embrace new ideas or norms. The death penalty has been abolished most rapidly in countries that have undergone the most radical changes of regime and thus could quickly implement legal reforms that would have taken much longer to accomplish under stable governments.

There was real progress toward democracy in Korea, but the transition process was not radical or revolutionary. Political change in South Korea has been slow and incremental, inheriting major socioeconomic policies from the previous authoritarian governments. In addition, the public's deep-rooted deference to authoritarian law and order hinders most requests for penal reform from below. A series of surveys have found that public opinion in favor of capital punishment is still dominant even after democratization. Most citizens allow their politicians to lock up more and more offenders and to impose strict control upon behavior that should not be socially tolerated. The majority of the public favors the death penalty in most countries, however, so these survey results are not peculiar to the Korean case. The difference is that Koreans' respect for the hierarchical, authoritarian social order goes as far as championing hard-core dictatorship. A great majority of Koreans over many years have supported the following survey statement: "The dictatorial rule led by a strong leader like Park Chung Hee is much better than a democracy to tackle the various problems facing our country" (61% in 1994; 53% in 1996; 67% in 1997).[63] This persistent attitude stems from long experience with undemocratic governance and its discipline, which have socialized the majority of Koreans to live under a false idea of security. As Shin and Shyu argue, this is comparable to the case in West Germany some decades ago when political ambivalence existed between democracy and order. People found themselves "desiring freedom from political oppression while simultaneously wanting to be ruled by a strong leader."[64] At any rate, it is more difficult for the abolitionist cause to gain wide support when most Koreans generally favor strong authority. A key constraint on penal reform in Korea lies in the "shadow of history," that is, the residual authoritarian institutions and mindset, which, due to the incremental nature of political transformation, has not been interrupted.

The Paradox of Democracy

Another important obstacle to penal reform is the weakness, or the conservative nature, of the South Korean democratic regime. President Kim Dae-jung owed his election triumph to an alliance with Kim Jong Pil, one of the most conservative politicians in South Korea and the founder of the Korean Central Intelligence Agency (KCIA) under the military dictatorship. This determined in large measure the ideological spectrum of Kim's leadership, making any bold liberal attempts at penal reforms politically risky. Although the sixteenth South Korean president, Roh Moo-hyun, is even more inclined to reform than Kim Dae-jung, Roh's progressive moves are consistently thwarted by the influential conservative camp, including the majority Grand National Party (*Hannara*) and mainstream press. Governmental and legislative leaders therefore fear that such gestures may become a serious political liability for them, especially when all major domestic judicial bodies—the Constitutional Court, the Department of Justice, and even lawyers' groups—oppose the abolition of capital punishment. When the leaders of the ruling party feel that they are in a politically weak position in domestic affairs, they are likely to maintain a cool attitude toward progressive policy reforms. The only "safe" attitude is one that is "tough on crime" and gives priority to security. The weakness of the regime means that the political leadership is also weak in its ability to advocate penal reforms.

A civilian government is more sensitive to the policy preferences of the public than are military dictators, who may feel freer to propose bold initiatives, partly because they need not worry about their legitimacy, and partly because their policies are likely to be interpreted as inherently conservative simply because they are initiated by dictators, no matter what the policies may be. Popularly elected governments are far more constrained by the public constituency. This is why the stringent National Security Law still persists even under democratic civilian governments, and even when it appears to conflict with the "sunshine policy" of engagement with North Korea.[65]

Weak Roles of Human Rights Groups

The principal obstacle to the abolition of capital punishment in Korea lies, ironically, within the Korean human rights groups themselves. While a large number of human rights organizations have been established in Korea and have performed key functions in the transition to democracy, their role in the abolitionist movement has not been conspicuous. Why the death penalty has not been actively opposed by human rights groups—with the single exception of Amnesty International's South Korean office—is a mystery.

The major human rights groups of Korea, such as Citizen's Solidarity for Human Rights and the Sarangbang Group for Human Rights, state that they oppose the death penalty because it violates basic human dignity.[66] People's Solidarity for Participatory Democracy, a prominent civic group, also opposes capital punishment, arguing that it is not an effective deterrent.[67] While they voice their opposition, however, they take no action. Two possible reasons for this can be advanced. First, from the perspective of human rights groups, capital punishment is very likely to be banned in Korea in a few years anyway, so that extra work toward this outcome is unnecessary.[68] Second, human rights groups apparently wish to avoid getting involved in an issue most Koreans have strong reservations about. Since many Korean civic groups are still young and inexperienced, they prefer, perhaps until they feel they are better established, an agenda that has broad public support. When the abolishing the death penalty does not appear to be "the will of the people," it is considered risky for civil groups, let alone the political leadership, to promote it.

Some have argued that grassroots support does not seem to be a necessary condition for abolition.[69] It did not seem so in Europe, where pro–capital punishment sentiment remained relatively high at the time of abolition. However, general public support for capital punishment does not necessarily mean that the anti–capital punishment movement must remain underdeveloped. South Africa, where robust anti–capital punishment organizations played a decisive role in expediting the progress of abolitionism, is a good example. Even when the majority of the public backed the retention of capital punishment, invoking the unprecedented growth of violent crime in the post-apartheid era, the South African human right organizations relentlessly promoted the legitimacy of abolition.[70]

Instead of nongovernmental organizations, it is in fact a governmental body that has taken the initiative for abolition in Korea. The newly established National Human Rights Commission, the most prestigious human rights body in Korea, confessed that it did not discuss the death penalty during the whole of the first year following its inauguration. When Amnesty International Korea asked, in 2002, about its stance on capital punishment, the answer from this most influential commission was: "There is no official position about that issue."[71] However, time has brought quite a change. In April 2005, the National Human Rights Commission issued a series of recommendations, including the abolition of the current death penalty system. The death penalty, according to the commission, "compromises the dignity of human beings."[72]

The temporary halting of executions came through the will of political leaders. Because Korea's political institutions still remain shallow and immature, even though its democracy has been in some minimal way consolidated, this moratorium can be lifted at any time in accordance with changes in the political configuration. In this regard, it is vital to emphasize that a moratorium is simply a stage on the road to full abolition. A moratorium can never be an end in itself.

CONCLUDING REMARKS

Reflecting the changes in the social and political atmosphere surrounding capital punishment, the Supreme Court, in February 2002, handed down a decision on a murder case in which the Military Court had twice ruled in favor of the death sentence. The court ruled: "The death penalty was too severe as the crime was committed on impulse, and the defendant has had no trouble with the law in the past and had been faithful to his military duties before committing the criminal act . . . he has ample potential to correct himself."[73] It was unprecedented for the Supreme Court to overturn the lower court's judgment on the ground that the defendant had the potential to reform. Similar rulings were made in the criminal courts. In February 2004, a person who committed a heinous murder was sentenced to life imprisonment instead of the death penalty. In the concurring opinion, the court stated: "If this crime had happened ten years ago, the death penalty might have been applied. Yet considering the growing social concerns about the death penalty and its relations with human rights, we sentence him to life imprisonment. Human rights are entitled to everyone including those who have committed the worst crimes."[74] In May 2005, the criminal court also sentenced a person who had committed multiple homicides to life imprisonment. The court stated: "It seems inevitable to impose the ultimate punishment on the most heinous crime like this. But the death penalty is a truly exceptional punishment that a civilized country's judicial system can present. It is allowed only to special and objective situations that can be justified by the responsibility of the crime and aim of the punishment."[75] A series of recent court cases and the suspension of executions for the past eight years suggest that the country has been gradually moving toward a death penalty–free society.

If Schabas is right in saying that the abolition of capital punishment is "generally considered to be an important element in democratic development for states for breaking with a past characterized by terror, injustice and repression," is the change in Korea's use of the death penalty related to its democratic progress?[76] Certainly a considerable shift has occurred in the sentiments of the leadership regarding the death penalty system in Korea. The experience of President Kim Dae-jung as a death row prisoner seemed to convince him that the death penalty is a relic of a barbarous past, and has no place in a civilized legal system. It may not be coincidental that Nelson Mandela and Kim Dae-jung, who both were once political prisoners facing execution, worked to put an end to the death penalty once they were in power, though Mandela's efforts were more determined and thus yielded a more tangible outcome than Kim's. Yet, the abolitionist endeavor in South Korea deserves credit, especially because it has occurred in the face of this country's special security concerns with regard to North Korea. The people working to end capital punishment know that security should not be an excuse or justification for denying fundamental human rights.

Efforts to abolish capital punishment have followed different paths. South Africa voluntarily outlawed capital punishment in 1995 as a result of changing ideas and the creation of a post-apartheid identity. In South Africa, human rights became a central part of the national self-image through a revolutionary political transformation that brought the end of apartheid. Ukraine's decision to abolish capital punishment in 2000 came only after a great deal of pressure and persuasion from the Council of Europe, which has made abolition of the death penalty a prerequisite for membership. South Korea, without the pivotal role of a regional body (as in the cause of Ukraine) or a revolutionary change from the past (as in the case of South Africa), is on the way to abolishing the death penalty. Is it possible that South Korea can follow in the footsteps of Ukraine and South Africa without favorable conditions for abolition? Will this country be the first in East Asia to hold up that beacon by joining the world trend away from capital punishment? South Korea's path is likely to be a significant alternative for study if this country chooses to comply with the international norm.

CHAPTER FIVE

THE UNITED STATES

> From this day forward, I no longer shall tinker with the machinery of death. For more than 20 years I have endeavored—indeed, I have struggled— along with a majority of this Court, to develop procedural and substantive rules that would lend more than the mere appearance of fairness to the death penalty endeavor. Rather than continue to coddle the Court's delusion that the desired level of fairness has been achieved and the need for regulation eviscerated, I feel morally and intellectually obligated simply to concede that the death penalty experiment has failed.
>
> —Justice Harry Blackmun, *Callins v. Collins* (1994)

In June 2001, at the time when the Council of Europe at Strasbourg was busy holding the first world congress against the death penalty, the federal government of the United States conducted the first two federal executions in Terre Haute, Indiana, after thirty-eight years: those of Oklahoma bomber Timothy McVeigh and alleged drug kingpin Juan Garza. When the United States Justice Department decided to seek the penalty for Zacarias Moussaoui in March 2002, a French Moroccan and an allegedly active participant in the conspiracy of the Sept. 11 attacks, the French government, which had until then pledged to support the United States in the fight against terrorism, was determined not to cooperate in producing data on the defendant or his associations that could be used in a capital trial.[1] Other European nations, including Germany, made it clear that they would not extradite suspects to be prosecuted in the United States, particularly before American military commissions, if these suspects would face the death penalty.[2] These episodes illustrate the current opposition between the United States and its European allies on the death penalty. The United States and the rest of the developed West "are now farther divided on the question of capital punishment than on any other morally significant question of government policy."[3]

During World War II, the number of executions surged on all sides, after long, execution-free periods in Western Europe. In its aftermath, the Nuremberg trials led to the mass hangings of wartime collaborators. War criminals were also executed following domestic prosecutions in Germany, France, the Netherlands, Norway, and Denmark.[4] After this dramatic increase in executions, however, further imposition of the death penalty declined substantially. Against popular opinion, Germany, in its Basic Law of 1949, abolished the death penalty. England abolished the death penalty for murder in 1969; Spain in 1978; France in 1981; Austria in 1984; Ireland in 1990; and Greece in 1993. In addition, countries that had already abolished the death penalty for murder before the 1960s moved to abolish it for all crimes throughout the period between the1970s and the 1990s: Sweden and Finland in 1972; Portugal in 1976; Denmark in 1978; Norway and Luxembourg in 1979; the Netherlands in 1982; Switzerland in 1992; and Italy in 1994.[5] The death penalty for ordinary crimes has at this point been abolished either de jure or de facto in Europe.

In contrast to Europe, the United States still actively imposes the death penalty. In 2005, Amnesty International ranked the United States fourth in the world in the number of executions, behind only China, Iran, and Saudi Arabia, countries that the United States defines as the least democratic and the worst abusers of human rights.[6] What the Council of Europe, the world's most robust international human rights organization, regards as an unacceptably inhuman and degrading punishment is the official legal policy of the national government of the United States and thirty-eight of its fifty states. Stephen Bright, capital defense lawyer and abolitionist activist, remarked: "If people were asked thirty years ago which one of the following three countries—Russia, South Africa, and the United States—would be most likely to have the death penalty at the turn of the century, few people would have answered the United States."[7] As it turns out, even South Africa and Russia—along with other former Soviet Union states—have abandoned the death penalty, while the United States has retained it.

Harold Koh, Assistant Secretary of State for Democracy, Human Rights, and Labor in the Clinton administration, was one of few outspoken critics of the death penalty among high administrative officials. After finishing his service, he stated that the issue of the death penalty had placed the United States and its closest allies—particularly the European Union and Latin American countries—on a collision course both in important bilateral meetings and in almost every multilateral human rights forum. He continued: "Capital punishment concretely diminishes America's reputation as a human rights leader and hence its ability to lead a coalition of nations founded on moral principle. For a country that aspires to be a world leader in human rights, the death penalty has become our Achilles' Heel."[8]

Why does the transnational norm concerning the prohibition of the death penalty, which is apparently so important for every other Western democracy, seem to have no impact on the contemporary United States? Why has capital punishment remained so strongly entrenched in the United States when it has disappeared from the penal codes of almost all the countries that share a common political heritage and culture? Why has the United States resisted the general international trend? What are the perceptual differences regarding the death penalty that separate the United States from its European peers? Do some values and institutional structures of the United States encourage a death penalty? The task of this chapter is to answer these questions.

The chapter has five major sections. The first presents a brief history of capital punishment in the United States since the 1970s, compared to its history in other developed Western countries. The second section examines the question of whether "American exceptionalism" relates to crime rates and whether capital punishment is causally connected to crime reduction. The third section focuses on the South's tradition of vigilante justice, discussing how and why the regional or state factor contributes to our understanding of the capital punishment system in the country. The fourth section addresses the movement to abolish the death penalty and the effect of public opinion, allegedly one of the most robust variables in explaining the persistent use of the death penalty in the United States. The final section seeks to identify the key factors that undermine political leadership in the attempt to embrace the norm that prohibits the death penalty.

"AMERICAN EXCEPTIONALISM" AND INTERNATIONAL PRESSURE

Before the late 1970s, the practice of capital punishment had declined in the United States, much as it had in Europe. England and France, the major European powers, retained the death penalty, and their occasional executions continued for decades after World War II. Yet the general trend beginning in the 1950s in Europe was either to abolish the death penalty or to restrict its practice. The trend was similar in the United States: whereas there were 1,289 executions in the 1940s, there were 715 in the 1950s, and the number fell even further, to only 191, from 1960 to 1976.[9] The abolitionist movement brought challenges to the fundamental legality of the death penalty, resulting in the Supreme Court's de facto moratorium imposed in *Furman v. Georgia* in 1972. In nine separate opinions, and with a vote of five to four, the United States Supreme Court ruled that the choices between imprisonment and execution for specific crimes without any clear guidelines were unconstitutional as they permitted arbitrary and capricious decision making by juries.[10] The high court held that the death penalty was a "cruel and unusual" punishment and often selectively used against minorities in violation of the Eighth Amendment.[11] This Supreme Court decision made forty death penalty statutes void, thereby commuting the sentences of 629 death row inmates around the country. Thus, it appeared at the time as if the

88 WHEN THE STATE NO LONGER KILLS

abolitionist movement would take the same course in the United States as in Europe.

The abolitionist victory did not last long, however. Against the *Furman* ruling, advocates of capital punishment began proposing new statutes that they believed would end arbitrariness in capital sentencing. Led by Florida, Georgia, and Texas, more than thirty states rewrote their death penalty statutes, including the guidelines that allowed for the introduction of aggravating and mitigating factors in determining sentencing. Four years later, in 1976, these guided-discretion statutes were approved by the Supreme Court in *Gregg v. Georgia*, which concluded that the new death penalty statutes in Florida, Georgia, and Texas were constitutional.[12] Reinstating the death penalty in those states, the Supreme Court held that "the death penalty is not per se unconstitutional."[13]

This landmark decision has separated the United States and the rest of the Western nations in action and in ideology regarding capital punishment for the last several decades. A couple of months after the *Gregg* ruling, two significant executions in different parts of the globe took place. The first execution in the United States after a decade-long hiatus, that of Gary Gilmore by firing squad in Utah in January 1977, was a sign of many more to come. In Southern France, on the other hand, Hamida Djandoubi, a Tunisian immigrant and a convicted murderer, was executed in September 1977 and became the last person executed by guillotine as well as the last executed on the Western European continent. The very moment that Western democracies ended state-sanctioned killing and began to institutionalize abolition was when the United States returned to it.

Since the death penalty was reinstated in 1976, the United States has carried out about 1,000 executions (see Figure 5.1). The condemned included prisoners who committed their crimes as juveniles aged sixteen or seventeen. From 1976 until the U.S. Supreme Court outlawed the execution of juvenile offenders in March 2005, twenty-two inmates had been executed—a record for the highest number of juvenile executions in the world.[14] Outside of the United States, only Iran and the Democratic Republic of Congo are reported to have executed juvenile offenders in the past five years. Even China, the world's leader in executions, has reportedly banned the execution of people with mental retardation since imperial times, as well as of people below eighteen years of age since 1997.[15] The juvenile death penalty is a violation of international law, as both the UN International Covenant on Civil and Political Rights and the American Convention on Human Rights prohibit capital punishment for juvenile offenders (Article 6, adopted December 16, 1966, entered into force on March 23, 1976). This view was reaffirmed when the Economic and Social Council of the United Nations, by Resolution 1996/15 of July 23, 1996, called upon retentionist states to apply effectively the safeguards that included the banning of juvenile executions: "[J]uvenile defendants never ever face the death penalty." The United

States is the only country to ratify the International Covenant on Civil and Political Rights with an outstanding reservation regarding the execution of juveniles. The Convention on the Rights of the Child also forbids such executions, but the United States is one of the few countries in the world that has failed to ratify this treaty.

The United States has neither signed nor ratified the two international legal instruments providing for the abolition of the death penalty: these are the Second Optional Protocol to the International Covenant Aiming at the Abolition of the Death Penalty, adopted by the UN General Assembly on December 15, 1989, and the Protocol to the American Convention on Human Rights to Abolish the Death Penalty, adopted by the Organization of American States on June 8, 1990. In April 1999, the UN Human Rights Commission passed the Resolution Supporting Worldwide Moratorium on Executions. The resolution calls on countries that have not abolished the death penalty to restrict their use of it, including not imposing it on juvenile offenders and limiting the number of offenses for which it can be imposed. The only countries that voted against the resolution were the United States and China.

While most European countries have ratified the two protocols, abolished the death penalty under their domestic law, and pressed neighboring countries to abandon it with missionary vigor, the United States seems out of step with a growing international sentiment against capital punishment as executions become routine. How can we explain this reservation, given the worldwide importance of the covenants named above and the leadership of the United States in promoting international awareness of the role of human rights in domestic law? As a leading power, does this country feel no sensitivity to international pressure, and does it not wish to avoid reprisals or any unfavorable international resolutions?

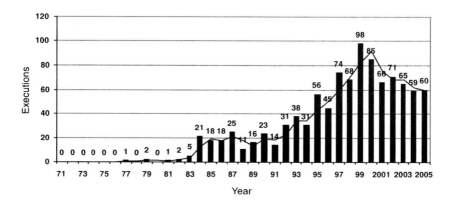

Source: U.S. Department of Justice, Bureau of Justice Statistics

Figure 5.1. Number of Executions in the United States, 1970–2005

It is true that the United States, unlike most European countries, did not experience direct pressure from its neighbors and thus could employ capital punishment as it saw fit. It is also true, however, that demands from across the Atlantic have significantly increased. The Council of Europe argues that it is unfair for the organization to urge some of its member states, such as Russia, to abolish the death penalty, while it does not penalize the United States, which enjoys observer status with the council. Convinced of the necessity to deal with the abolition of the death penalty in observer states, the Council of Europe nevertheless tabled a motion for a resolution in February 1998 on the abolition of the death penalty in the United States.[16] The Council of Europe considers observer states that still apply the death penalty to be violating human rights and therefore in contravention of Statutory Resolution (93) 26 on observer status: "Any state willing to accept the principles of democracy, the rule of law and the enjoyment by all persons within its jurisdiction of human rights and fundamental freedoms, . . . may be granted . . . observer status with the Organization."[17] The Council of Europe has since passed a number of resolutions calling for revocation of the United States' observer status unless it makes "significant progress" toward abolishing the death penalty.[18] Similar pressure has also come from the European Union, which has called for a moratorium on federal executions in the United States. Canada and Mexico have officially declared that they would refuse to extradite criminal suspects to the United States if those people would be subject to capital punishment.[19]

While international pressure has been increasing against the continuing practice of capital punishment in the United States, American behavior worries those who believe it may have a contagious effect on neighboring nations. As Martine Jacot notes, some of the Caribbean countries tend to follow the United States. For instance, Trinidad and Tobago, the Bahamas, and Jamaica resumed executions in the late 1990s after a pause of several years.[20]

Some recent evidence indicates that the U.S. Supreme Court has begun to look beyond national shores in interpreting its judgment on whether the death penalty violates "evolving standards of decency." In *Atkins v. Virginia*, in June 2002, the Supreme Court held that the execution of any individual with mental retardation violated the Eighth Amendment's prohibition on cruel and unusual punishment, referring not only to the number of U.S. states that had abolished the death penalty for the mentally retarded, but also to international opinion on the matter. The Court's opinion made specific reference to the *amicus curiae* brief filed by the European Union supporting such a ban. In March 2005, when the Supreme Court ruled that imposing the death penalty on convicted murderers who were younger than eighteen at the time of their crimes was unconstitutional, international opinion seemed to contribute even more forcefully to the decision. In the Court's majority opinion in *Roper v. Simmons*, Justice Anthony Kennedy wrote, "It is proper that we acknowledge the overwhelming weight of international opinion against the juvenile death penalty, resting in large part on the understanding that the instability and emotional imbalance of young people may often be a factor in the crime," adding that there was an emerging national consensus against juvenile execution. The Court further noted that the execution of juvenile offenders violated several international treaties, including the United Nations Convention on the Rights of the Child and the International Covenant on Civil and Political Rights. The Court also pointed out that the UN Convention on the Rights of the Child, which prohibits the juvenile death penalty, has been ratified by every country except Somalia and the United States.[21]

In a dissent, Justice Antonin Scalia rejected the Court's use of international law to confirm its finding of a national consensus, stating that " '[a]cknowledgement' of foreign approval has no place in the legal opinion of this Court." He wrote: "The court thus proclaims itself sole arbiter of our nation's moral standards."[22] This opinion was shared by many others around the nation. Dianne Clements, president of the Houston-based victims' rights group Justice for All, criticized the decision to end juvenile executions, stating that "the Supreme Court has opened the door for more innocent people to suffer by 16 and 17 year olds. I can't wait for the Supreme Court to have judges more concerned with American values, American statutes and American law than what the Europeans think."[23]

Where will the process end after these Supreme Court decisions banning the execution of the mentally retarded and juvenile offenders? Can we regard them as early steps toward prohibiting the death penalty under all circumstances? It might be too early to predict that the Court's recent decisions in these cases are leading inexorably to complete abolition of capital punishment. The decisions may be intended to prohibit it in situations that would make ordinary people uncomfortable. Like the belief that the use of DNA evidence prevents the execution of the innocent, the ban on juvenile executions might be another safeguard against controversy over the death penalty. When those uncomfortable and unattractive features of the death penalty are eliminated, in other words, as long as there is no execution of the innocent, the mentally retarded, and juvenile offenders, the core of the system may remain stronger ever.

DO CRIME RATES MATTER?

The most common theory on the issue of U.S. capital punishment is that the crime problem is far worse in the United States than in other comparable countries, even though there have been some substantial fluctuations in violent crime rates since the 1960s. During the 1960s and 1970s, the homicide rate was much higher in the United States than it was in most Western countries. The rate dropped substantially in the early 1980s but increased again later in the decade. In 1990, the homicide rate in the United States was four and one-half times that in Canada, nine times that in France or Germany, and thirteen times that in England. Although the rate fell precipitously in the 1990s, the United States still has a homicide rate two to four times higher than most other Western industrialized nations.[24]

Given this fact, we might ask whether the difference in violent crime rates across nations determines crime policy. According to Michael Tonry and Richard Frase, national differences in imprisonment rates and patterns— which we can extend by conjecture to rates of capital punishment—result not from differences in crime rates but from differences in policy. For instance, in the United States, Germany, and Finland, very similar rates of change in violent crimes have been found from the 1960s to the early 1990s, yet these are associated with utterly dissimilar penal policy responses. Crime rates are not viewed as the primary determinant of punitiveness in penal policy.[25] Likewise, it is a puzzle that countries with extremely high rates of homicide such as South Africa, Russia, and Mexico have abolished the death penalty, while Japan, where the homicide rate is comparatively low, continues to retain it. In the late 1990s, the U.S. murder rate per one hundred thousand people was only 50 percent of Russia's, yet the total number of death sentences was twice as high.[26]

Even within the United States, homicide rates are not responsive to execution rates. From the mid-1960s to the mid-1970s, the homicide rate roughly doubled, while the execution rate fell to zero for several years preceding the Supreme Court's temporary invalidation of the death penalty in 1972. Fluctuations in execution rates during the 1970s and 1980s are not mirrored by substantial fluctuations in homicide rates. The year 1984 saw the lowest number of murders of the last two decades in the United States, while in 1985 and in 1986 the number of death sentences was the highest. More significantly, homicide rates fell significantly throughout most of the 1990s, while execution rates soared, reaching the highest level since the 1950s. At the local level as well, we find that homicide rates do not determine death sentencing rates. In the state of Georgia, for example, the rate ranges from four death verdicts per one thousand homicides in Fulton County (Atlanta) to thirty-three death verdicts per one thousand homicides in rural Muscogee County. In Pennsylvania, Allegheny County (Pittsburgh) returns twelve verdicts per one thousand homicides, while Philadelphia County (Philadelphia) returns twenty-seven death verdicts per one thousand homicides.[27]

A number of studies have produced convincing evidence that the presence or absence of the death penalty has no effect on the pattern of murders or other serious crimes, challenging the general claim that crime policy is determined primarily by crime rates. The institution of the death penalty has no criminological significance in terms of general deterrence, and thus there is no logical connection or statistical correlation between them.[28] Since resuming judicial killing in 1977, the United States has seen a continuing rise in the rate of violent crimes, including murder, while in neighboring Canada

the homicide rate has fallen continually since the abolition of capital punishment in 1976. In Canada, the homicide rate has fluctuated over the past
three decades (between 2.2 and 2.8 per 100,000), but the general trend has
clearly been downward. It reached a thirty-year low in 1995 (1.98), and in
2003 the homicide rate dipped below 1.73 per one hundred thousand, the
lowest rate since the 1960s.[29]

Not only does the United States have the highest murder rate in the
industrialized world, but murder rates are highest in the Southern states,
where most executions occur. Federal Bureau of Investigation data shows
that half the states with the death penalty have homicide rates above the
national average, while ten of the twelve states without capital punishment
have homicide rates below the national average. According to F.B.I statistics
for 1998, the homicide rate per one hundred thousand in North Dakota,
which does not have the death penalty, was lower than the homicide rate in
South Dakota, which does have it. The homicide rate in West Virginia,
which has no death penalty, is 30 percent below that of Virginia, which has
one of the highest execution rates in the country. The dozen states that have
chosen not to enact the death penalty since the Supreme Court's ruling in
1977 do not have higher homicide rates than states with the death penalty.
In short, it is safe to say that the death penalty as a penal policy and institution neither reflects nor deters the crime rate.

THE VIGILANTE TRADITION

At present, thirty-eight states provide for the death penalty in law, yet actual
executions vary extensively state-by-state. As Hugo Adam Bedau points out,
death penalty policy among U.S. states is regionally divided into three tiers:
(1) in "the northern tier," running from Maine to Alaska, the death penalty
plays little or no visible role; (2) "the middle tier," from Pennsylvania to
California, still retains the death penalty, but actual executions have been
few; (3) "the lower tier," from Virginia and the Carolinas to Texas and
Arizona, are at the extreme in the distribution of executions; hence, this is
called "the death belt."[30] Of the first 1,009 executions since 1976, 824 were
carried out by only a few states located in the South, while 117 were in the
Midwest, 64 in the West, and 4 in the Northeast. Nearly half occurred in
only two states, Texas and Virginia, where 451 people were executed.[31] With
the exception of Arizona and Missouri, all of the highest levels of execution
are in the South.

The fact that only a few states in the U.S. South carry out the most
executions suggests that there is no single unifying or universal policy regarding the imposition of the death penalty in the United States. As Franklin
Zimring notes, "[A]ppreciating the absence of a single national profile is the
first step in understanding the causes and meanings of variation between the
states."[32] This also invites the following questions: Why is the death penalty

so deeply rooted in Southern culture? Why are Texas and Virginia so much more likely to execute criminals than Michigan and Vermont? Numerous studies have focused on an interesting relation between historically high rates of institutionalized vigilante behavior and high current rates of execution in the United States.[33] Zimring argues that the legacy of lynching and the vigilante tradition has had a significant impact on national character and culture that is most evident in the South and Southwest.[34] Dominating emotions and beliefs concerning punishment, the vigilante mentality seems to have a strong influence on the contemporary imposition of the death penalty in the South.

Figure 5.2 shows the regional percentage distributions of lynching from 1889 to 1918: 88 percent in the South; 7 percent in the Midwest; 5 percent in the West; and 0.03 percent in Northeast. The region with the most lynching, that is, the highest level of vigilante violence, a century ago has the highest percentage of executions, both in the earlier and contemporary time periods, while there are fewer executions in the regions that lack any substantial history of extreme vigilante behavior. The death penalty has thus been described as "the first cousin of lynching" or "a socially acceptable form of the old Black Codes and the lynch law enforced by Ku Klux Klan."[35]

According to Zimring, the South, where lynching was a peculiarly social method of crime control that had no government sanction, now views official executions "as expressions of the will of the community rather than the power of a distant and alien government."[36] Although circumstantial evidence supports a strong association between the "lynch mob" and the current "lethal injection," it is difficult to infer a causal relation. More research would be necessary before we could reliably assert that vigilante values are the cause of variations in execution among the U.S. states.[37]

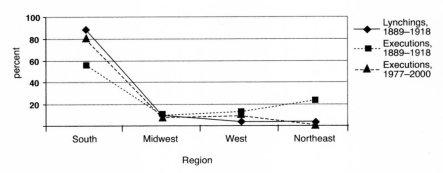

Source: Franklin E. Zimring, The Contradictions of American Capital Punishment (New York: Oxford University Press, 2003), 94.

Figure 5.2. Regional Distribution of Lynchings and Executions

RACIAL PREJUDICE AND INJUSTICE

Eighty-three percent of lynchings from 1882 to 1962 involved African American victims.[38] The foregoing discussion of the influence of a vigilante tradition on capital punishment naturally suggests that the death penalty in the South today is largely a relic of the system of racial injustice and violence. The historical link between executions and the status of minorities, especially African Americans, may in part explain why the impact of the transnational norm against capital punishment has been substantially disregarded in the United States. According to Tony Poveda, the persistent use of the death penalty in the United States derives partly from the institution of slavery before the Civil War, arising from "the legalized discrimination that followed, and the implications of this legacy for the incorporation of African-Americans into the larger society."[39] Compared to slavery in other nations, slavery in the United States was considered distinctive and more influential for the social system because the division between free persons and slaves was sharper and because, in a sense, slavery became a permanent status that persisted even after the institution was formally abolished.[40] Despite the sudden emancipation of slaves, the legacy of slavery irrevocably marked the character of the United States, particularly in the South, where the way to punish the criminality of ex-slaves was a significant issue of criminal justice. Because of the unique position of ex-slaves in society, the majority of the U.S. population and its leaders have more willingly accepted capital punishment, which until now has disproportionately affected African Americans and other minorities. Indeed, numerous empirical studies show that racial prejudice is significantly linked to greater support for the death penalty as well as for tougher crime control polices.[41] Such prejudice remains stronger among native white Southerners than among whites who were born and live elsewhere.[42]

African Americans account for 11 percent of the American population, but more than 40 percent of death row prisoners and one in three of those executed. Most murders in the United States involve perpetrators and victims of the same race, but studies consistently show that defendants who kill a white person are many times more likely to be executed than those who kill a black person.[43] Since judicial killing resumed in 1976, 209 black defendants have been executed for the murder of a white victim, but only twelve white defendants have been executed for the murder of a black victim.[44] A study of potentially capital murders in Philadelphia from 1983 to 1993 found that black defendants were 38 percent more likely than other defendants to receive a death sentence, even after controlling for crime severity and the defendant's criminal history.[45]

Race has been the focus of the criminal justice debates in the United States Supreme Court on several occasions. An important case in 1987, McCleskey v. Kemp, raised the issue of racial discrimination in the application of Georgia's death penalty. McCleskey presented a statistical analysis based on the race of the victim showing a pattern of racial disparities in death sentences. The Supreme Court held, however, that racial disparities would not be recognized as a constitutional violation of "equal protection under the law" unless intentional racial discrimination against the defendant could be shown. In contrast, Justice Harry Blackmun, who voted to uphold the death penalty both in 1972, when it was halted, and in 1976, when it was reinstated, asserted that racial discrimination continued to infect the practice of the death penalty: "Even under the most sophisticated death penalty statutes, race continues to play a major role in determining who shall live and who shall die."[46]

Disproportionate application of capital punishment for minorities is related not only to the prejudice of prosecutors or jurors but also to the legal representation appointed for the defendant. According to Lane and Tabak, about 90 percent of those facing capital charges cannot afford their own lawyer.[47] For that reason, the death penalty is often imposed not on those who have committed the worst crimes but on those given the worst lawyers. Indigent defendants must rely on court-appointed lawyers who are often not competent to try capital cases. There have been documented cases of lawyers who had just graduated from law school, who had never handled a criminal case, or who had racist attitudes toward their own clients. In several cases, lawyers were drunk and fell asleep during the trial while representing a man or woman whose life was at stake, giving a new meaning to the term *dream team*.[48]

WHY MORE AFTER THE 1980S? THE ERA OF HEIGHTENED INEQUALITY AND PUNITIVENESS

Even though the aforementioned factors—an enduring historical legacy of vigilante activity and racial discrimination—have influenced the way in which the modern system of capital punishment was generated and reinforced in the United States, they do not explain why executions were more common in the late twentieth century, notably in the 1980s and 1990s. In fact, American exceptionalism regarding the death penalty appears to be a relatively recent phenomenon, given that abolitionism worldwide is essentially a post–World War II trend.

Poveda describes a series of social and political events in the tumultuous decade of the 1960s that resulted in the "demise of liberalism." As the liberal line represented by Kennedy and Johnson was defeated by the conservative backlash, Republican hardliners seized hegemony, setting up and advancing the "get-tough" approaches to crime.[49] In a similar vein, another study of the U.S. criminal justice system over the past three decades maintains that conservatives started to mobilize the system of law and order in the 1960s in an effort to discredit the civil rights movement and the welfare state, which influenced support for capital punishment in the following decades.[50] Under this circumstance, Southern governors, law enforcement officials, presidential candidate Barry Goldwater, and the other conservative politicians who followed his lead were instrumental in mobilizing the crime issue in order to redefine poverty as the consequence of individual failure. Richard Nixon and a large number of Republicans who wanted to please their Southern white constituencies, pursued further the rhetoric of law and order, which is summarized as "the Republican southern strategy."[51] The law and order discourse became central to the Grand Old Party's electoral strategy.

The salience of the crime and drug issues declined dramatically following President Nixon's departure from office. Neither Republican President Ford nor Democratic President Carter took much legislative action on crime-related issues, which therefore largely disappeared from the national political discourse in the latter part of the 1970s. During and after the 1980 election campaign, however, the crime issue regained a central place on the national political agenda. Throughout the Reagan era, the state's control apparatus was revived and strengthened. It helped to legitimate the contraction of welfare programs and the dramatic expansion of the penal system. In this process, the state's objective changed from "the war on poverty" to "the war on crime."

On the other hand, Congress did not enact broad death penalty legislation until 1988, when it made some drug offenses subject to capital punishment. Despite its institutional ability to enact gradual measures such as a moratorium, Congress "was characterized by consistent timidity . . . lacking a tradition of moral leadership such as that evinced in the British Parliament."[52] During the 1990s, however, its attitude went beyond mere "consistent timidity." Through a series of legislative changes, Congress actively strengthened the institution of capital punishment. In the 1994 omnibus anticrime bill, Congress expanded the number of crimes subject to the death penalty to about sixty.[53] In 1995, Congress eliminated funding for a federal judiciary program that paid for Death Penalty Resource Centers, where attorneys in capital cases could get legal advice from experts on complicated capital punishment law. In 1996, Congress passed legislation dramatically limiting the appeals process for state and federal prisoners convicted of capital crimes. The law set time limits for appeals and forbade federal judges from overturning a state court verdict if it was "reasonable."

ANTI—DEATH PENALTY ACTIVISM

The effort to abolish the death penalty, as a coordinated social movement, is not a recent development in the United States. Opposition to capital punishment has existed in one form or another since the eighteenth century. Before the American Revolution, such opposition was fostered primarily by religious groups such as the Quakers and some vocal critics who argued that the death penalty violated scriptural dictates, that it was an inefficient deterrent, or that it was a disproportionately severe punishment for crimes other than murder.[54] Anti–death penalty sentiment became stronger and more visible during the post-Revolution years, as widespread liberal ideology undermined biblical justifications for capital punishment. Organized opposition to capital punishment by that time came not only from religious leaders but from secular groups, which established a variety of abolitionist organizations: the Anti–Capital Punishment Society of America, the American League to Abolish Capital Punishment (ALACP), the American Civil Liberties Union (ACLU), and the National Coalition to Abolish the Death Penalty.

Until recent years, the history of organized abolitionism has been cyclical. It gained or lost its momentum in relation to the effects of wars, the abolition of slavery, the hardship of economic conditions, and even the introduction of new means of execution. The increasing number of lawyers in the abolitionist camp during the 1960s, along with the relentless mission of the National Association for the Advancement of Colored People (NAACP) and the American Civil Liberties Union, have been extremely important in the anti–death penalty movement. The movement subsided somewhat in the 1980s and early 1990s not only because of the decline of political liberalism at all levels and branches of government, as well as in the electorate, but also because of "a sharp rise in the *visibility* of crime."[55] The movement seems to have revived only in recent years. A growing number of religious bodies, such as the World Council of Churches, the American Friends Service Committee, the American Jewish Committee, and the U.S. Catholic Conference, have campaigned to abolish capital punishment. In addition, in 1997, the American Bar Association took the unprecedented step of calling for a moratorium on executions, arguing that issues of racial inequality in capital sentencing, inadequate legal representation for capital defendants, and evidence of wrongly convicted persons necessitated a rethinking of the issue.[56]

Like capital punishment itself, the social movement to abolish the death penalty varies extensively state-by-state in the United States. Anti–death penalty activism in the 1960s was promoted by the same institutional actors who promoted the end of racial segregation in the South, and by the same means—appeals to the federal Constitution through litigation. The National Association for the Advancement of Colored People and the Legal Defense and Education Fund (LDF) litigated both the major desegregation cases and the death penalty cases. Activists found that the movement's robust national organizations, including Amnesty International USA, were not able to prevail in battles fought largely at the state level, where such movements are typically weak. In contrast, the Kansas anti–death penalty movement helped create its own political opportunities during 1986 when it successfully framed the issue in terms of the costs of executions, which are known to be higher than the costs of imprisonment for life without parole.[57]

In this regard, a strong anti–death penalty movement does not seem enough to bring capital punishment to a quick end, yet it is "a necessary precondition."[58] This is especially true when the general public lacks accurate knowledge about the actual administration of capital punishment.

Nonetheless, the anti–death penalty movement in the United States has never been considered very effective compared to other political or social campaigns. Both Michael Kroll and Eric Muller point out that it employs the wrong strategy, namely, that of working through the courts rather than the political processes.[59] Herbert Haines, in his detailed analysis of anti–death penalty activism in the United States, characterizes the political opposition to capital punishment as having "too few members, too little money . . . and too little broad appeal in the messages the movement has tried to deliver."[60] He argues that no nationally organized protest is less promising than the anti–death penalty movement. Not only are those who would benefit destitute and unable to organize themselves from cells on death row, but its conscience rests with a tiny coalition of predominantly middle-class whites, who, in Haines's words, "do not feel comfortable working with poor and minority people on the latter's own turf and in their own terms."[61] Its primary goal is especially difficult to frame persuasively for a public increasingly frustrated with crime. This distinguishes the anti–death penalty movement from other human rights activism, and makes it less likely to earn wide public support than other human rights movements. Since they confront the state, on the other hand, anti–death penalty organizations are not welcomed, and are thus much less likely to receive governmental aid than are the many community crime prevention and victim rights organizations. This is not surprising, since the movement seeks to restrict the authority and power of the state and its criminal justice agencies. Opposition to capital punishment, therefore, is supported neither from below (public) nor from above (state).

PUBLIC SUPPORT FOR THE DEATH PENALTY: A CONSTANT VARIABLE

As it is in other societies, the death penalty is a highly divisive issue in the United States. A substantial minority of the people, including religious leaders who work with prisoners on death row and their families and lawyers who specialize in capital defense, opposes capital punishment entirely, and a quite a few favor a moratorium on its use. Death penalty opponents originally considered their cause as a twin of that other great Enlightenment project, the abolition of slavery, and worked to end both age-old practices simultaneously.[62] Yet winning agreement to eliminate the death penalty proved more difficult than abolishing slavery. Even many liberal reformers who loathed slavery found the death penalty acceptable under the right circumstances. Unlike slavery, the death penalty has generally enjoyed widespread public support, as it continues to do today.

In the 1976 *Gregg v. Georgia* decision that approved the constitutionality of the death penalty, the United States Supreme Court noted public
opinion polls that indicated a majority of the public favored the death penalty. Coping with massive protests on his first visit to Europe in June 2001,
President George W. Bush commented on the death penalty: "Democracies
represent the will of the people. The death penalty is the will of the people
in the United States."[63] Despite some fluctuation, there is little doubt that
a majority of the U.S. public supports the death penalty in principle as a
legitimate punishment for heinous crimes. Several polls conducted at the
time when President Bush was speaking about the "will of the people" indicated that he was not wrong. A Gallup poll in February 2001 found that 67
percent of Americans favored capital punishment when asked, "Do you favor
or oppose the death penalty for persons convicted of murder?" Similar results
were found in other polls: 60 percent favored it in a survey by Peter D. Hart
Research Associates in March 2001; 59 percent in a survey by *USA Today*
in May 2001; and 67 percent in a Harris poll in August 2001.[64] Support for
the death penalty is high despite the common public assumption that innocent people have been put to death in the past five years. A growing percentage of the public believes the death penalty is applied fairly, and by a
two-to-one margin, the U.S. public says the death penalty is not imposed
often enough rather than imposed too often.[65] For most Americans, what
makes them support the death penalty is not the utilitarian argument of
whether the death penalty is a deterrent; the death penalty is, rather, a moral
argument as its practice is believed to indicate how much a community
values life, in that when one takes one unjustly, one sacrifices one's own.[66]

In the twenty years between 1936 and 1957 in the United States, the
percentage supporting the death penalty declined from 61 percent to 47
percent.[67] Death penalty support fell to the lowest level ever, 42 percent, in
1966. Over the next six years, and until the death penalty became unconstitutional in 1972, this figure hovered around 50 percent. After 1976, when
the U.S. Supreme Count changed its ruling and declared the death penalty
constitutional, the number of supporters increased steadily for the next twenty
years: 66 percent in 1976; 70 percent in 1986; and 80 percent in 1994, which
is a record high for death penalty support in the United States. Public support had increased an average of more than 1 percentage point per year since
1976, but it has recently begun to drop, falling back to 64 percent in 2005.

Death penalty policy varies enormously by state in the United States,
yet public support is spread fairly evenly across regions. According to a Gallup
poll released in May 2001, 72 percent of the respondents in the East answered "yes" to the question, "Are you in favor of the death penalty for a
person convicted of murder?" Seventy-two percent answered affirmatively in
the Midwest; 59 percent in the South; and 60 percent in the West. In the
South, where executions are clustered, the percentage of the public that
supports the death penalty is actually lower than in the East and the Midwest. Whatever separates the South from other regions, it is not the propor-

tion of citizens in public opinion polls who favor the death penalty. The level of public support, therefore, may not be an important predictor of death penalty policy in regions of the United States.

U.S. public opinion on the death penalty is far from being exceptional. The general support of the populace for capital punishment does not distinguish the United States from other nations that have abolished the death penalty. Survey outcomes in Europe show a pattern similar to that in the United States: public opinion on the death penalty tracks national political decisions rather than the reverse. The level of public support for the death penalty in France, Germany, and the United Kingdom just prior to abolition was in the same range as is currently found in the United States. An English poll found 82 percent in favor of reintroducing the death penalty in 1975, a larger majority than any U.S. poll of the modern era.[68] Not until the last decade of the twentieth century did the majority of the population in at least some European countries became abolitionist. Even at present, a significant portion of the population in England, France, and elsewhere would prefer to reinstate capital punishment. As Joshua Marshall remarked, worldwide public opinion has been conservative with regard to criminal policies: "[A]ll over the industrialized world, it turns out that the men and women on the street like the death penalty."[69]

Nonetheless, the public's attitude toward the death penalty is not taken seriously by European political leaders who must know that, once the death penalty is abolished, public support for it is generally muted, and pressure to restore it weakened. For this reason, political elites in abolitionist states, even in the United States, can be relaxed about this issue. Republican Governor John Engler of Michigan was free to assert: "We're pretty proud of the fact that we don't have the death penalty," saying that he "opposed the death penalty on moral and pragmatic grounds."[70]

What separates the United States from other Western democracies, therefore, is not public opinion but the lack of efforts from the political leadership. In many countries, the death penalty was abolished before consensus was reached or a vote taken. Individual leaders, in the name of the government, made the decision that capital punishment did not further the goals of either their nation or the global community. When a solid majority supports the death penalty, are elected leaders required to follow suit? President Bush is right in saying that the death penalty is largely "the will of the people," and yet whether a democratic leader is obliged to accede to all wishes of the public is a different subject.

THE PECULIARITY OF THE U.S. POLITICAL INSTITUTIONS

Survey results cannot explain why American policy has taken its exceptional course. Popular support for the death penalty is a constant variable in cross-national research on capital punishment. Given the political system of the United States, however, active opposition to the death penalty by a politician would be tantamount to political retirement. Two major features of American political organization make death penalty policy less receptive to international standards and more responsive to domestic populist impulse: federalism and electoral politics. Not all U.S. political structures tend to be populist, yet certain features of federalism and its electoral politics can fairly be described as populist, especially in comparison to most Western democracies. In the U.S. context, the influence of the federal government on matters of criminal justice has been minimal. In several Western democracies certain autonomous spheres of authority are allocated to discrete governmental units within the larger federal nation-states, as in Canada, Germany, and Switzerland. However, the United States is the only country that gives full criminal legislative power to individual federal units.[71] Most criminal justice responsibilities, including execution policy, are vested in individual state governments, which have carried out more than 95 percent of all executions since 1977. The federal system of government that grants each state extraordinary powers to make its own policy is a defining element of the unique policy environment of capital punishment in the United States. The level of vigilante conduct, for instance, is a matter for the state rather than national control of punishment policy, making citizens believe that "official punishments are an extension of the community rather than a function of the government."[72]

That tradition is now evident in the fact that most executions are not carried out by the national government but by state governments. Thus, the United States, as distinct from the unitary state systems, is more likely to be immune from the enforcement of the international standard. State governments seem isolated from, and indifferent to, international norms relating to the death penalty. In sharp contrast with executions at the state level, no federal executions in the United States were carried out in between 1963 and 2001. Hence, it is safe to argue that the state-level domination of execution policy has inhibited the United States from joining the global trend toward abolition.

Second, the criminal justice system in the United States is inextricably intertwined with electoral politics. Far more public officials, including police chiefs and prosecutors, are directly elected in the United States than in Europe. District attorneys, who decide whether to seek the death penalty in a given case, are elected. Judges, too, are directly elected or otherwise politically accountable in a large number of states. Prosecutors, who are overwhelmingly elected officials in the United States, face heavy political pressure on the issue of capital punishment. While federal judges are appointed for life, they face a grueling congressional confirmation battle.[73] Judges recently removed from office because of their unpopular death penalty decisions have included Chief Justice Rose Bird of the California state supreme court, Tennessee Supreme Court Justice Penny White, Mississippi Supreme Court Justice James Robertson, Justice Charles Campbell of the

Texas Court of Criminal Appeals, and Texas district court judge Norman Lanford, to name few.[74]

"Crime" and "punishment" were not always such powerful political issues, even though some politicians strongly wanted them to be. In the 1984 presidential election, Walter Mondale was against the death penalty, while President Reagan was strongly in favor of it, but the difference was not a major issue. The death penalty issue surfaced in the late 1980s, and became a fully developed issue in the social and political debates of the 1990s. That people care more intensely about capital punishment relates to the simple fact that crime and punishment have risen to the top of the political agenda at all levels of government. The more salient the issue of capital punishment became, the greater was the influence of the leadership in the federal executive and legislative branches regarding its resolution. For instance, a 1988 presidential election exit poll of twenty-three thousand voters revealed that the issue of the death penalty was "very" important to them—more important than social security, health care, education, or even the candidates' political party. Concerning the question of "an issue that was very important to them in choosing between George Bush and Michael Dukakis," the candidates' positions on the death penalty scored 27 percent, which made it the second most important issue for voters. The only item that scored higher was abortion, which 33 percent of voters checked.[75] A Gallup exit poll found that 57 percent of Bush voters and 38 percent of Dukakis voters cited capital punishment as the "most important" issue in the race.[76] To this date, Dukakis remains as the last presidential candidate who publicized his anti–death penalty stance. Others came to realize the significance of this issue in U.S. electoral politics, noting that opposition to the death penalty could be viciously exploited by their political opponents, who would promise more executions. Political leaders assume that support for capital punishment is politically safe, while opposition is seen as eroding political popularity.

Even though Republicans are in general more enthusiastic about the death penalty, most Democrats do not seem willing to oppose it. Since the public is accustomed to and in favor of a "get-tough" attitude toward criminal offenders, it became difficult and politically dangerous for politicians to take a firm stand against the death penalty. During the 1992 presidential campaign, Bill Clinton expressed strong support for expanded police efforts, more aggressive border interdiction programs, and tougher penalties for drug offenders. The drive for tougher punishment prompted him, when he was still a governor, to return to Arkansas in the midst of the campaign to approve and oversee the execution of a convicted murderer so mentally retarded he hid a piece of pie to eat when he came back from the death chamber.[77] By endorsing the execution of a person with an IQ in the 70s, Clinton attempted to signal and demonstrate his tough "law and order" credentials. During his presidency, Clinton signed the Violent Crime Control and Law Enforcement Act (1994), which expanded the federal death penalty to some sixty crimes, three of which do not involve murder—espionage, treason, and high-volume drug trafficking. In addition, he refused to nominate anyone to the federal bench who was opposed to the death penalty in all circumstances.[78]

After Clinton, Democratic candidates embraced virtually all of the components of conservative law and order rhetoric and policy. The 2000 presidential election is notable for the fact that each of the initial eleven candidates for president, despite other ideological differences, made clear his support for the death penalty. Al Gore declared clearly that he favored the death penalty to counter any possible assertion that he was soft on crime. On the heated issue of capital punishment, a change in stance for a politician is not uncommon. Former governor Roy Romer of Colorado was "an avowed foe of the death penalty." Yet as the support of a majority of Colorado citizens for capital punishment grew, so did the governor's.[79] As recently as the primary election for the 2004 presidency, former Governor Howard Dean of Vermont, the liberal maverick in the field of nine Democratic contenders and once an outspoken opponent of the death penalty, discarded his previous position, and extended his endorsement of the death sentence for those who kill children or police officers to include those who commit terrorist acts. To voters alarmed about crime, and with an appetite for retribution, the death penalty has become a litmus test that few candidates, national or local, dare to fail.

The influence of conservative Republicans on death penalty policies is even stronger. Senate Republicans, in 1993, pledged opposition to judicial nominees they considered insufficiently committed to the death penalty. Senator Orrin Hatch of Utah, the ranking Republican on the Judiciary Committee, remarked: "Where the death penalty is warranted, we don't need judges who look for excuses not to carry it out."[80] Missouri state judge Ronnie White was denied a federal judgeship in 1999 by Senate Republicans, mainly led by then-Senator John Ashcroft, who declared Judge White "pro-criminal," in part because he opposed the death penalty.[81] Most prominently, George W. Bush oversaw 152 executions in the state of Texas during his five-year governorship. In proportion to the population, the number of executions carried out in Texas surpasses that in China. In June 1995, Governor Bush signed a bill aimed at reducing the time spent on death penalty appeals by two-and-one-half years. The new law was reported to save taxpayers an estimated $50,000 per inmate in overall costs. Legislative changes across the United States resulted in a dramatic increase in the number of executions, from thirty-one in 1994 to ninety-eight in 1999.[82] After taking office, President Bush also allowed federal executions to resume after nearly four decades without them. Even though the number of federal death row inmates is very small compared to the number of prisoners awaiting execution by the states, Bush's action carries substantial symbolic meaning.[83]

The separation of powers system of the United States is less resistant to raw public opinion than European parliamentary governments. In parliamentary systems, people tend to vote for parties, which have more ideological variety, rather than for individuals. As a result, parties are less influenced by every reaction of the electorate, so that raw public opinion does not necessarily translate into legislative action. U.S. candidates are less insulated from populist impulses, and this feature of the U.S. political structure allows popular support for capital punishment to translate more easily and more directly into public policy.

IS POLITICAL LEADERSHIP A REMAINING VIRTUE?

As Zimring aptly notes, "[T]he prospect of abolition creates the potential for opposition from citizens who are politically conservative or authoritarian in their orientation, who place high values on community punishment in the vigilante tradition or who revere the claim of states' rights in a federal system."[84] This makes the United States different from its Western peers: capital punishment has a special and enduring political salience given the U.S. political and cultural context. Support for the death penalty seems to be beneficial to politicians: "[P]olitically, it's easier for any governor to execute a criminal than spare him."[85]

It is interesting to compare this situation with what happened in France when the death penalty was an important issue in the presidential election campaign in the early 1980s. During *Cartes sur la table*, a French television program on the election campaign, candidate François Mitterrand spelled out his conviction:

> As with the other issues, I will not hide my views on the death penalty. And I have no intention of going to the country in this race and pretending to be something that I am not. In my innermost conscience, like the churches, the Catholic church, the Reformed churches, Judaism, and all the important national and international humanitarian associations, in my heart of hearts, I am opposed to the death penalty. . . . I am standing for the presidency of the French Republic, and in asking for a majority of French people's votes, I do not hide what I think. I say what I think, what I hold to, what I believe in, and what my spiritual beliefs and concern for civilization are based on: I am not in favor of the death penalty.[86]

Despite Mitterrand's strong opposition to the death penalty, he was elected as president in May 1981. Several months later, in October 1981, the death penalty was abolished in France for all crimes, both civilian and military. If a candidate for president of the United States were to oppose capital punishment so explicitly and forcefully, would the same result occur? Are there even any prominent politicians in the United States who refuse to follow the public fever in terms of capital punishment? In that regard, the role of Republican Governor George Ryan of Illinois is noteworthy. When he pardoned four death row prisoners and commuted all 167 other death sentences in Illinois in January 2003, Governor Ryan energized the death penalty debate, setting up a special bipartisan commission to investigate the state's capital punishment system. He is one of very few models for this sort of bravery in the recent U.S. experience.

CONCLUDING REMARKS

According to FBI statistics, between twenty thousand and twenty-one thousand criminal homicides were recorded annually in the United States for the ten years preceding 2000.[87] Of these, only three thousand cases on average were egregious enough to qualify for the death penalty, and three hundred actually resulted in a death sentence. Only fifty people, on average, were executed annually during this period.[88] The chances of a murderer being caught, prosecuted, convicted, and then executed are about one in a thousand, implying that a murderer has to be very unlucky indeed to end up being executed. Furthermore, race, economic status, location of the crime, and a host of other factors dictate who is executed and who is spared. This raises the question whether it is possible to achieve fairness in executions given these odds and the vagaries of the criminal justice system. The practice of capital punishment remains a lottery—or it applies only to defendants who are put at a disadvantage by race, sex, poverty, and other unjust factors.

Each country has its own peculiar death penalty story. The recognition of the complex singularity of each nation's experiences with capital punishment reveals the simplistic homicide rate hypothesis to be fundamentally incomplete or inadequate. The homicide rate, or the crime rate in general, is neither a necessary nor sufficient cause for the retention or abolition of capital punishment. The argument that the death penalty remains in force because of public support runs into bigger problems. Given that similar levels of public support for capital punishment exist everywhere in the world, we can assume that public opinion hardly explains American exceptionalism with regard to the ongoing practice of the death penalty. In addition, the credibility of public opinion surveys is called into question when we see that they yield different results depending on the amount of accurate knowledge respondents have about the death penalty, as well as on the way in which questions regarding the death penalty are asked.

Capital punishment in the United States is located within several broader contexts: cultural, political, and historical. A cultural variable has a strong potential to explain the historical pattern of current behavior surrounding capital punishment. The gross disproportions in executions across

U.S. states have no parallel in the distribution of death penalty statutes, rates of murder, or even death sentences. The sentiments and values associated with a vigilante past are linked to current regional differences in the practice of capital punishment, as the Southern inclination toward high rates of execution is closely linked to the vigilante tradition itself.

Although there are many other nations where vigilante behaviors and attitudes were once pervasive, it is peculiar to the United States that such values and sentiments are much stronger and still influential in the twenty-first century. Countries that share an extensive frontier tradition with the United States, such as Australia, Canada, or Mexico, got rid of capital punishment a long time ago, suggesting that the continued practice of the death penalty in the United States cannot be merely explained as a legacy of the country's frontier past. The vigilante tradition and values are strongly generated by and reinforced within the populist nature of U.S. electoral politics, which makes capital punishment more responsive to the public will. In addition, its federalism allows capital punishment to be mostly a matter of state law and state politics, which largely insulates the nation from international pressure. State governments are much less likely to be interested in or influenced by international conventions.

Few U.S. politicians are willing to ignore the preferences of most of their constituents. Elsewhere, however, we see that action by courageous political leaders has been needed to overcome local public opinion that has remained mostly in favor of the death penalty. These leaders have somehow managed to denounce the death penalty in opposition to the populace's view. In the United States, it may well require an extremely brave political initiative by presidential or congressional leadership to turn the tide of public perception and lead the change. Political leadership seems to be the only answer. When we calculate the political costs and risks in a society so sensitive to public opinion, however, the prospect of strong political leadership in opposition to the tradition of capital punishment is highly unlikely. Here is the central dilemma of American capital punishment.

CHAPTER SIX

CONCLUSION

"Punishment," despite this singular generic noun, is not a singular kind of entity. We need to remind ourselves, again and again, that the phenomenon which we refer to, too simply, as "punishment," is in fact a complex set of interlinked processes and institutions, rather than a uniform object or event.

—David Garland, *Punishment and Modern Society*

Death is different from other punishments practiced in our society—different in its morality, its politics, and its symbolism. My belief and hope is that once these differences are truly understood, support for punitive killing will lessen and eventually subside.

—Hugo Adam Bedau, *Death Is Different*

The death penalty is unique among human rights issues. Compared with other policies considered to be human rights violations, including torture, slavery, arbitrary arrest and detention, and extrajudicial executions, the death penalty is different in that it takes place within authorized or legal procedures, and, partly owing to this reason, it has been widely supported by the vast majority of the public in most countries. Unlike other "easy" norms that are generally buttressed by popular opinion and thus find it relatively easy to influence domestic policy change, the norm against the death penalty is a "hard" case that provokes domestic resistance.

Yet, despite public opposition, a change has been made. In not much more than fifty years, a remarkable number of countries in different parts of the world have complied with this difficult and unpopular international human rights norm that bans the death penalty in all its forms, no matter how awful the crime or how savage the criminal. Europe, where the death penalty remained in the penal codes of most countries at the end of World War II, has completely· abolished the death penalty. Countries that had already abandoned the death penalty for ordinary crimes abolished it for all crimes, including terrorism and treason, as well as for military offenses. And this movement toward the universal abolition of the death penalty is under way in many countries outside of Europe. Altogether, by January 2007, one hundred twenty-nine countries had abolished the death penalty in law and practice. Sixty-eight other countries and territories retain the death penalty, but the number of countries that actually carry out executions is much smaller.[1] This trend demonstrates that, despite the partial match or mismatch between the international norm and prevailing domestic understanding, abolition of the death penalty in compliance with the norm has nonetheless become a central political phenomenon worldwide.

This study aims to expand our understandings of how, why, and under what conditions the state complies with unpopular international human rights norms. It focuses on two central questions: How does the state comply with international norms, especially those that lack popular support? By what mechanisms or pathways do international norms affect the state's domestic politics? Much of this research involves a detailed look at the political and cultural determinants of capital punishment policy, but its point of departure is international relations theory about the ways in which international norms become translated into domestic politics. I begin with a summary of each case considered in this research. Then I present in some detail the hypothesized processes that mediate between the existence of the international norm and its impact on domestic politics and policy choice. I attempt ultimately to identify plausible conditions and mechanisms that lead to state compliance with the norm against the death penalty. Finally, I discuss the wider implications of the research.

WAYS OF NORM COMPLIANCE: UKRAINE, SOUTH AFRICA, SOUTH KOREA, AND THE UNITED STATES

Ukraine

International human rights organizations play a significant role in persuading and coercing their member states to embrace transnationally promoted norms and values. The Council of Europe, a loose grouping of countries that often serves as a stepping-stone for those aspiring to join the European Union, has explicitly demanded that prospective members drop the death penalty as a nonnegotiable prerequisite to accession. Since the abolition of the death penalty became a formal condition for membership, the abolition issue has figured significantly as a measure of human rights probity during accession negotiations between the Council of Europe and applicant states. As a result, the admission criteria called the *acquis communautaire* have acted as a powerful spur to former Soviet states to eliminate their death penalty laws in the past few years.

Until Ukraine finally abolished capital punishment in early 2000, this country had been a serious "project" of the Council of Europe. Ukraine, having joined the council in 1995 and eager to be a "good neighbor" in the European community, kept executing its citizens nonetheless. The year after joining the council, 1996, Ukraine carried out 167 executions, the second-highest number worldwide in that year (China had the highest number).[2] Yet the ongoing persuasion ("You will be a good neighbor in our European community") and threats ("We will annul your membership otherwise") orchestrated by both the Parliamentary Assembly and the Committee of Ministers of the Council of Europe finally led Ukraine to make the crucial decision to abolish the death penalty. Ukrainian discourse and laws on the death penalty have since changed in ways consistent with new international understandings promoted by the Council of Europe.

Quite a few research projects have highlighted elite learning processes in explaining how and why states comply with international norms.[3] I agree that Ukrainian elites "learned" a great deal from the Council of Europe, and that the socialization and learning process played an important role in encouraging this country to adhere to unwanted norms. Yet it is equally important to note that when norms are backed by primary material incentives, learning and persuasion are more likely to be successful and politically feasible. For Ukraine, it was evident that being a part of the European community would guarantee its survival. Put differently, international norms are likely to be embraced if they are perceived to support important domestic material interests, whether economic or security-related. Ukraine had to choose between joining the Western world by abolishing the death penalty or retaining a strong penal policy in order to try to tame a society that was crime-stricken and undergoing radical transformation. The latter course, however, would lead to eventual expulsion from the Council of Europe. Ukraine's choice seemed to serve the state's interest better in the given situation. The benefits of joining Europe far exceeded the benefits that Ukraine might have gained from the routine use of the death penalty. Clearly, Ukraine's policy change regarding the death penalty was mainly based on strategic means-ends considerations at both domestic and international levels.

South Africa

A dramatic change with regard to the death penalty was made in South Africa, beginning with the release of Nelson Mandela in 1990. By 1992, all executions were suspended pending the introduction of a Bill of Rights for the new South Africa. It was indeed a sudden decision, given this country's long-standing history of the practice of the death penalty: about 2000 people were executed between 1971 and 1990.[4] Between 1978 and the end of the 1980s, the number of executions was greater than one hundred per year in all but one year. The number reached a stunning 172 in 1987, the highest annual figure since 1910.[5] Hence, when the Constitutional Court of South Africa proclaimed the death penalty unconstitutional in June 1995, Roger Hood wrote: "Who, a decade ago, would have predicted the abandonment of capital punishment in South Africa?"[6] It was acclaimed: "Even South Africa drops death penalty!"[7]

In the landmark judgment of *State v. Makwanyane*, the South African court declared that the death penalty was incompatible with the "human rights culture," including protection of the right to life and prohibition of cruel, inhuman, and degrading treatment or punishment, on which the post-apartheid constitution was based. The court, actively looking up international and foreign law precedents and quoting the worldwide campaign against the death penalty, made it clear that to repeal capital punishment was to join the international human rights movement. Facing a situation of endemic violence, the Constitutional Court maintained that the way to reduce violence is not to practice "uncivilized" punishment, but to create a culture where human rights are respected. At present, a soaring crime rate has produced a noisy pro-restoration campaign backed by opposition parties, but the South African government has adamantly, and so far successfully, refused to consider such a move.

The new South Africa has shown that a country may follow international norms even when such behavior does not necessarily serve political interests, including responding to dominant public opinion and getting tough on crime. This directly challenges rationalist thinking about the self-interested behavior of states. While no obvious material incentives or interests existed, a prevailing set of normative ideas played an important role in policy change. Those ideas included collective memories of injustice under past policy and a shared conception about the appropriate role of the new government, which together constituted the political discourse of this country.[8]

Domestic policymakers in South Africa were motivated by the logic of appropriateness, rather than the logic of consequences, and voluntarily complied with the tenets of the international human rights norm.[9] Whereas Ukraine adopted the international norm when pressures raised the cost of keeping the death penalty higher than the benefit, South Africa based its policy choice on what it believed to be the correct rules of behavior. The impact of human rights norms in South Africa reached deeper and thus reconstituted the elites' identities and preferences regarding humanitarian issues. Human rights principles became a central part of the national self-image through the revolutionary political transformation that brought the end of apartheid.

South Korea

Across many parts of Asia, capital punishment is on the rise, with China, Vietnam, Bangladesh, and, most recently, the Philippines making international headlines because of their enthusiastic support for the death penalty.

They appear to emulate each other in adopting a zero-tolerance approach to crime and robustly embracing the death penalty. While more than 90 percent of all executions in the world take place in Asia, South Korea is apparently taking a different path from its neighbors both in terms of the social attitude surrounding the death penalty and its actual practice. No death row inmates have been executed since 1998, and legislation to abolish the death penalty has been submitted to the National Assembly three times in six years. The growing abolitionist movement in Korea stands in marked contrast to this country's authoritarian past when the death penalty was imposed not only on common criminals but also on those who refused to support government policy.

Yet formal abolition of the death penalty does not seem to come easily. Legislative initiatives to remove the death penalty from the penal codes have failed, and a series of Constitutional Court decisions confirmed the constitutionality of the death penalty. Compared to other countries that abolished the death penalty relatively quickly, South Korea seems to lack two important elements. First, at the international level, Korea never experienced any regional enforcement mechanisms to protect human rights. Asia is the only continent that has no regional human rights enforcement agency, and thus Korea, like its neighbors, has been immune from direct influence of international human rights norms, including the norm against the death penalty. With no outside pressure, Korea, surrounded by countries that support capital punishment, has no incentives to expedite the process of abolition. Second, Korea's political transformation has been incremental, with no drastic breaks from the past. The death penalty was abolished more quickly in many countries, including South Africa and Ukraine, that experienced radical regime changes and thus could expedite legal reforms that might have taken much longer to accomplish in times of stable government. Korea's political continuity, despite meaningful democratic progress, has kept previous legal or penal institutions almost intact. When there is neither international pressure nor a revolutionary change from the past, a state finds it more difficult to change in order to adopt a norm, especially when the norm is not popular domestically. The continuing suspension of executions in Korea, without any actual move to formal abolition, seems to confirm this hypothesis.

United States

The U.S. position on the death penalty provides an illuminating case study of the maintenance of sovereignty in the face of organized international human rights campaigns against capital punishment. It symbolizes the U.S. determination to interpret human rights in accordance with the U.S. Constitution and public opinion, rather than in harmony with internationally recognized and promoted principles and rules. The United States stands alone among Western industrial democracies in imposing the death penalty, in contrast to the global trend toward abolition. U.S. allies of long standing, including the members of the European Union, Canada, and Australia, have increasingly criticized the practice of executions, with particular emphasis on the execution of juvenile offenders and the mentally retarded. Despite the declaration of a "war on terror" by the United States, major European countries have announced that they will not extradite alleged terrorists if the suspects are threatened by a death sentence. In addition, they will not provide specific intelligence information on defendants charged with the murder.[10] As Roger Hood points out, the European initiative to influence so-called third world countries toward rejection of the death penalty has been criticized, mainly because the United States "continues to reject human rights arguments on the death penalty as defined by international consensus or treaty unless they are endorsed by its own Supreme Court."[11]

Why is the United States, or at least thirty-eight of its states and the federal government, which maintain the death penalty, so out of step with international opinion among countries with whom it shares similar social and political values? Why do "Americans not pay decent respect to the world opinion with regard to capital punishment"?[12] I argue that the retention of the death penalty in the United States closely relates to the nature of the domestic institutional systems. Major features of U.S. federalism and its electoral policies can fairly be described as populist. Political leadership in the United States is less resistant to raw public opinion, especially given that most public officials, such as district attorneys, prosecutors, and judges, are directly elected. Public officials, subjected to the popular vote, fear to voice their opposition to the death penalty, while European political elites are more likely to enjoy the autonomy to pursue liberal human rights norms in the face of political controversies and public opposition. Given such conditions, political leaders in the United States can take advantage of the symbolic politics of the death penalty by which they can acquire other benefits, including promoting the political message of being tough on crime.

Indeed, political leadership seems to be the most plausible explanation for how a norm that does not resonate with popular beliefs can be adopted domestically. Yet the nature of U.S. political institutions limits the political leverage and possibilities available to leaders. The sensitivity of U.S. political leaders to public sentiment also implies that once public opinion changes, political leaders are likely to react to the public's new attitude. Unlike most countries, which abolished the death penalty through political initiatives that went against public beliefs, the United States may abolish it only after a change in public opinion.

CONDITIONS FOR NORM COMPLIANCE

Cultural Match: Crime Rate and Social Inequality

As discussed in chapter 1, the "cultural match" between the international norm and domestic cultural settings refers to the conditions that determine the impact of an international norm once it enters the national arena. In the case of capital punishment, the impact of crime rates and social inequality has been addressed. Does the death penalty exist because of the prevalence of social and political violence in a given country? The most common, and most commonsensical, argument for the death penalty—that it deters crime more effectively than any other punishment—has been widely discredited by the lack of scientific evidence. The lesson from the deterrence literature is that there is no causal connection between the use of capital punishment and reduction in crime. The literature argues that the death penalty is an illusory or ineffective solution to controlling the problem of violent crime. Crime rates are more influenced by various social factors, including the effectiveness of police in bringing perpetrators to justice, than by the distant threat of execution.[13] According to death penalty opponents, what is ultimately at stake is the articulation of state policy toward bodily integrity and toward the sanctity of life. Renate Wohlwend, European parliamentarian, states: "In fact, it could be argued that by institutionalizing death, we create a more violent society."[14] Since the United States routinely carries out lethal injections, electrocutions, and hangings, the legal structure clearly endorses the idea that killing the criminal is an appropriate response to certain crimes. From this perspective, the reduction or abolition of capital punishment would demonstrate a commitment by the state to nonviolence, and would affirm its recognition of each citizen's inviolable right to physical integrity.

Crime is not deterred by the death penalty, nor do high crime rates necessarily determine the existence of the death penalty or the frequency of executions. The death penalty was abolished both in South Africa and Ukraine during dramatic surges in crime rates after their regime changes.[15] These two countries outlawed the death penalty at a time when fighting crime was the leading challenge for their governments. Over the last five years, the U.S. murder rate per one hundred thousand people has been one-half that of Russia, although the total number of death sentences was almost twice as high. Likewise, the death penalty is widely practiced in Japan and India, where violent crime rates are in no way exceptional. There are many examples that seem to deny the link between crime rates and the death penalty.

The hypothesis of social inequality looks more compelling, especially in the cases of South Africa and the United States. In South Africa, once known as "the capital punishment capital of the world," the death sentence was imposed disproportionately on the black population by an almost entirely white judiciary. As is still true in many states of the United States, black defendants stood a greater chance of being sentenced to death than white defendants, especially when the victim was white. The U.S. states with the largest death row populations and the highest numbers of executions annually include Texas, Florida, and Virginia, which have long and strong histories of racial disparity. It is difficult to totally reject the historical connection between the administration of capital punishment and the legacy of racial discrimination.

Studies have denied the "cultural match" principle as an explanatory variable for some internationally promoted norms such as democracy and human rights.[16] The people of postindependence Ukraine did not all share normative values with respect to human rights, and yet newly empowered national elites were able to institutionalize the norm against the death penalty espoused by the regional human rights organization. As Gerald Curtis aptly notes, "the varieties of political experience are not experienced by 'culture,' which at best constitutes a broad and changing framework within which a great variety of political regimes and behaviors are possible."[17] Given that there is no clear link in most countries between capital punishment and other elements of the core culture of the communities governed, as discussed in chapter 1, we should remain skeptical of the cultural explanation.

International Organization and Neighbors: Contagious Effects

International pressure has not been a necessary condition for the abolition of capital punishment. Through all the years of suspension and abolition of the death penalty in Western Europe, there was no international organization or government-to-government pressure animating the change in policy. It was almost exclusively a matter of the internal politics of each nation, as the issue of the death penalty was considered part of state sovereignty. During the last few decades, however, transnational pressure has been significant for "new democracies." The norm against capital punishment, once confined largely to the domestic arena, has become increasingly internationalized and transnationalized. In an increasingly united Europe, in particular, pressure from neighboring states has had a great impact on domestic decision making.

Interactions between states and the international organizations regarding human rights are characterized not only by strategic pressures and threats but also by diplomatic persuasion. Transnational organizations such as the Council of Europe played a key role in death penalty decisions in Central and Eastern Europe, where a pattern of decline of capital punishment has prevailed. Member states of the organization share a political culture that includes internationally accepted standards of human rights and humanitarian law to inhibit abuse. Governments altered their agendas, behavior, and institutions in an attempt to comply with widespread standards of human rights, which many of them view as morally right. In some cases governments made changes to conform with prevailing norms simply because doing so was of great help to their interests. Yet international pressure in support of the abolition of the death penalty is by no means limited to the European community. Whether or not transnational human rights organizations are active in their region, nations in Asia, America, and Africa do not seem to respond to pressure from their neighbors or

regional organizations on this issue; they continue to pursue capital punishment according to their own judgment.

Public Opinion and Moral Leadership

Mass public opinion has been considered to play a crucial role in determining state policy on the death penalty. Strong public support appears to be
the main reason for retaining capital punishment.[18] Yet this explanation
runs into a number of anomalous problems. First of all, most people who
respond to public polls are generally uninformed about the death penalty,
which suggests that in most instances they formulate their attitudes without a clear understanding of the salient issues. When specific issues are
raised, such as executing the mentally retarded, juvenile murderers, criminals of a particular race and economic status, and those who are in fact
innocent, most people have strong reservations about the ultimate punishment. People's attitude toward the death penalty changes as they gain more
knowledge of the facts.[19] Public support for the death penalty is widespread,
yet also quite shallow. Compared to other social and political issues, support for the death penalty is more common but less intense. Accordingly,
Herbert Haines characterizes death penalty support as "a mile wide and an
inch deep."[20]

Second, public sentiment in favor of the death penalty is similar across
countries, regardless of political and social backgrounds. Regarding the arguments of both supporters and opponents of the death penalty, and in many
of the determinants of public opinion, countries have many more similarities
than differences. Public sentiment on criminal policy in general has been
conservative everywhere. Across the world, including in Europe and other
advanced industrial abolitionist nations, large segments of the public support
capital punishment, which suggests that such support is not closely linked to
the likelihood of governmental action.[21] According to the findings of a *Le
Figaro-Sofres* survey, 62 percent of the French population favored maintaining the guillotine when President François Mitterrand decided to ban the
death penalty in 1981.[22] It was only in 1999 that poll support in France
dipped below 50 percent for the first time.[23] In Britain—the world headquar-
ters of Amnesty International—between two-thirds and three-quarters of
those responding to public opinion polls favored the death penalty, which is
about the same as in the United States.[24] Similarly, at least 70 percent of the
German population was in favor of retaining the death penalty at the time
of its abolition.[25] Despite the abolition of the death penalty in the mid-1970s
in Canada, public support for it is only slightly lower there than in the
United States; opinion polls consistently show that between 60 percent and
70 percent of Canadians want the death penalty reinstated.[26] Canada's low
crime rates make an association between high crime rates and public support
for the death penalty unlikely.

It is hard to find any country around the globe that banned capital punishment in response to public opinion rather than in spite of it. A public support level of 70 percent or more in favor of the punishment is not a significant barrier to its abolition. States, if in compliance with international and regional treaties banning capital punishment, are clearly not following popular demand, or responding to internal pressure: "[S]uccessful and sustained abolition [of the death penalty] has never been a result of great popular demand."[27] A majority in opposition to capital punishment is neither a necessary nor a sufficient condition for abolition.

Third, what value and significance should we give to opinion polls on the death penalty? One example proves noteworthy. Two institutes polled the French people on the very same date. One institute stated: "54% of those questioned said that they did not wish the death penalty to be restored," but the other announced: "50% are in favor of the death penalty and 46% against."[28] How can we interpret these results? Does a majority of the French population favor the death penalty but oppose its restoration? According to the questionnaires, the first question was "Are you in favor of restoring the death penalty?" and the second was "Are you in favor of the death penalty?" To be sure, the contrasting answers may reflect the differences in the wording of the questions. As many studies suggest, if the questions were more sophisticated, the polls would probably give a better sense of the complexities of public opinion with regard to the death penalty.[29] Death penalty support may even become a minority opinion when the public is presented with a variety of alternative sentences.[30]

Public opinion in the abolitionist countries appears to follow elite behavior and policy outcomes rather than lead them. In the mid-1970s public opinion on the death penalty was similar in the United States and Western Europe: In both cases, public support was slightly over 50 percent. European governments outlawed capital punishment and the number of supporters decreased steadily in Europe, while the U.S. Supreme Court reinstated the death penalty and public support increased an average of more than one percentage point per year over the next few decades, reaching 80 percent in 1994, which is a record high in the United States.[31] Abolition of capital punishment usually provokes no great public outcry or political backlash. With a few exceptions, public reaction to abolition is muted, and pressure to restore capital punishment weakens; only four countries in the world have reinstated the death penalty after abolition. This must mean that even when the majority of people in a given country favors the death penalty, abolition is accepted. As Zimring points out, "[T]he presence or absence of a death penalty may not be a very important issue to the man in the streets."[32] Polls that ask respondents to state their position on the death penalty, however, do not usually reveal the low degree of intensity of public opinion on this issue. Politicians in abolitionist nations might have known this and thus did not rest their case solely on opinion polls. The fact that opposition to abolition has been short-lived and ineffectual suggests that the death penalty is not of enduring political significance to those who favor it.

Policy changes precede opinion changes, suggesting that the former cause the latter rather than vice versa. Strong political leadership has therefore been an important channel for transmitting international norms to the domestic agenda. When the vast majority of the public everywhere is in favor of capital punishment, the decision to abolish it must be taken by the nation's government, legislators, and courts. What matters more for abolition is political willingness to act against public opinion and to choose a more civilized and humane political order over a fully popular and participatory one.[33] In fact, when the death penalty was abolished in Western European countries, most governments persuaded a reluctant public to learn and accept the fact that the death penalty not only violates fundamental human rights but is also not the most effective means for combating crime. The norm that promotes the abolition of the death penalty is not only ethical but also practical and logical.

This invites an interesting question, however, as to whether the demand for abolition contradicts the basic principles of democracy: Should not any policy under democratic governments be made or reformed in accordance with the will of the majority? According to Joshua Marshall, "[I]f these [abolitionist] countries' political cultures are morally superior to America's, it's because they're less democratic. . . . Europe doesn't have the death penalty because its political systems are less democratic, or at least more insulated from populist impulse."[34] If democracy is defined as majoritarian rule narrowly conceived, the attempt to abolish the death penalty against the dominant opinions and values of the general public is certainly not democratic. Yet liberal democratic theory has long maintained that democracy means more than a solely procedural, majoritarian rule. Protections of civil liberties and minority rights are also an important component of most definitions of democracy.

Political leaders in any society cannot be entirely immune to the influence of public sentiment. Perhaps it is wrong to give no credit to public opinion when states come to embrace norm-inspired policy commitments. Nonetheless, in all successful cases of abolition, political elites, including the executives, legislators, and judges, were active in shaping public opinion. As Richard Buxton predicted a few decades ago, the usual process for ending the death penalty begins "from the front."[35] The case of South Africa, in particular, illustrates that abolition occurs through a combination of judicial leaders' efforts and sympathetic political support, even as it goes against public wishes. The South African Constitutional Court and Nelson Mandela's ANC demonstrated that the pattern of public opinion regarding the death penalty was difficult to determine because many people were conflicted, ambivalent, and uncertain about the morality of the death penalty. The court argued that if public support cannot be determined with any certainty, and if it waxes and wanes in response to arbitrary events, it should not decide government policy, particularly not one that determines life and death.[36] This also suggests the important distinction between the wishes of the majority, on the one hand, and the role of the state and political elites in protecting the rights of the minority and others who cannot defend their rights adequately through the democratic process, on the other. Even if this stance is unpopular, the "trustee" model of political leadership suggests that it is the inescapable duty of honest politicians to explain to the electorate what stance they would take.[37] In the decisions to abolish the death penalty, both the South African and Ukrainian courts maintained that the state might take the lead in determining what part of public opinion is relevant and what weight to attach to it in assessing the validity of a policy. Once the relevance and weight of public opinion have been determined, the courts play a role in educating citizens as to why such a determination was made. They, after all, have the capacity to inform public opinion rather than following its lead. Again, abolition of capital punishment requires courageous political leadership.

Domestic Political Institutions

Similarities in public attitudes toward the death penalty across different countries do not necessarily lead to similar policy outcomes. The death penalty has been retained in some countries in accordance with public support, while in others, with similar public support, it has been abolished. Thus, if public attitudes cannot explain differences in death penalty policies, one has to look at the features of domestic political institutions by which the significance of public opinion is highly conditioned. The centralized unitary systems in South Africa and Ukraine made it relatively easier to reach a political decision with regard to the death penalty. Centralized state institutions strongly helped political elites to impose unpopular norm-based policy on society against domestic resistance. By contrast, the comparatively decentralized and fragmented nature of American political institutions, which grants each state extraordinary power to set its own policies, weakens political autonomy. Even as compared with other Western democracies that have a long tradition of federal government, such as Canada, Germany, or Switzerland, the United States is the only country that gives full criminal legislative power to individual states. This is indeed a defining element of the unique policy environment of American capital punishment. In the United States, most criminal justice responsibilities, including execution policy, are vested in individual state governments, under which more than 95 percent of all executions since 1977 have been conducted. Moreover, the United States has more elected officers per capita than any country in the world, providing public opinion with ample opportunity to affect policy.[38] It is certainly true that national policy on the death penalty is heavily screened by American public sentiment.

The United States has been less susceptible to international pressure and far more responsive to domestic populist impulse. The fact that the individual states impose death sentences and carry out the actual executions, rather than the federal government, helps to explain why the international campaign against the U.S. death penalty proves difficult.[39] International pressure cannot effectively target a single governmental authority; instead, it is weakly dispersed against those thirty-eight retentionist states.[40] Zimring and Hawkins are right when they note: "[P]otentially unpopular steps are more often taken at the national level than by state or local governments; more often by the judiciary than the executive; and still less frequently by the legislature."[41] This may also explain the broader issue of "American exceptionalism" in matters pertaining to human rights. As Andrew Moravcsik points out, conservative opponents of international human rights norms tend to be empowered by the decentralized federal political institutions in the United States.[42] The impact of public opinion on policy does not depend so much on the specific issues involved or on the particular pattern of public attitudes as on the domestic institutional structure.

Clean Break with the Past

At the end of World War II, the first major nations to abolish capital punishment were the losing powers (except for Japan). Italy abandoned it first in 1944, followed by the Federal Republic of Germany in 1949. Those defeated nations abolished the death penalty sooner than the major victorious powers, such as England and France, which kept the death penalty for decades after the war's end. The defeated nations abolished the death penalty more quickly than the victorious nations because the former experienced radical changes of regime when the war ended, which enabled them to push through legal reforms that might have taken much longer to accomplish under stable governments. The pace of change was more rapid largely because of radical political change in transitional governments.

The relatively prompt reform in death penalty policy both in South Africa and Ukraine is explained by the same line of logic. New democratic elites in these countries promulgated a new, postauthoritarian constitution when the political context allowed them leverage to ponder and decide what kind of government they would create and to avoid succumbing to public opposition. The political moment was a crucial catalyst in embodying the political will in policy changes. If the right moment for abolition had been missed, the death penalty would probably still exist, especially considering the ongoing mass protest against abolition in both countries.

Korea's historical experience is similar to that of many other newly democratized countries, including South Africa and Ukraine, in that political and social resistance was crushed for decades under a hard-core, authoritarian regime. Yet the difference in the pattern of transition is rather clear:

the demise of apartheid (South Africa) and the gaining of independence (Ukraine) entailed revolutionary social and political change, whereas the political transition of South Korea was incremental. Despite its progress toward democracy, Korea lacks a clean break with the past, so that the age-old state institutions and public mindset remain largely intact. The argument that reform of the penal system, including abolition of capital punishment, is dangerous and detrimental to the country's own military and societal concerns still finds majority support in Korea. It is therefore difficult for political leaders to find an opportunity to decide on monumental changes. Progressive political action requires a "moment of decision."

CAUSAL MECHANISMS OF NORM COMPLIANCE

Figure 6.1 illustrates the mechanism of norm adoption in the case of the death penalty. Political leadership is significant because the norm against the death penalty does not resonate with public opinion. The leadership is either internal, coming from the government, the legislators, and the courts, or external, as with the pressuring and persuading roles of leaders of regional institutions and neighboring countries. The leverage of this leadership is mediated both by the nature of domestic political institutions and by the political "opportunities" created by radical political transformations. A more centralized decision-making process allows leadership to be more autonomous from the predominant public will, which usually opposes abolition of the death penalty. Political elites are then more likely to take a countermajoritarian stance on issues. The process of abolition is also expedited when a radical political transformation provides a favorable climate for more rapid change. Radical political transformation, which often entails a drastic regime change, is a critical factor in the state's adoption of controversial norms.

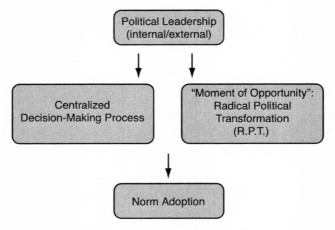

This figure can be generalized as following:

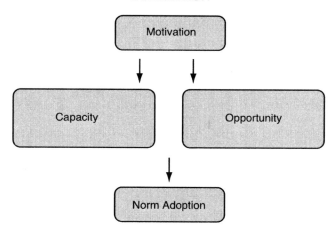

Figure 6.1. Causal Mechanisms of Norm Adoption[43]

Table 6.1 explains the trajectory of norm compliance in each case considered in this book. Strongly influenced by external leadership of the Council of Europe, Ukraine's adoption of the norm was made possible by its centralized political decision-making process and under the new political structure that emerged at a time of radical political transformation. South Africa saw determined internal political leadership from the ANC and Nelson Mandela. Their roles were successfully supported by two major features of the domestic political setting: a fairly autonomous decision-making process and the radical political transformation as the apartheid era ended. In South Korea, two of the elements necessary for norm adoption are present: a strong

Table 6.1. Pathways of Norm Compliance in Four Cases

Country	Source of Political Leadership		Attributes of Domestic Political Institutions/ Nature of Political Transformations		Outcome of Norm Compliance
Ukraine	External	→	Centralized/R.P.T.	→	Strong Compliance
South Africa	Internal	→	Centralized/R.P.T.	→	Strong Compliance
South Korea	Internal	→	Centralized/Incremental	→	Weak Compliance
United States	Not Applicable	→	Decentralized/no R.P.T.	→	Noncompliance

political willingness among elites to implement the international human rights norm in domestic law and a centralized decision-making process. Yet without a radical political change, the traditional penal policies remain deeply embedded in the status quo. Korea's slow political evolution lacks "moments of decision," that is, turning points of political significance. This has resulted in weak compliance with the norm against capital punishment (moratorium instead of abolition), even though the "right" person was in power. The United States is not responsive to external leadership. Domestic political leadership that might favor abolition is stymied by sensitivity to public opinion and the decentralized political setting. Moreover, when there is no process of radical political transformation in this well-established democracy, the prospect of norm compliance is dim.

CONCLUSION: EXTENDING THE ARGUMENT

The conditions of norm compliance discussed above are neither competing nor mutually exclusive explanations. State compliance with norms is too complex a political phenomenon to have only a single cause. A particular case of norm compliance may be a function of one or more of these factors. In other words, there may be multiple sufficient causes or mechanisms producing norm compliance. My hope is that the empirical investigation of this research to identify those causes and mechanisms will lead to the formulation of more precise hypotheses regarding the interaction of international norms and domestic factors in shaping state behavior. Despite the fact that every case is unique, we can make useful generalizations about why and under what conditions states comply with international norms.

I conclude with three major points derived from the foregoing discussion. First, in the process of norm compliance, the nature and features of domestic political institutions shape the circumstances under which political agents pursue policy reform with support from, or in opposition to, public opinion. The norm prohibiting the death penalty is unique, because its interpretation is so closely related to public beliefs and attitudes. A national populace resists embracing any international norm when its tenets are seen as inconsistent with prevailing values and traditions. When an international norm is in conflict with understandings and values established in the domestic sphere, political actors are likely to find that appeals to the international norm are ineffective in garnering support for a particular policy. Yet this research suggests that states can nonetheless endorse an international human rights norm even when it does not resonate with widely held public beliefs and opinions. In a liberal democracy, democratically elected representatives, who obviously should carry out the people's wishes, must also protect the rights of individuals and minorities. Leaders have the prerogative and obligation to affirm human rights for everyone. Thus, elite leadership may be as significant as widespread domestic beliefs and understanding—and often more important—in bringing the international norm into the domestic arena and bringing about policy change.

Determined political leadership is empowered when directed by either regional values or a change in national identity. A key concern in analyzing the balance between public beliefs and determined political leadership is to understand that this balance is conditioned, but not simply determined, by political institutional settings. An explanation based on political decentralization seems accurate with regard to policy choice in the United States. The U.S. political system is so "democratic" that state politicians respond strongly to populist, local, preferences, which provides a plausible explanation of American exceptionalism with regard to the death penalty. Yet this logic does not seem adequate to account for centralized, nonfederal democratic political systems in which the death penalty is nonetheless widely used, as in East Asia, South Asia, the Middle East, and northern Africa. Nor does it explain decentralized, federal systems such as Germany, Belgium, and Canada where the death penalty has long been abolished. The political institutional features are an intervening variable, and the key "agent" factors—such as changes in ideology among elites or the presence of international pressure—should be considered a prerequisite for setting the agenda and initiating policy change.

Second, moments of opportunity created by the presence of radical political change are a worthwhile subject of analysis. Undoubtedly the role of political leadership is crucial in a government's compliance with an international norm, especially when it is unpopular among the majority of the public. Perhaps the differences between the United States and other countries are due partly to historical circumstances—certainly the United States has never had a president who, like Nelson Mandela and Kim Dae-jung, faced the possibility of a death sentence during his life. Through their experience, both presidents seemed to realize that certain tasks require the state to take the lead. If the issue concerns human life and dignity, in particular, the state should uphold such values, whether the general public supports them or not.

A political moment of opportunity that arises out of urgent circumstances plays a positive role in putting new ideas into practice. Both South Africa and Ukraine experienced a radical political transformation that was the catalyst for elites' moments of decision. Fully established democracies (the United States) or pseudo-established ones (South Korea) are reluctant to comply with international norms. As Bryan Jones points out, it is very likely that the sudden flurry of interest caused by "discontinuous and non-incremental" transformation leads to and influences changes in a nation's political agenda.[44] The broad implications and results of political and legal decision making cannot be solely explained as a direct reflection of changing social structure. However, the nature of political transformation is another important intervening force, along with the structural aspects of domestic political institutions, that affects the choices of strong political leadership in the face of public opposition. States respond to international norms in complex ways that relate not only to actor-centered factors such as transnational pressure, dominant domestic beliefs, and elite leadership but also to context-centered factors such as the nature of domestic political structures and their transformation.

Third, it is important to understand what drives state policy changes. The fundamental reasons for state compliance with international rules and norms are either that compliance serves state's material goals or that it is appropriate behavior given the national identity formation, or both. States may comply because of a cost-benefit analysis, as in the case of Ukraine, which ultimately abolished the death penalty in spite of popular support for the punishment as it desired membership in the Council of Europe. But states may also comply with norms even when such norms provide them with no clear benefits, as in the case of South Africa, which, in the face of rising crime rates and little external pressure to do so, abolished the death penalty in its post-apartheid constitution. It is empirically obvious that much of everyday social interaction is about strategic exchange and self-interested behavior; yet, we often observe evidence of nonstrategic social learning through which decision makers, in the presence of a norm, acquire a new understanding of interests. In reality, it is not always easy to separate one effect from the other because the two strands of logic often interact to produce the same outcome: "States pursue appropriate behavior in part because it helps them achieve their goals of peaceful, stable interaction with other states. On the flip side, when calculating the costs and benefits of different actions, states favor some means over others precisely because they are widely accepted as appropriate behaviors."[45]

It is true that moral principles alone rarely determine political behavior. But it is also true that we should not ignore the increasingly complex interaction of morality and norms in state policy. States follow both forms of logic: the logic of consequences and the logic of appropriateness. Compliance with international norms is an outcome of strategic considerations of the material interests held by state or societal groups. It also occurs when compliance simply seems to be the right thing to do. States may obey international norms because doing so is right and moral, helps to shape and maintain an ordered international environment, and gains them respect in the eyes of the world. It is evident that both logics matter in explaining the complex political phenomenon of norm compliance, which certainly has more than a single cause. The more important and perhaps more challenging task, then, is to develop ways to foresee when and under what conditions the interaction of these two logics leads to norm compliance.

NOTES

CHAPTER 1. INTRODUCTION

1. Michael H. Reggio, "History of the Death Penalty," in *Society's Final Solution : A History and Discussion of the Death Penalty*, edited by Laura E. Randa (Lanham, MD: Rowman and Littlefield, 1997), 3.

2. Throughout this book, I use the terms, *death penalty, capital punishment,* and *executions* to refer to judicial executions, that is, legal killings by state agents. The open employment of judicially sanctioned execution as a matter of public policy is different from the use of military terror and death squads, practices that even the harshest regimes usually have enough shame to deny. Although I believe that a substantial number of executions worldwide are extrajudicial, the scope of this research is limited to judicial killings sanctioned by the legal system.

3. Immanuel Kant, *The Metaphysical Elements of Justice*, translated by John Ladd (New York: Bobbs-Merrill, [1797] 1965).

4. William A. Schabas, *The Abolition of the Death Penalty in International Law* (Cambridge: Cambridge University Press, 1997), 295–301.

5. Resolution 32/61, adopted on 8 December 1977, Resolutions and Decisions adopted by the General Assembly (A/32/45), 1978, paragraph 136.

6. United Nations, "Safeguards Guaranteeing the Protection of the Rights of Those Facing the Death Penalty," E.S.C. Res.1984/50, U.N. Doc. E/1984/84, 1984.

7. William A. Schabas, "Invalid Reservations to the International Covenant of Civil and Political Rights: Is the United States Still a Party?" *Brooklyn Journal of International Law* 21 (1995): 278–82.

8. Council of Europe, "Recommendation 1246 on the Abolition of Capital Punishment." See http://assembly.coe.int/Documents/AdoptedText/TA94/EREC 1246.HTM.

9. Amnesty International, "Abolitionist and Retentionist Countries." See http://web.amnesty.org/pages/deathpenalty-countries-eng.

10. Rome Statute of the International Criminal Court, Part 7, Article 77.

11. Caroline Ravaud and Stefan Trechsel, "The Death Penalty and the Case-law of the Institutions of the European Convention on Human Rights," in *The Death Penalty: Abolition in Europe*, edited by the Council of Europe (Strasbourg: Council of Europe Publishing, 1999), 79–90.

12. Roberto Toscano, "The United Nations and the Abolition of the Death Penalty," in *The Death Penalty: Abolition in Europe* (Strasbourg: Council of Europe Publishing, 1999), 91–104.

13. Ronald L. Jepperson, Alexander Wendt, and Peter J. Katzenstein, "Norms, Identity, and Culture in National Security," in *The Culture of National Security: Norms and Identity in World Politics*, edited by Peter Katzenstein (New York: Columbia University Press, 1996), 54.

14. Janice E. Thomson, "Norms in International Relations: A Conceptual Analysis," *International Journal of Group Tension* 23, no. 1 (1993): 72. For a good summary on the various definitions of international norms, see Gregory A. Raymond, "Problems and Prospects in the Study of International Norms," *Mershon International Studies Review* 41, no. 2 (1997): 216–22.

15. See, for example, Thomas Risse, Stephen C. Ropp, and Kathryn Sikkink, eds., *The Power of Human Rights: International Norms and Domestic Change* (Cambridge: Cambridge University Press, 1999); Jeffrey T. Checkel, "Norms, Institutions, and National Identity in Contemporary Europe," *International Studies Quarterly* 43, no. 1 (1999): 83–114; Andrew P. Cortell and James W. Davis Jr., "Understanding the Democratic Impact of International Norms: A Research Agenda," *International Studies Review* 2, no. 1 (2000): 65–87.

16. Susan Strange, "*Cave! hic dragones*: A Critique of Regime Analysis," in *International Regimes*, edited by Stephen D. Krasner (Ithaca: Cornell University Press, 1983), 345.

17. John J. Mearsheimer, "The False Promise of International Institutions," *International Security* 19, no. 3 (1994/95): 5–49.

18. See, for example, Robert Axelrod and Robert O. Keohane, "Achieving Cooperation under Anarchy: Strategies and Institutions," *World Politics* 38, no. 1 (1985): 226–54; Robert O. Keohane, *After Hegemony: Cooperation and Discord in the World Political Economy* (Princeton: Princeton University Press, 1984); Robert O. Keohane, "International Institutions: Can Interdependence Work?" *Foreign Policy* 110 (1998): 82–94; Robert O. Keohane and Lisa Martin, "The Promise of Institutionalist Theory," *International Security* 20, no. 1 (1995): 39–51; Ann-Marie Slaughter, "International Law and International Relations Theory: A Dual Agenda," *American Journal of International Law* 87 (1993): 205–39; Kenneth A. Oye, ed., *Cooperation under Anarchy* (Princeton: Princeton University Press, 1986).

19. Krasner, *International Regimes*, 3.

20. Ibid.

21. Mearsheimer, "False Promise of International Institutions," 8.

22. Robert O. Keohane, "The Demand for International Regime," in *International Regimes*, edited by Stephen Krasner (Ithaca: Cornell University Press, 1983), 158.

23. Ibid., 387.

24. On human rights, see Ann Marie Clark, *Diplomacy of Conscience: Amnesty International and Changing Human Rights Norms* (Princeton: Princeton University Press, 2001); Darren Hawkins, *International Human Rights and Authoritarian Rule in Chile* (Lincoln: University of Nebraska Press, 2002); Andrew Moravcsik, "Explaining International Human Rights Regime: Liberal Theory and Western Europe," *European Journal of International Relations* 1, no. 2 (1995): 157–89; Risse, Ropp, and Sikkink, *Power of Human Rights*; on national security, see Brian Frederking, "Constructing Post–Cold War Collective Security," *American Political Science Review* 97, no. 3 (2003): 363–78; Peter Katzenstein, ed., *The Culture of National Security: Norms and Identity in World Politics* (New York: Columbia University Press, 1996); Janice Bially Mattern, "The Power Politics of Identity," *European Journal of International Relations* 7, no. 3

(2001): 349–97; on environmental policy, see John W. Meyer, David John Frank, Ann Hironaka, Even Schofer, and Nancy Brandon Tuma, "The Structuring of a World Environmental Regime, 1870–1990," *International Organization* 51, no. 4 (1997): 623–51; Leigh S. Raymond, *Private Rights in Public Resources: Equity and Property Allocation in Market-Based Environmental Policy* (Washington, DC: Resources for the Future, 2003); Paul Wapner, "Politics Beyond the State: Environmental Activism and World Civic Politics," *World Politics* 47, no. 3 (1995): 311–40; on immigration, see Amy Gurowitz, "Mobilizing International Norms: Domestic Actors, Immigrants, and Japanese State," *World Politics* 51, no. 1 (1999): 413–51; on economic policy, see Andrew P. Cortell and James W. Davis Jr., "How Do International Institutions Matter? The Domestic Impact of International Rules and Norms," *International Studies Quarterly* 40, no. 4 (1996): 451–78; Andrew P. Cortell and James W. Davis Jr., "When International and Domestic Norms Collide: Japan and the GATT/WTO," paper presented at the Annual Meeting of the International Studies Association, Chicago, IL, February 2001; John Jacobsen, "Much Ado About Ideas: The Cognitive Factor in Economic Policy," *World Politics* 47, no. 2 (1995): 283–310; on nationalism, see Michael Barnett, "Sovereignty, Nationalism, and Regional Order in the Arab States System," *International Organization* 49, no. 3 (1995): 479–510; on decolonization, see Neta C. Crawford, *Argument and Change in World Politics: Ethics, Decolonization, and Humanitarian Intervention* (Cambridge: Cambridge University Press, 2002); on regional integration, see Thomas Christiansen, Knud Erik Jørgensen, and Antje Wiener, eds., *The Social Construction of Europe* (Thousand Oaks, CA: Sage, 2001); and on terrorism, see Erica Chenoweth and Jessica Teets, "Constraining U.S. Policy: Adherence to International Norms Post 9/11," paper presented at the Annual Meeting of the Western Political Science Association, Portland, OR, March 2004; Eric Patterson, "Just War on Terror? Reconceptualizing Just War Theory in the 21st Century," paper presented at the Annual Meeting of the Western Political Science Association, Portland, OR, March 2004.

25. Audie Klotz, *Norms in International Relations: The Struggle against Apartheid* (Ithaca: Cornell University Press, 1995), 19.

26. Alexander Wendt, "Constructing International Politics," *International Security* 20, no. 1 (1995): 76.

27. Nicholas G. Onuf, "Constructivism: A User's Manual," in *International Relations in a Constructed World*, edited by Vendulka Kubalkova, Nicolas Onuf, and Paul Kowert (Armonk, NY: M.E. Sharp, 1998), 59.

28. Raymond, "Problems and Prospects in the Study of International Norms": 216.

29. The definition of learning used mostly commonly is "a change of beliefs (or the degree of confidence in one's beliefs) or the development of new beliefs, skills, or procedures as a result of the observation and interpretation of experience." See Jack S. Levy, "Learning and Foreign Policy: Sweeping a Conceptual Minefield," *International Organization* 48, no. 2 (1994): 283.

30. Ted Hopf, "The Promise of Constructivism in International Relations Theory," *International Security* 23, no. 1 (1998): 177.

31. Christian Boulanger, "Book Review: Mary McAuley, Russia's Politics of Uncertainty," *Comparative Political Studies* 32, no. 2 (1999): 278.

32. Jeffrey T. Checkel, "Sanctions, Social Learning, and Institutions: Explaining State Compliance with the Norms of the European Human Rights Regime," ARENA Working Paper 99/11 (Oslo: ARENA/Universitetet i Oslo, 1999); Jeffrey T. Checkel, "Compliance and Conditionality," ARENA Working Paper 00/18 (Oslo:

130 NOTES TO CHAPTER ONE

ARENA/Universitetet i Oslo, 2000); Lloyd S. Etheridge, *Can Governments Learn?*
(New York: Free Press, 1985); Peter A. Hall, "Policy Paradigms, Social Learning, and
the State," *Comparative Politics* 25, no. 3 (1993): 275–96; Hawkins, *International Human
Rights and Authoritarian Rule in Chile*; John Gerard Ruggie, "What Makes the World
Hang Together?: Neo-Utilitarianism and the Social Constructivist Challenge," *International Organization* 52, no. 4 (1998): 855–85.

33. Martha Finnemore and Kathrýn Sikkink, "International Norm Dynamics
and Political Change," *International Organization* 52, no. 4 (1998): 887–917.

34. Cortell and Davis, "How Do International Institutions Matter?" 453.

35. Checkel, "Norms, Institutions and National Identity in Contemporary
Europe."

36. Jan Egeland, *Impotent Superpower—Potent Small State: Potentials and Limitations of Human Rights Objectives in the Foreign Policies of the United States and Norway*
(Oxford: Norwegian University Press, 1988), 3.

37. Moravcsik, "Explaining International Human Rights Regime."

38. Thomas Risse-Kappen, ed., *Bringing Transnational Relations Back In: Non-State Actors, Domestic Structures, and International Institution* (Cambridge: Cambridge
University Press, 1995), 25–28.

39. Jeffrey T. Checkel, "International Norms and Domestic Politics: Bridging
the Rationalist-Constructivist Divide," *European Journal of International Relations* 3,
no. 4 (1997): 473–95.

40. Stephen van Evera, *Guide to Methods for Students of Political Science* (Ithaca:
Cornell University Press, 1997), 55.

41. Paul Kowert and Jeffrey Legro, "Norms, Identity, and Their Limits: A Theoretical Reprise," in *The Culture of National Security: Norms and Identity in World Politics*,
edited by Peter Katzenstein (New York: Columbia University Press, 1996), 485.

42. Checkel, "Norms, Institutions, and National Identity in Contemporary
Europe," 86.

43. A suggestion for controlling this bias is to focus on varying degrees in a
single continuum of norm compliance by either looking at different degrees of norm
implementation in a country over time, or reviewing variations in norm impact
across countries during the same period of time.

44. See, for example, Erika S. Fairchild and Harry R. Dammer, *Comparative
Criminal Justice Systems* (Belmont, CA: Wadsworth, 1993); Jonathan Fletcher, *Violence and Civilization: An Introduction to the Work of Norbert Elias* (Malden, MA :
Blackwell, 1997); Hans-Gunther Heiland and Louise Shelley, "Civilization, Modernization, and the Development of Crime and Control," in *Crime and Control in Comparative Perspectives*, edited by Hans-Gunther Heiland, Louise Shelley, and Hisao
Katoh (Berlin: Walter de Gruyter, 1992), 1–19; Helmut Kuzmics, "The Civilizing
Process," in *Civil Society and the State: New European Perspectives*, edited by John
Keane (London/New York: Verso, 1998), 149–76.

45. Jeffrey Reiman, "Justice, Civilization, and the Death Penalty: Answering
van den Haag," in *Punishment and the Death Penalty: The Current Debate*, edited by
Robert Baird and Stuart Rosenbaum (Amherst: Prometheus Books, 1995), 175.

46. Robert Badinter, "Preface—Moving Towards Universal Abolition of the
Death Penalty," in *The Death Penalty Beyond Abolition* (Strasbourg: Council of Europe
Publishing, 2004), 11.

47. Ibid.

48. Bertil Dunér and Hanna Geurtsen, "The Death Penalty and War," *The International Journal of Human Rights* 6, no. 4 (2002): 13.

49. Ibid., 19.

50. In the case of the United States, not all states have the death penalty. At present, twelve states do not permit the death penalty under any circumstances: Alaska, Hawaii, Iowa, Maine, Massachusetts, Michigan, Minnesota, North Dakota, Rhode Island, Vermont, West Virginia, and Wisconsin. The differing death penalty policies of the various states in the United States make it difficult to generalize about a "U.S. phenomenon." Nonetheless, I consider the United States "retentionist" because a significant majority of states—thirty-eight out of fifty—along with the federal government and the legal system of the American armed forces apply the death penalty. To compare different political and social conditions between "abolitionists" and "retentionist" states within the United States will be another project.

51. van Evera, *Guide to Methods for Students of Political Science*, 86.

52. Victor E. Kvashis, "The Death Penalty and Public Opinion," *Russian Social Science Review* 40, no. 1 (1999): 77.

53. On norm emergence, see Clark, *Diplomacy of Conscience*; Ann Florini, "The Evolution of International Norms," *International Studies Quarterly* 40, no. 3 (1996): 363–89; Margret E. Keck and Kathryn Sikkink, *Activists Beyond Borders: Advocacy Networks in International Politics* (Ithaca: Cornell University Press, 1998); Kenneth R. Rutherford, "The Evolving Arms Control Agenda: Implications of the Role of NGO's in Banning Antipersonnel Landmines," *World Politics* 53, no. 1 (October 2000): 74–114; on norm development, see Kathryn Sikkink, "Human rights and Issue-Networks in Latin America," *International Organization* 47, no. 3 (1993): 411–42; and on norm internalization, see Klotz, *Norms in International Relations*; Risse, Ropp, and Sikkink, *The Power of Human Rights*.

54. Margaret Keck and Kathryn Sikkink distinguish three stages of a norm's life cycle: (1) emergence, (2) cascade, and (3) internalization; see Keck and Sikkink, *Activists Beyond Borders*. Jeffrey Checkel calls the early stages of norm emergence "empowerment," defined as when "the prescriptions embodied in a norm first become, through discourse or behavior, a focus of domestic political attention or debate"; see Checkel, "International Norms and Domestic Politics," 476.

55. Robert M. Bohm, *Deathquest: An Introduction to the Theory and Practice of Capital Punishment in the United States* (Cincinnati: Anderson, 1999); Phoebe C. Ellsworth and Lee Ross, "Public Opinion and Capital Punishment: A Close Examination of the Views of Abolitionists and Retentionists," *Crime and Delinquency* 29 (1983): 116–69; Kimberly Gross and Donald R. Kinder, "Ethnocentrism Revisited: Explaining American Opinion on Crime and Punishment," paper presented at the Annual Meeting of the American Political Science Association, Washington, DC, September 2000; Mark Warr, "Poll Trends: Public Opinion on Crime and Punishment," *Public Opinion Quarterly* 59, no. 2 (1995): 296–310.

56. The Gallup organization has conducted extensive death penalty surveys since 1953. Results are available at www.gallup.com//poll/indicators/inddeath_pen.asp.

57. See Risse, Ropp, and Sikkink, *The Power of Human Rights*.

58. Checkel, "Sanctions, Social Learning, and Institutions": 5–6.

59. Keck and Sikkink, *Activists Beyond Borders*, 201–204.

60. Clark, *Diplomacy of Conscience*. Also see Richard Price, "Reversing the

Gun Sights: Transnational Civil Society Targets Land Mines," *International Organization* 52, no. 3 (1998): 613–44; James Ron, "Changing Methods of Israel State Violence," *International Organization* 51, no. 1 (1997): 275–300; Wapner, "Politics Beyond the State": 311–40.

61. Clark, *Diplomacy of Conscience*; Keck and Sikkink, *Activists Beyond Borders*; Price, "Reversing the Gun Sights: Transnational Civil Society Targets Land Mines"; Risse-Kappen, *Bringing Transnational Relations Back In*.

62. Andrew Moravcsik, "The Origins of Human Rights Regimes: Democratic Delegation in Postwar Europe," *International Organization* 54, no. 2 (2000): 217–52.

63. Martha Finnemore, "International Organizations as Teachers of Norms: The United Nations Educational, Scientific, and Cultural Organization and Science Policy," *International Organization* 47, no. 4 (1993): 565–97.

64. John T. S. Keeler, "Opening the Window for Reform: Mandates, Crises, and Extraordinary Policy-making," *Comparative Political Studies* 25, no. 4 (1993): 433–86; Levy, "Learning and Foreign Policy."

65. Keeler, "Opening the Window for Reform": 441.

66. Ibid., 434.

67. Checkel, "International Norms and Domestic Politics": 10.

68. Checkel, "Norms, Institutions and National Identity in Contemporary Europe."

69. Andrew P. Cortell and James W. Davis Jr., "Understanding the Democratic Impact of International Norms: A Research Agenda."

70. Hawkins, *International Human Rights and Authoritarian Rule in Chile*.

71. Warren Young and Mark Brown, "Cross-national Comparisons of Imprisonment," in *Crime and Justice: A Review of Research*, edited by Michael Tonry (Chicago: University of Chicago Press, 1993), 1–49.

72. Theda Skocpol, *Protecting Soldiers and Mothers: The Political Origins of Social Policy in the United States* (Cambridge: Harvard University Press, 1992), 17.

73. Note, however, that extrajudicial executions in those Catholic countries, regardless of the formal abolition of the death penalty, were not uncommon under the authoritarian regimes.

74. Isaac Ehrlich, "The Deterrent Effect of Capital Punishment: A Question of Life and Death," *American Economic Review* 65 (1975): 397–417.

75. William Bailey and Ruth Peterson, "Murder, Capital Punishment, and Deterrence: A Review of the Evidence and an Examination of Police Killings," *Journal of Social Issues* 50, no. 2 (1994): 53–74; Bohm, *Deathquest*; Lawrence R. Klein, Brian Forst, and Victor Filatov, "The Deterrent Effect of Capital Punishment: An Assessment of the Estimate," in *Deterrence and Incapacitation: Estimating the Effects of Criminal Sanctions on Crime Rates*, edited by A. Blumstein, J. Cohen, and D. Nagin (Washington, DC: National Academy of Science, 1978); Raymond Paternoster, *Capital Punishment in America* (New York: Lexington Books, 1991); Ruth D. Peterson and William C. Bailey, "Is Capital Punishment an Effective Deterrent for Murder? An Examination of Social Science Research," in *America's Experiment with Capital Punishment*, edited by James R. Acker, Robert M. Bohm, and Charles S. Lanier (Durham: Carolina Academic Press, 1998), 157–82; Michael L. Radelet and Ronald L. Akers, "Deterrence and the Death Penalty: The Views of the Experts," *Journal of Criminal Law and Criminology* 86 (1996): 1–16.

76. Bailey and Peterson, "Murder, Capital Punishment, and Deterrence": 72.

77. The authors define "incomplete incorporation" as "the extent to which local, regional, ethnic, and class identities and interests take precedence over national citizenship rights and commitments, and thus deprive diverse social elements of full membership status in the national community." See William Bowers, Glenn Pierce, and John McDevitt, *Legal Homicide: Death as Punishment in America, 1864–1982* (Boston: Northeastern University Press, 1984), 149. Their analysis highlights two other societal characteristics—"political centralization" and "political coerciveness"—as the important variables predicting the retention of the death penalty.

78. James Marquart, Sheldon Ekland-Olson, and Jonathan Sorensen, *The Rope, the Chair, and the Needle: Capital Punishment in Texas, 1923–1990* (Austin: University of Texas Press, 1994).

79. Tony Poveda, "American Exceptionalism and the Death Penalty," *Social Justice* 27 (2000): 252–67.

80. David Baldus, George Woodworth, David Zuckerman, Neil Alan Weiner, and Barbara Broffitt, "Symposium: Racial Discrimination and the Death Penalty in the Post-*Furman* Era: An Empirical and Legal Overview, With Recent Findings from Philadelphia," *Cornell Law Review* 83 (1998): 1638–1770; Michael Mitchell and Jim Sidanius, "Social Hierarchy and the Death Penalty: A Social Dominance Perspective," *Political Psychology* 16, no. 3 (1995): 591–619; Glenn Pierce and Michael Radelet, "The Role and Consequences of the Death Penalty in American Politics," *New York University Review of Law and Social Change* 18 (1990/91): 711–28; Leslie T. Wilkins, *Punishment, Crime, and Market Forces* (Aldershot, UK: Dartmouth, 1991); Leslie T. Wilkins and Ken Pease, "Public Demand for Punishment," *The International Journal of Sociology and Social Policy* 7, no. 3 (1987): 16–29.

81. Rosalee Clawson, "White Support for Capital Punishment: The Impact of Anti-Black Prejudice and Pro-White Identity," Unpublished Manuscript. 2000. Available upon request from the author.

82. Gross and Kinder, "Ethnocentrism Revisited: Explaining American Opinion on Crime and Punishment"; Franklin E. Zimring and Gordon Hawkins, *Capital Punishment and the American Agenda* (New York: Cambridge University Press, 1986). The issue of racism in the application of capital punishment has raised serious doubts about the death penalty. As Austin Sarat comments, "[E]ven as we are reassured about the legitimacy of state killing and its difference from violence outside the law, the racialization of that difference arouses other fears that encourage an acceptance, if not a warm embrace, of state violence as a necessary tool in a struggle between 'us' and 'them.' " See *When the State Kills: Capital Punishment and the American Condition* (Princeton: Princeton University Press, 2001), 92.

83. Harald Müeller, "The Internalization of Principles, Norms, and Rules by Governments: The Case of Security Regimes," in *Regime Theory and International Relations*, edited by Volker Rittberger (Oxford: Oxford University Press, 1993), 361–88. Similarly, Thomas Risse-Kappen's explanation based on the power relationship between states and societies provides a plausible account of norm diffusion. In his view, domestic structure has two components: the key political institution of the state and the nature of civil society. Political institutions are either "centralized" or "fragmented," and societies are conceptualized as either "strong" or "weak." See Risse-Kappen, *Bringing Transnational Relations Back In*, 14–33.

84. Andrew Moravcsik, "Why Is U.S. Human Rights Policy So Unilateralist?" in *The Cost of Acting Alone: Multilateralism and US Foreign Policy*, edited by Shepard

Forman and Patrick Stewart (Boulder: Lynne Riener Publishers, 2001): 345–76. For alternative conceptualizations see Checkel, "International Norms and Domestic Politics"; Cortell and Davis, "Understanding the Democratic Impact of International Norms."

CHAPTER 2. UKRAINE

1. The last execution in Western Europe took place in France in 1977. Turkey's executions continued until 1984. It took Eastern European countries longer to stop executions: Croatia in 1987, Hungary 1988, Poland 1988, Bulgaria 1989, Moldova 1989, Estonia 1991, Armenia 1991, Azerbaijan 1993, Georgia 1994, Lithuania 1995, and finally Ukraine in 1997.

2. Council of Europe, "About the Council of Europe," see http://www.coe.int/T/e/Com/about_coe.

3. Preamble of the European Convention on Human Rights, Rome, 4 November 1950.

4. Walter Schwimmer, "We are Condemned to Life," *Rossijskaja Gazeta*, 20 March 2002.

5. Article 1 of Protocol No. 6 to the European Human Rights Convention states, "The death penalty shall be abolished. No-one shall be condemned to such penalty or executed."

6. Council of Europe Press Service, "Protocol No. 6 to the Convention for the Protection of Human Rights and Fundamental Freedoms Concerning the Abolition of the Death Penalty: The turning point," 2001.

7. Council of Europe, "Resolution 1179 (1999): Honouring of Obligations and Commitments by Ukraine," 1999.

8. Council of Europe Press Service, "Council of Europe Secretary General Supports Vladimir Putin's Position on Death Penalty Moratorium," March 2002.

9. When Turkish officials captured Kurdish rebel chief Abdullah Ocalan in 1999, public sentiment ran high for his quick execution. The Ocalan case caused widespread public and diplomatic protest among the council's member states. Nationalist leaders pressed for Ocalan's execution, arguing that his crimes fell under the treason or near-war exceptions. As the extensive diplomatic threats against Turkey continued for several years, Turkey complied with the stay of execution issued while the Ocalan case was being heard before the European Court of Human Rights. Furthermore, Turkey agreed to lift the death penalty even for terrorism crimes.

10. Franklin E. Zimring, *The Contradictions of American Capital Punishment* (New York: Oxford University Press, 2003), 25.

11. Canada and Mexico, the other two observer states, do not impose the death sentence. In Japan, forty-one executions took place during the last ten years, many of them carried out in secrecy. See van der Lugt, "*Japan verheimelijkt doodstraf* [Japan Hides Executions]," *NRC Handelsblad* (Dutch), 25 March 2002.

12. Personal interview, David Cupina, Parliamentary Assembly secretariat, Council of Europe, 11 June 2002.

13. Council of Europe Press Service, "Assembly Committee on Legal Affairs and Human Rights Adopts Report on the Abolition of the Death Penalty in Council of Europe Observer States," 6 June 2001.

14. Personal interview, David Cupina, 11 June 2002.

15. Don Hill, "World: Death Penalty on the Decline, Despite High-Profile Cases," Radio Free Europe/Radio Liberty (RFE/RL) News, 20 August 2002. Unlike its neighboring East Asian countries, where the death penalty is still extensively used, the Republic of Korea (South Korea) appears to be taking a different path both in terms of the social attitude toward the death penalty and its actual use over the last few years. Since 1998, there have been no executions in Korea, resulting in a de facto moratorium. A strenuous legislative effort has been made to abolish capital punishment: a major number of legislators presented special bills to the National Assembly in both 1999 and 2001.

16. Council of Europe Press Service, "European Parliamentarians to Engage US Congressmen and Senators in Debate over Death Penalty," 4 April 2003; Council of Europe, "An Assembly Conference on the Death Penalty Opens in Springfield, Illinois," April 2003.

17. Don Hill, "World: Death Penalty on the Decline, Despite High-Profile Cases."

18. Council of Europe Press Service, "Mr Kuchma, President of the Republic of Ukraine, Made the Following Statement," 1997.

19. Roman Solchanyk, *Ukraine and Russia: The Post-Soviet Transition* (Oxford: Rowman and Littlefield, 2001), 93.

20. Paul D'Anieri, Robert Kravchuk, and Taras Kuzio, *Politics and Society in Ukraine* (Boulder: Westview, 1999), 40.

21. Serhiy Holovatiy, "Point of View of an Abolitionist Against Public Opinion," in *The Death Penalty: Abolition in Europe* (Strasbourg: Council of Europe Publishing, 1999), 144.

22. Elliot Currie, "Market, Crime, and Community: Toward a Mid-Range Theory of Post-Industrial Violence," in *The Crime Conundrum: Essay on Criminal Justice*, edited by Lawrence M. Friedman and George Fisher (Boulder: Westview, 1997), 25.

23. Todd S. Foglesong and Peter H. Solomon Jr., *Crime, Criminal Justice, and Criminology in Post-Soviet Ukraine* (Washington, DC: National Institute of Justice, 2001), 27.

24. The World Bank, "Ukraine at a Glance," 23 September 2002. See http://www.worldbank.org/data/countrydata/aag/ukr_aag.pdf.

25. See the Global Competitiveness Report. http://www.weforum.org. I am grateful to Fiona J. M. Paua of the Global Competitiveness Programme of the World Economic Forum for providing the data for 1997 and 1998.

26. D'Anieri, Kravchuk, and Kuzio, 176–77.

27. Holovatiy, 148.

28. D'Anieri, Kravchuk, and Kuzio, 44.

29. Council of Europe, "Recommendation 1395 Honouring of Obligations and Commitments by Ukraine," 1999.

30. Russia executed 140 people in 1996, accounting for the third highest number of executions worldwide. Amnesty International, "Death Sentences and Executions in 1996," AI index: ACT 51/01/97.

31. Renate Wohlwend, "The Efforts of the Parliamentary Assembly of the Council of Europe," in *The Death Penalty: Abolition in Europe* (Strasbourg: Council of Europe Publishing, 1999), 60; Amnesty International, "Ukraine: Secret Mass Executions in Ukraine Called 'Barbaric,' " AI index: EUR 50/16/96; *Los Angeles Times*,

"Ukraine: Executions Held, Ex-minister alleges," Part A; page 10; Foreign Desk, 24 September 1997.

32. Khadine L. Ritter, "The Russian Death Penalty Dilemma: Square Pegs and Round Holes," *Case Western Reserve Journal of International Law* 32, no. 1 (2000): 141; Council of Europe, "Ukraine: Decision-time for the Assembly," *The Europeans*, 1998.

33. Holovatiy, 144.

34. Ibid., 143–47.

35. Checkel, "Sanctions, Social Learning, and Institutions": 20.

36. D'Anieri, Kravchuk, and Kuzio, 142.

37. Ibid., 146; Sarah Mendelson and John Glenn, "Democracy Assistance and NGO Strategies in Post-Communist Societies," Democracy and Rule of Law Project, Carnegie Endowment Working Paper (2000):16–17, 23–25.

38. Council of Europe, "Resolution 1112: On the Honouring of the Commitment Entered Into by Ukraine Upon Accession to the Council of Europe to Put into Place a Moratorium on Executions," 1997; Council of Europe Press Service, "Monitoring Committee Warning to Ukraine," 2 December 1998; Council of Europe, "Honouring of Obligations and Commitments by Ukraine," Doc.8424, 1 June 1999.

39. Council of Europe Press Service, "Parliamentary Assembly Gives Ukraine a Stern Warning," 28 January 1999.

40. Council of Europe, "Resolution 1179 (1999): Honouring of Obligations and Commitments by Ukraine," 1999.

41. Personal interview, David Cupina, 11 June 2002.

42. Personal interview, Johan Friestedt, Monitoring Department Directorate of Strategic Planning, Council of Europe, 10 June 2002.

43. Personal interview, Johan Friestedt, 12 June 2002.

44. Council of Europe, "Monitoring: Awaiting Significant Progress in Ukraine," *The Europeans: The Electronic Newsletter of the Council of Europe Parliamentary Assembly*, June 1999.

45. The Constitutional Court of Ukraine, Case No. 1-33/99, "Decision of the Constitutional Court of Ukraine on the Case Based on Constitutional Appeal of 51 People's Deputies of Ukraine Regarding Conformity with the Constitution of Ukraine (Constitutionality) of the Provisions of Articles 24, 58, 59, 60, 93, 190 of the Criminal Code of Ukraine Which Envisage Death Penalty as a Kind of Punishment" (29 December 1999), paragraph 1.

46. The Constitutional Court of Ukraine, Case No. 1-33/99, paragraphs 3; 4; 6.

47. "Kuchima Signs New Criminal Code, Finalizing Abolition of Death Penalty," Associated Press, 22 May 2001; Patrick E. Tyler, "World Briefing Europe: Ukraine: No More Executions," *New York Times*, 22 May 2001.

48. Checkel, "Compliance and Conditionality": 19.

49. Andrei Chernikov, "Incarceration Will Be Different in Ukraine," *Current Digest of the Post Soviet Press* 53, no. 36 (2001): 17.

50. Personal interview, Johan Friestedt, 10 June 2002.

51. Checkel, "Compliance and Conditionality": 19.

52. The Constitutional Court of Ukraine, Case No. 1-33/99, paragraph 6.

53. The Constitutional Court of South Africa, Case No. CCT/3/94, *The State v. T Makwanyane and M Mchunu* (6 June 1995), paragraphs 87–88.

54. For an overview of the tiers of Ukrainian government, see D'Anieri, Kravchuk, and Kuzio, 102–105.

55. Fred Weir, "Storm Clouds over Ukraine's Fragile Democracy," *The Christian Science Monitor*, 18 July 2000.

56. Solchanyk, 118–21.

57. D'Anieri, Kravchuk, and Kuzio, 105.

58. Checkel, "International Norms and Domestic Politics": 487. Emphasis added.

59. BBC Monitoring International Reports, "Ukrainian Prosecutor-General's Office Wants Death Penalty Reinstituted," 18 June 2002; BBC Monitoring International Reports, "Not Ready to Outlaw Death Penalty—Top Interior Official," 19 June 2002.

60. Lord Russell-Johnson in his keynote at the Council of Europe Conference, "Justice and Human Rights in Council of Europe Observer States: The Abolition of the Death Penalty," Springfield, Illinois, 9 April 2003.

CHAPTER 3. SOUTH AFRICA

1. Howard W. French, "South Africa's Supreme Court Abolishes Death Penalty," *New York Times*, 7 June 1995.

2. Michael Hamlyn, "Death Sentence is Abolished by South Africa," *The Times*, 7 June 1995.

3. "Pretoria has more than confirmed its status this week as the hanging capital of the world with the execution of 21 people here in the last three days" (*Pretoria News*, 10 December 1987), quoted in Janos Mihalik, "The Moratorium on Executions: Its Background and Implication," *South African Law Journal* 108 (1991): 133.

4. Solomon Ngobeni, hanged on 14 November 1989, was the last person executed in South Africa.

5. Austin Sarat and Christian Boulanger, eds., *The Cultural Lives of Capital Punishment: Comparative Perspectives* (Stanford: Stanford University Press, 2005).

6. Julia Sloth-Nielsen, "Legal Violence: Corporal and Capital Punishment," in *People and Violence in South Africa*, edited by Brian McKendrick and Wilma Hoffmann (Cape Town: Oxford University Press, 1990): 89.

7. This number includes only judicial executions carried out within the "proper legal system." See Ellison Kahn, "The Relaunch of the Society for the Abolition of the Death Penalty in South Africa" (Speech delivered at the University of the Witwatersrand), *The South African Law Journal* (1989): 39–52.

8. Julia Sloth-Nielsen, Roelien Theron, and Hugh Corder, *Death by Decree: South Africa and the Death Penalty* (Cape Town: University of Cape Town Press, 1991).

9. D. M. Davis, "Extenuation—an Unnecessary Halfway House on the Road to a Rational Sentencing Policy," *South African Journal of Criminal Justice* 2 (1989): 205–18; Jan H. van Rooyen, "Toward a New South Africa Without the Death Penalty—Struggles, Strategies, and Hopes," *Florida State University Law Review* 20 (1993): 737–99.

10. Sixty-nine peaceful protesters were killed by the South African government, stirring an international outcry.

11. Ellison Kahn, "Remarks at the Symposium on Capital Punishment," in *Proceedings of the Conference on Crime, Law, and the Community* 220/221 (1976): 222.

12. Barend van Niekerk, ". . . Hanged by the Neck until You are Dead: Some Thought on the Application of the Death Penalty in South Africa," *The South African Law Journal* 86 (1969/1970): 87.

13. Nathan V. Holt Jr., "Human Rights and Capital Punishment: The Case of South Africa," *Virginia Journal of International Law* 30, no. 1 (1989): 298.

14. Mihalik, "The Moratorium on Executions,"139.

15. Holt, "Human Rights and Capital Punishment," 315. The death sentences were again handed down at a time of increasing debate in South Africa about the death penalty and sparked mass rallies against capital punishment.

16. Holt, "Human Rights and Capital Punishment," 301–302; van Rooyen, "Toward a New South Africa without the Death Penalty," 737–43.

17. Amnesty International, *When the State Kills . . . The Death Penalty: A Human Rights Issue* (New York: Amnesty International, 1989), 263.

18. Holt, "Human Rights and Capital Punishment," 303; emphasis in original.

19. Report of the Penal and Prison Reform Commission U.G. No. 47 of 1947, paragraph 457; cited in Holt, "Human Rights and Capital Punishment," 300.

20. John Dugard, *Human Rights and the South African Legal Order* (Princeton: Princeton University Press, 1978), 126–27.

21. Graeme Simpson and Lloyd Vogelman, "The Death Penalty in South Africa," CSVR (Centre for the Study of Violence and Reconciliation) Working Paper, Johannesburg, South Africa, 1989.

22. Dugard, *Human Rights and the South African Legal Order*, 128.

23. See Holt, "Human Rights and Capital Punishment," 300.

24. Michael L. Radelet and Margaret Vandiver, "Race and Capital Punishment: An Overview of the Issues," *Crime and Social Justice* 25 (1986): 94–113.

25. Herman Giliomee, "Hanging Question over SA," *Sunday Times*, 22 August 1988.

26. Ellison Kahn, "The Death Penalty in South Africa," *Tydskrif vir Hedendaagse Romeins-Hollandse Reg* (1970): 12.

27. Etienne Mureinik, "Caring about Capital Punishment," in *Essays in Honour of Ellison Kahn*, edited by Coenraad Visser (Johannesburg: University of the Witwatersrand, 1989), 221.

28. Dugard, *Human Rights and the South African Legal Order*, 415.

29. Mihalik, "The Moratorium on Executions,"125.

30. See Holt, "Human Rights and Capital Punishment," 273–318. The regionally based organizations in Africa, in contrast, did not function well in supporting any human rights issues. Since the establishment of the Organization of African Unity (OAU, currently African Union) in 1963, a system of ad hoc arrangements has dealt with interstate conflict in Africa, while intrastate conflict has been largely left to each member state to handle as it chose. The OAU Charter of 1964 provided for a Commission of Mediation, Conciliation and Arbitration to encourage OAU members to settle their disputes peacefully. The commission, however, remained unused, as the OAU sought merely to maintain the inviolability of its interstate boundaries at all costs and ignored the gross violations of human rights that characterized many African governments. As Claude Welch points out, the organization seemed to function as a club of presidents who tacitly agreed not to inquire into each other's domestic practices: "The O. A. U. . . . historically considered human rights largely in the guise of self-determination, through the ending of alien or settler rule . . . 'Hear no evil, speak no evil, see no evil,' typified the views of most O. A. U. summiteers." See Claude E. Welch Jr., "The Organization of African Unity and the Promotion of Human Rights." *The Journal of Modern African Studies* 29, no. 4 (1991): 537–38.

31. See Holt, "Human Rights and Capital Punishment," 298.

32. Mihalik, "The Moratorium on Executions," 134–35.

33. Mureinik, "Caring about Capital Punishment"; Holt, "Human Rights and Capital Punishment."

34. Kahn, "The Relaunch of the Society for the Abolition of the Death Penalty in South Africa," 39–52; van Rooyen, "Toward a New South Africa Without the Death Penalty," 763–765.

35. Mihalik, "The Moratorium on Executions," 127.

36. Ibid., 128.

37. Ibid., 126–29.

38. Klotz, *Norms in International Relations*.

39. Hermann Giliomee, "Democratization in South Africa," *Political Science Quarterly* 110, no. 1 (1995): 90.

40. Sloth-Nielsen, Theron, and Corder, *Death by Decree*.

41. Christopher S. Wren, "South Africa's New Era: South Africa's President Ends 30-year Ban on Mandela Group; Says It Is Time for Negotiation," *New York Times*, 3 February 1990. In the same month, de Klerk terminated the nuclear weapons program. South Africa's nuclear policy would become part of his strategy to normalize relations with the West.

42. BBC, "South Africa: President de Klerk's Address at Opening of Parliament," BBC Summary of World Broadcasts, 1 February 1993.

43. van Rooyen, "Toward a New South Africa Without the Death Penalty," 781–82.

44. Technical Committee on Fundamental Rights, "Fifth Report: Death Penalty Agenda," Unpublished Report, Technical Committee on Fundamental Rights in Johannesburg, 11 June 1993.

45. Christopher S. Wren, "White Supremacist Sentenced to Death by a Pretoria Court," *New York Times*, 26 May 1989.

46. BBC, "Mandela on White Perceptions of the ANC, the Death Penalty and Education," Summary of World Broadcasts, 27 November 1993.

47. Mark Shaw, ed., *Policing the Transformation* (Halfway House, South Africa: Institute for Security Studies, 1997), 8.

48. Corinna Schuler, "South Africans Back 'Horrific' Cops," *Christian Science Monitor* 91, no. 111, 10 May 1999.

49. Shaw, *Policing the Transformation*.

50. Anthony Ginsberg, *South Africa's Future: From Crisis to Prosperity* (London: Macmillan, 1998), 39.

51. Schuler, "South Africans Back 'Horrific' Cops."

52. Ginsberg, *South Africa's Future*, 39.

53. Greg Mills, *War and Peace in Southern Africa: Crime, Drugs, Armies, and Trade* (Cambridge: World Peace Foundation, 1996), 1.

54. Schuler, "South Africans Back 'Horrific' Cops."

55. Corinna Schuler, "Mob-rule Justice Rises in South Africa," *Christian Science Monitor* 91, no. 176, 6 August 1999, 176.

56. Jamie Frueh, *Political Identity and Social Change: The Remaking of the South African Social Order* (Albany: State University of New York Press, 2003), 142.

57. Kimberley J. Cook, *Divided Passions: Public Opinions on Abortion and the Death Penalty* (Boston: Northeastern University Press, 1998); Angina Parekh and

Cheryl de la Rey, "Public Attitudes Toward the Death Penalty in South Africa: A Life or Death Decision," *Acta Criminology: Southern African Journal of Criminology* 9, no. 1 (1996): 108–13; Marla Sandy, "Attitudes Toward Capital Punishment: Preference for the Penalty or Mere Acceptance?" *Journal of Research in Crime and Delinquency* 32, no. 2 (1995): 191–213.

58. Parekh and de la Rey, "Public Attitudes toward the Death Penalty in South Africa."

59. The factual background of the case is discussed in the Appellate Division opinion, *S v. Makwanyane en n Ander* 1994 (3) SA 868 (A).

60. As a member of the Johannesburg bar, Chaskalson had been involved in the defense of Nelson Mandela during the Rivonia trial that ended in his conviction and sentence to life imprisonment on Robben Island.

61. The justices include seven whites, three blacks, and one Indian. Two of them are women. For more information about the justices of the Constitutional Court, see Patrick McDowell, "Death Penalty First Big Test for New Constitutional Court," *Associated Press*, 11 February 1995.

62. The Constitutional Court of South Africa, Case No. CCT/3/94, *The State v. T Makwanyane and M Mchunu* (6 June 1995) (hereafter cited as CCT/3/94), paragraph 151.

63. Ibid., paragraph 146.

64. Ibid., paragraph 278.

65. Ibid., paragraph 182.

66. Ibid., paragraph 119–20.

67. Ibid., paragraph 51.

68. Ibid., paragraph 49.

69. Ibid., paragraph 54.

70. French, "South Africa's Supreme Court Abolishes Death Penalty."

71. CCT/3/94, paragraph 87.

72. Ibid., paragraph 87.

73. Ibid., paragraph 88.

74. Ibid., paragraph 33–39.

75. *New York Times*, "South Africa Shows the Way," 10 June 1995.

76. Jan H. van Rooyen and LC Coetzee, "How Easily Could the Death Sentence be Introduced in South Africa?" *Codicillus* (Pretoria) 37, no. 1 (1996): 10.

77. Zimring and Hawkins, *Capital Punishment and the American Agenda*, 10–15; 21–22.

78. Schuler, "South Africans Back 'Horrific' Cops," 5.

79. Voice of America, "Interview with Nelson Mandela," 9 September 1996.

80. John Carlin, "Nelson Mandela: My Life; Fifty Years after the Universal Declaration of Human Rights, the President of South Africa Talks to John Carlin about Reconciliation," *Independent*, 6 December 1998.

81. van Rooyen and Coetzee, "How Easily Could the Death Sentence be Introduced in South Africa?"

82. Timothy D. Sisk, *Democratization in South Africa: The Elusive Social Contract* (Princeton: Princeton University Press, 1995).

83. Mihalik, "The Moratorium on Executions": 132.

84. Ibid., 137.

85. Christian Boulanger, "Between the Rule of Law and the Rule of the Majority: Can Courts Bring about Abolitionism?" Unpublished Manuscript.

86. William A. Schabas, "South Africa's New Constitutional Court Abolished the Death Penalty," *Human Rights Law Journal* 16, no. 4 (1995): 147.

87. CCT/3/94, paragraph 12–28.

88. Ibid., paragraph 40.

89. Zimring, *The Contradictions of American Capital Punishment*, 39.

90. CCT/3/94, paragraph 387.

91. Amnesty International, "Africa: A New Future without the Death Penalty," AI index: AFR, 3 January 1997, 3.

92. Amnesty International, "Abolitionist and Retentionist Countries," see http://web.amnesty.org/pages/deathpenalty_countries_eng.

CHAPTER 4. SOUTH KOREA

1. *Xinhua News*, 18 May 2003.

2. Amnesty International, "China: Execution Is Not a Solution. Amnesty International Condemns 46 Executions in Two Days," 2002; Amnesty International, "1,526 Executed in 2002," News Service. ACT 50/007/2003; Amnesty International, "The Death Penalty Worldwide: Developments in 2003"; Amnesty International, "The Death Penalty Worldwide: Developments in 2004."

3. In one particular death frenzy, at least 150 accused drug criminals were executed across China in June 2002 to mark International Drugs Day.

4. The Death Penalty Issue Research Group, "The Taiwan Human Rights Report 2000: The Taiwan Death Penalty Issue in International Perspective." At present, a significant change is occurring in Taiwan. In spite of public opinion polls that show 70 percent of Taiwanese favor the death penalty, President Chen Shui-bian has repeatedly remarked that death sentences should be replaced by life sentences without parole. The Taiwanese presidential office and the cabinet have jointly drafted legislation to abolish the death penalty, resulting in the Criminal Code amendment in January 2005 that bans the execution of people under the age of eighteen or over the age of eighty. A major amendment to the entire death penalty sections of the Criminal Code will take effect on 1 July 2006. *Taipei Times*, 8 September 2003; 3 October 2003; 8 January 2005.

5. Agence France Presse, "Capital Punishment Soars in Singapore," 24 September 2003.

6. United Nations, "Conference's Committee Continues Adoption of Drafting Committee Texts on International Criminal Court Statute," UN Press Release L/ROM/21, 16 July 1998.

7. Zimring, *The Contradictions of American Capital Punishment*, 37–38.

8. I use "Korea" to refer to the Republic of Korea or South Korea unless otherwise indicated. "North Korea" refers to the Democratic People's Republic of Korea.

9. Of the 278 executions that took place between 1970 and 1990, 121 were based on political grounds. In-sup Han, "*Yeoksajuk Youmoolroseoui Sahyung* [The Death Penalty as a Historical Artifact]," *Samok* (Seoul: Catholic Bishops' Conference of Korea, 1999).

10. Frank Gibney, *Korea's Quiet Revolution: From Garrison State to Democracy* (New York: Walker and Company, 1992), 68.

11. Hawkins, *International Human Rights and Authoritarian Rule in Chile*, 4.

12. Address at the sixth anniversary of the proclamation of the Charter for Education, May 1974, quoted in Sohn Hak-kyu, *Authoritarianism and Opposition in South Korea* (London: Routledge, 1989), 102.

13. South Korean economic growth deserves the word *miracle*. During the three decades preceding the late 1990s, South Korea's GNP grew by more than 8 percent per annum, and per capita GNP increased from US $79 in 1960, $243 in 1970, and $1589 in 1980 to $10,548 in 1996 (*Kyongje Tongge Nyonbo* [Annual Economic Statistics]).

14. John Kie-chiang Oh, *Korean Politics: The Quest for Democratization and Economic Development* (Ithaca: Cornell University Press, 1999), 51–52; emphasis in original.

15. David I. Steinberg, "Continuing Democratic Reform: The Unfinished Symphony," in *Consolidating Democracy in South Korea*, edited by Larry Diamond and Byung-Kook Kim (Boulder: Lynne Rienner, 2000), 218.

16. *Inhyugdang* was one of the major cases reinvestigated in 2002 by Kim Dae-jung's Presidential Truth Commission on Suspicious Deaths.

17. Martin Hart Landsberg, *Korea: Division, Reunification, and U.S. Foreign Policy* (Berkeley: University of California Press, 1998), 190.

18. Sang-jin Han, "Popular Sovereignty and a Struggle for Recognition from a Perspective of Human Rights," *Korea Journal* 39, no. 2 (1999): 191–93.

19. The role of the United States in the bloody Kwangju massacre has been disputed. Under the Freedom of Information Act, journalist Tim Shorrock obtained declassified U.S. State Department and Defense Intelligence Agency documents, and released the fact that the Carter administration was informed in advance of Chun's coup in 1980. Yet the Carter administration, believing that South Korea was not ready for democracy and that the Korean military was the only institution capable of holding the country together, allowed Chun to use whatever military force necessary to quell the Kwangju uprising and later treated the Chun group as legitimate holders of power. Tim Shorrock, "U.S. Knew of South Korean Crackdown: Ex-Leaders Go on Trial in Seoul," *Journal of Commerce* 27 (1996): 21–47.

Oh explains Carter's decision to support the Chun military regime as follows: "The Carter administration was concerned that the 1980 wholesale demonstrations against the Chun authorities might lead to a situation similar to that in Iran. There the Shah had been forced to leave the country following violent and massive demonstrations despite a declaration of martial law, thus leading to the establishment in early 1979 of the Ayatollah Khomeini regime, which was decidedly anti-American." John Kie-chiang Oh, *Korean Politics*, 84. President Reagan welcomed Chun's visit to the White House right after the massacre.

20. Kim Dae-jung, "Interview: Kim Dae-jung—Democracy and Dissidence in South Korea," *Journal of International Affairs* 38 (1985):188–89.

21. A presidential amnesty in December 1988 commuted the death sentences of these two students.

22. To this date, these were the last executions carried out in South Korea.

23. Hyuk-chol Kwon and Jae-sung Lee, "*Machimak Ipsenun Thulgo Itnayo* [Are the Last Leaves Trembling?]," *Hankyoreh 21* 432, 31 October 2002.

24. Amnesty International, *When the State Kills*, 162–63.

25. Dai-chul Chyung, "Capital Punishment Abolition Campaign in Korea and Its Prospect," paper presented at a seminar entitled "Justice and Human Rights in Council of Europe Observer States: The Abolition of the Death Penalty," Tokyo, Japan, 4–5 May 2002.

26. The Constitutional Court of Korea, Case No. 89 *Hunma* 36 (25 November 1989); Case No. 90 *Hunba* 13 (1 May 1990); Case No. 95 *Hunba* 1 (28 November 1996).

27. South Korean Constitution. Adopted: 17 July 1948; Status: 29 October 1987.

28. The Constitutional Court of Korea, Case No. 95 *Hunba* 1.

29. Ibid.

30. Ian Neary, *Human Rights in Japan, South Korea, and Taiwan* (New York: Routledge, 2002); Steinberg, "Continuing Democratic Reform."

31. Byung-Kook Kim, "Electoral Politics and Economic Crisis, 1997–1998," in *Consolidating Democracy in South Korea*; David I. Steinberg, "Korea: Triumph Amid Turmoil," *Journal of Democracy* 9, no. 2 (1998): 76–90.

32. Steinberg, "Continuing Democratic Reform," 211.

33. Oh, *Korean Politics*, 232.

34. Amnesty International, "Republic of Korea (South Korea): Summary of Concerns and Recommendations to Candidates for the Presidential Elections in December 2002," ASA 25/007/2002 (11 June 2002); Korea Solidarity for Conscientious Objection, "Recognition of Conscientious Objectors Declaration of 1000 People Urging Alternative Military Services." See http://www2.gol.com/users/quakers/korea_solidarity_for_CO.htm.

35. Asian Human Rights Commission, "Korea: South Korea Marks Human Rights Anniversary," *Asia Human Rights News*, 11 December 2001; United Nations Economic and Social Council, "Consideration of Reports Submitted by States Parties under Articles 16 and 17 of the Covenant: Republic of Korea," reported by the Committee on Economic, Social and Cultural Rights, E/C.12/1/Add.59, 11 May 2001.

36. Kim Dae-jung, "A Response to Lee Kuan Yew: Is Culture Destiny? The Myth of Asia's Anti-Democratic Values," *Foreign Affairs* 73 (1994): 189–95; Farred Zakaris, "A Conversation with Lee Kuan Yew," *Foreign Affairs* 74 (1994): 109–27.

37. The president is required to authorize executions under Korean law.

38. *Pyonghwa Shinmun*, 20 July 1997.

39. Andrew Eungi Kim, "Christianity, Shamanism, and Modernization in South Korea," *Cross Currents*, Spring/Summer 2000.

40. Eric Dwyer, "Teen Life in South Korea," in *Teen Life in Asia*, edited by Judith Slater (Westport, CT: Greenwood Press, 2004), 217–18.

41. *Korea Herald*, "Anti-Death Penalty: A Prayer for the Dying," 4 December 2001.

42. *Chosun Ilbo*, "Religions Start Campaign to Abolish Death Penalty," 24 May 2001. In her report following her participation in a death penalty symposium held in Korea in 2002, Sister Helen Prejean, author of *Dead Man Walking*, wrote, "I was deeply touched by the witness and good work for justice of the Catholic Church in Korea." She expected that Korea's example would exert a strong influence on other Asian countries, quoting Father Paul Lee: "If the Korean National Assembly votes to abolish the death penalty, Japan will follow because they hate for Korea to surpass them in anything." See Sister Helen Prejean's official Web site, http://www.prejean.org.

43. *Weekly Christian News*, April 2002.

44. *Chosun Ilbo*, "Anti–Capital Punishment Movement Grow," 26 January 2001.

45. *Asia Times*, 23 April 1999.

46. Amnesty International, "USA: Arbitrary, Discriminatory, Cruel, Futile—25 Years of Judicial Killing," News Service, AMR 51/007/2002 7/02, 6.

47. This number exceeded the 137 needed to pass a bill in the 273-seat unicameral National Assembly. For a bill to be enacted, however, it must first be approved by a majority of the fifteen-member Legislative and Judiciary Committee before being sent to a floor vote in the assembly.

48. About this bill, Justice Minister Kim Seung-gyu commented that the death penalty must be maintained for social peace and safety. Referring to cases of serial murder, he asked, "Should the life of those committing such crimes be respected at the risk of jeopardizing the safety of so many innocent citizens?" He urged respect for the fact that two-thirds of the public is opposed to the abolition of the death penalty. *Hangyereh*, 18 February 2005; 29 March 2005.

49. *Korea Times*, 15 November 2001.

50. Personal interview, David Cupina, Parliamentary Assembly Secretariat, Council of Europe (Strasbourg), 11 June 2002. Mr. Cupina, as a Council of Europe delegate, participated in the seminar on the death penalty held in the Japanese Diet in May 2002.

51. *Korea Herald*, "Anti-Death Penalty: A Prayer for the Dying," 4 December 2001.

52. Dai-chul Chyung, "Capital Punishment Abolition Campaign in Korea and Its Prospect," 11.

53. Gallup Korea, "Gallup Poll: Should the Death Penalty be Abolished?" 27 September 2003.

54. Public support for the death penalty understandably waxes and wanes in response to arbitrary events. When serial murder suspect Yoo Young-chul confessed in July 2004 that he killed at least twenty-one innocent people, countless Internet articles called for immediate executions of death row prisoners. It happens worldwide that opinion polls taken at the time of well-publicized violent crimes show a peak in support for the death penalty, perhaps distorting the true figures.

55. On the debates over the correlation between Confucianism and democratic development, see Daniel A. Bell, *East Meets West: Human Rights and Democracy in East Asia* (Princeton: Princeton University Press, 2000); Fred Dallmayr, " 'Asian Values' and Global Human Rights," *Philosophy East & West* 52, no. 2 (2002): 173–89; Francis Fukuyama, "Confucianism and Democracy," *Journal of Democracy* 6, no. 2 (1995): 22–30; Francis Fukuyama, "The Illusion of Exceptionalism," *Journal of Democracy* 8, no. 3 (1997): 146–49; Rhoda Howard, "Cultural Absolutism and the Nostalgia for Community," *Human Rights Quarterly* 15, no. 2 (1993): 315–38; Kyong-dong Kim, "Confucianism, Economic Development, and Democracy," *Asian Perspective* 21 (1997): 77–97; Adamantia Pollis, "Cultural Relativism Revisited: Through a State Prism," *Human Rights Quarterly* 18, no. 2 (1996): 316–44; Alison Dundes Renteln, *International Human Rights: Universalism Versus Relativism* (Newbury Park, CA: Sage, 1990); Edward Shils, "Reflections on the Civil Society and Civility in the Chinese Intellectual Tradition," in *Confucian Traditions in East Asian Modernity*, edited by Tu Wei-ming (Cambridge: Cambridge University Press, 1996), 3–20.

56. Steinberg, "Continuing Democratic Reform," 218.

57. Erich Fromm, "The State as Educator: On the Psychology of Criminal Justice," in *Erich Fromm and Critical Criminology: Beyond the Punitive Society*, edited by Kevin Anderson and Richard Quinney (Urbana: University of Illinois Press, [1930] 2000), 126.

58. Howard Palley, "Social Policy and the Elderly in South Korea: Confucianism, Modernization, and Development," *Asian Survey* 32, no. 9 (1992): 796.

59. Kim, "A Response to Lee Kuan Yew": 195.

60. Zehra F. Kabasakal Arat, "The Women's Convention and State Reservations: The Lack of Compliance by Muslim States," paper presented at the Annual Meeting of International Studies Association, New Orleans, LA, March 2002: 22.

61. European Parliament, "Debate on the Abolition of the Death Penalty in Japan, South Korea, and Taiwan," News Release, 13 June 2002; Monique Chu, "Europeans Want Taiwan to Scrap the Death Penalty," *Taipei Times*, 22 June 2002.

62. European Parliament, "Debate on the Abolition of the Death Penalty in Japan, South Korea and Taiwan."

63. Doh Chul Shin, *Mass Politics and Culture in Democratizing Korea* (Cambridge: Cambridge University Pres, 1999), 31.

64. Doh Chul Shin and Huoyan Shyu, "Political Ambivalence in South Korea and Taiwan," *Journal of Democracy* 8, no. 3 (1997): 117.

65. The "Sunshine Policy" favors engagement with North Korea and encourages greater business and civilian links with North Korea, including family contact, rail and road links, tourist trips, and the importation of North Korean literature.

66. Personal interview, Oh Chang-ik, Secretary General of the Citizen's Solidarity for Human Rights, Seoul, Korea, 6 January 2003; interview, Lyu Eun-sook, human rights activist, Seoul, Korea, 10 January 2003.

67. *Korea Herald*, "Anti-Death Penalty: A Prayer for the Dying," 4 December 2001.

68. Oh Chang-ik, leader of the influential Citizen's Solidarity for Human Rights stated: "The death penalty agenda is not our priority. The Catholic Church is doing a good job in the abolitionist campaign, and that is enough. The death penalty will be eventually abolished anyway." Interview, Oh Chang-ik, Seoul, Korea, 6 January 2003.

69. Roger Hood, "Introduction—The Importance of Abolishing the Death Penalty," in *Death Penalty: Abolition in Europe* (Strasbourg: Council of Europe Publishing, 1999); Zimring and Hawkins, *Capital Punishment and the American Agenda*.

70. Charles Abugre, "NGOs, Institutional Development, and Sustainable Development in Post-Apartheid South Africa," in *Sustainable Development for a Democratic South Africa*, edited by Ken Cole (New York: St. Martin's Press, 1994); Mihalik, "The Moratorium on Executions": 118–42.

71. Interview, Kim Chulhyo, director of the Death Penalty Abolition Campaign, Amnesty International's South Korean Section, Daegu, Korea, 28 December 2002; 6 January 2003. After receiving a number of letters from the Korean branch office of Amnesty International that called for addressing the issue of capital punishment, in January 2003 the National Human Rights Commission added the death penalty to the list of "The Ten Most Serious Human Rights Problems Facing the New Government." NHRC Press Release, 28 January 2003.

72. *Korea Times*, "Presidential Body Calls for Abolition of Death Sentences," 6 April 2005; *Korea Times*, "Rights Panel Causes Outcry Over Key Issues," 15 April 2005.

73. *Hankyoreh*, 23 February 2002.

74. *Donga Ilbo*, "Life Imprisonment for Murderers," 5 February 2004.

75. *Hankyoreh*, 13 May 2005.

76. Schabas, *The Abolition of the Death Penalty in International Law*.

CHAPTER 5. UNITED STATES

1. The jury in Alexandria, Virginia, on 3 May 2006, declined to put Moussaoui to death.

2. Joel Blocker, "France/U.S.: Criticism Tempered on Decision to Seek Death Penalty for Moussaoui," Middle East News Online, 2 April 2002; Philip Shenon and Neil A. Lewis, "A Nation Challenged: The Conspiracy Trial; U.S. to Seek Death Penalty For Moussaoui in Terror Case," *New York Times*, 28 March 2002; The Associated Press, "Germany Sets Terms for Sharing Evidence Against Terror Suspect: Moussaoui Charged in Sept. 11 Conspiracy," 1 September 2002.

3. Zimring, *The Contradictions of American Capital Punishment*, 181.

4. Zimring and Hawkins, *Capital Punishment and the American Agenda*, 9–12.

5. Amnesty International, "Abolitionist and Retentionist Countries."

6. In 2005, 94 percent of all known executions took place only in these four countries. Amnesty International, "Death Sentences and Executions in 2005." see http://web.amnesty.org/pages/deathpenalty-sentences-eng.

7. Stephen B. Bright, "Will the Death Penalty Remain Alive in the Twenty-First Century?: International Norms, Discrimination, Arbitrariness, and the Risk of Executing the Innocent," *Wisconsin Law Review* 2001, no. 1 (2000): 2.

8. Harold Hongju Koh, "Paying 'Decent Respect' to World Opinion on the Death Penalty," *U.C. Davis Law Review* 35, no. 5 (2002): 1108.

9. Bohm, *Deathquest*, 7.

10. All three cases, *Furman v. Georgia*, *Jackson v. Georgia*, and *Branch v. Texas*, were consolidated under 408 U.S. 238, 1972, and are referred to as the *Furman* decision.

11. In the 1958 *Trop v. Dulles* case, the Supreme Court ruled that the Eighth Amendment contained an "evolving standard of decency that marked the progress of a maturing society." Even though *Trop v. Dulles* was not a death penalty case itself, abolitionists applied the Court's logic to the death penalty and maintained that the United States had progressed to a point that its "standard of decency" should no longer tolerate the death penalty. Bohm, *Deathquest*, 11–12.

12. The Supreme Court rulings in *Gregg v. Georgia*, 428 U.S. 153, *Jurek v. Texas*, 428 U.S. 262, and *Proffitt v. Florida*, 428 U.S. 242 are collectively referred to as the *Gregg* decision.

13. *Gregg v. Georgia*. 1976. 428 U.S. 153.

14. The Associated Press, "High Court Ends Death Penalty for Youth," 1 March 2005.

15. Stephen B. Davis, "The Death Penalty and Legal Reform in the PRC," *Journal of Chinese Law* 1, no. 3 (1987): 303–34; Death Penalty Information Center. http://www.deathpenaltyinfo.org.

16. Wohlwend, "The Efforts of the Parliamentary Assembly of the Council of Europe," 65.

17. Council of Europe, "Statutory Resolution (93) 26 on Observer Status," adopted by the Committee of Ministers at its 92nd Session, on 14 May 1993. http://cm.coe.int/ta/res/1993/93x26.htm.

18. Council of Europe Resolution 1253 (2001); Recommendation 1522 (2001); Resolution 1349 (2003); Recommendation 1627 (2003).

19. The Associated Press, "Mexico Extradition Policy Highlighted," 25 June 2003.

20. Martine Jacot, "The Death Penalty: Abolition Gains Ground," *UNESCO Courier* (October, 1999): 37–38.

21. *Roper v. Simmons*, 543 U.S. 551 (2005), *Ante*, at 22.

22. Ibid., *Ante*, at 9.

23. Hope Yen, "High Court Ends Death Penalty for Youths," *Associated Press*, 1 March 2005.

24. Stuart Banner, *The Death Penalty: An American History* (Cambridge: Harvard University Press, 2003), 300–301. With the exception of homicide, however, the crime rate in the United States is considered neither rising nor exceptionally high in comparison to other industrial countries. The International Crime Surveys consistently found that the overall victimization rate was lower in the United States than in Canada, France, Switzerland, England, and the Netherlands and was actually slightly below the norm. In contrast, incarceration rates in the United States were second highest after Russia, much higher than those in any other Western countries. See Katherine Beckett and Theodore Sasson, *The Politics of Injustice: Crime and Punishment in America* (Thousands Oaks, CA: Pine Forge Press, 2000), 15–25.

25. Michael Tonry and Richard S. Frase, eds., *Sentencing and Sanctions in Western Countries* (New York: Oxford University Press, 2001).

26. Kvashis, "The Death Penalty and Public Opinion": 81–82. At present, Russia has a moratorium on death sentences.

27. James Liebman, Jeffrey Fagan, and Valerie West, "A Broken System: Error Rates in Capital Cases, 1973–1995," *Texas Law Review* 78 (2002): 1839–67.

28. Anthony G. Amsterdam, "Capital Punishment," in *The Death Penalty in America*, edited by Hugo Adam Bedau (New York: Oxford University Press, 1982), 346–58; William C. Bailey and Ruth D. Peterson, "Police Killings and Capital Punishment: The Post-*Furman* Period," *Criminology* 25, no. 1 (1987): 1–25; Bailey and Peterson, "Murder, Capital Punishment, and Deterrence": 53–74; William Bowers, "The Effect of Executions is Brutalization, Not Deterrence," in *Challenging Capital Punishment: Legal and Social Science Approaches*, edited by. K. C. Haas and J. A. Inciardi (Newbury Park, CA: Sage, 1988), 49–89; Ellsworth and Ross, "Public Opinion and Capital Punishment": 116–69; Victoria Schneider and John Ortiz Smykla, "A Summary Analysis of Executions in the United States, 1608–1987: The Espy File," in *The Death Penalty in America: Current Research*, edited by Robert M. Bohm (Cincinnati: Anderson, 1991), 1–19.

29. Allison Dunfield, "Homicide Rate Lowest in Three Decades," *Globe and Mail*, 29 September 2004.

30. Hugo Adam Bedau, ed., *The Death Penalty in America: Current Controversies* (New York: Oxford University Press, 1997), 21.

31. Death Penalty Information Center, "Number of Executions by State and Region Since 1976." http://www.deathpenaltyinfo.org/article.php?scid=8&did=186#region.

32. Zimring, *The Contradictions of American Capital Punishment*, 7.

33. Bedau, *The Death Penalty in America*; Stephen B. Bright, "The Politics of Crime and the Death Penalty: Not 'Soft on Crime,' But Hard on the Bill of Rights," *Saint Louis University Law Journal* 39 (1995): 479–505; Margaret Werner Cahalan and Lee Anne Parsons, *Historical Corrections Statistics in the United States, 1850–1984*

(Boston: Northeastern University Press, 1986); Robert Johnson, *Death Work: A Study of the Modern Execution Process* (Belmont, CA: West/Wadsworth, 1998); Marquart, Ekland-Olson and Sorensen, *The Rope, the Chair, and the Needle.*

34. Zimring, *The Contradictions of American Capital Punishment*, 89–90.

35. Bright, "The Politics of Crime and the Death Penalty": 483; Bedau, *The Death Penalty in America*, 23.

36. Zimring, *The Contradictions of American Capital Punishment*, 89.

37. Ibid., 118.

38. Cahalan and Parsons, *Historical Corrections Statistics in the United States*, 16.

39. Poveda, "American Exceptionalism and the Death Penalty": 256.

40. Stanley Elkins, *Slavery: A Problem in American Institutional and Intellectual Life* (Chicago: University of Chicago Press, 1968).

41. Steven E. Barkan and Steven F. Cohn, "Racial Prejudice and Support for the Death Penalty by Whites," *Journal of Research in Crime and Delinquency* 31, no. 2 (1994): 202–209; Christopher G. Ellison, "Southern Culture and Firearms Ownership," *Social Science Quarterly* 72 (1991): 267–83; Gregory D. Russell, *The Death Penalty and Racial Bias: Overturning Supreme Court Assumptions* (Westport, CT: Greenwood Press, 1994); Robert L. Young, "Race, Conceptions of Crime and Justice, and Support for the Death Penalty," *Social Psychological Quarterly* 54, no.1 (1991): 61–75.

42. Ellison, "Southern Culture and Firearms Ownership."

43. David Baldus and George Woodworth, "Race Discrimination and the Death Penalty: An Empirical and Legal Overview," in *America's Experiment with Capital Punishment: Reflections on the Past, Present, and Future of the Ultimate Penal Sanction*, edited by James Acker, Robert Bohm, and Charles Lanier (Durham: Carolina Academic Press, 1998), 385–415; Richard Dieter, *The Death Penalty in Black and White: Who Lives, Who Dies, Who Decides* (Washington, DC: Death Penalty Information Center, 1998); Marquart, Ekland-Olson, and Sorensen, *The Rope, the Chair, and the Needle*; Radelet and Vandiver, "Race and Capital Punishment": 94–113.

44. Death Penalty Information Center, "Race of Death Row Inmates Executed Since 1976." http://www.deathpenaltyinfo.org/article.php?scid=5&did=184.

45. Baldus et al., "Symposium: Racial Discrimination and the Death Penalty in the Post-*Furman* Era": 1638–1770. Public polls in the United States have consistently shown higher support for the death penalty among whites than among blacks.

46. *Callins v. Collins*, 510 U.S. 1141, 1994.

47. J. Mark Lane and Ronald J. Tabak, "The Execution of Injustice: a Cost and Lack-of-Benefit Analysis of the Death Penalty," *Loyola of Los Angeles Law Review* 23 (1989): 59–129.

48. Stephen B. Bright, "Counsel for the Poor: The Death Penalty Not for the Worst Crime but for the Worst Lawyer," *Yale Law Journal* 103 (1994): 1840–43.

49. Poveda, "American Exceptionalism and the Death Penalty": 259.

50. Beckett and Sasson, *The Politics of Injustice*, 47–74. It is instructive to note that the U.S. South was exceptional in the strength and depth of its resistance to the civil rights movement of the 1950s and 1960s, to which the movement for the abolition of capital punishment has had strong connection.

51. Beckett and Sasson, *The Politics of Injustice*, 55.

52. Zimring and Hawkins, *Capital Punishment and the American Agenda*, 153.

53. Congressional Quarterly Almanac (Washington, DC: CQ Press, 1988), 85; Congressional Quarterly Almanac (Washington, DC: CQ Press, 1994), 273.

54. Louis P. Masur, *Rites of Execution: Capital Punishment and the Transformation of American Culture, 1776–1865* (New York: Oxford University Press, 1989), 4–5.

55. Herbert H. Haines, *Against Capital Punishment: The Anti–Death Penalty Movement in America, 1972–1994* (New York: Oxford University Press, 1996), 148–61. In contrast, violent crime has actually fallen from its early 1980s peak. With the help of the news and entertainment media, which highlight dramatic but relatively uncommon forms of murder, the issue of crime in U.S. politics and culture, despite the decrease in the actual crime rate, has strongly affected the policy-making process.

56. George Anderson, "Organizing Against the Death Penalty," *America* 178 (1998): 10–11.

57. Romoda Jones, "Senate Votes Against Executions," *Wichita Eagle-Beacon*, 4 April 1987.

58. Haines, *Against Capital Punishment*, 5.

59. Michael Kroll, "Florida Day," in *Organizing Against the Death Penalty: A Handbook*, 3rd edition, D4–D9 (Washington, DC: National Coalition to Abolish the Death Penalty, 1988); Eric Muller, "The Legal Defense Fund's Capital Punishment Campaign: The Distorting Influence of Death," *Yale Law and Policy Review* 4 (1985): 158–87.

60. Haines, *Against Capital Punishment*, 194.

61. Ibid., 115.

62. Haines, *Against Capital Punishment*; Schabas, *The Abolition of the Death Penalty in International Law*.

63. Ewen MacAskill, "Bush Talks a Different Language: President Rebuffs Critics on First Stop of Europe Tour," *Guardian*, 13 June 2001.

64. Gallup News Service, "Plurality of Americans Believe Death Penalty Not Imposed Often Enough Basic Support for Death Penalty at 70%," 12 March 2003; Peter D. Hart Research Associates, "Study # 6292 Death Penalty Update," March 2001; Harris Poll, "Support For Death Penalty Still Very Strong In Spite Of Widespread Belief That Some Innocent People Are Convicted Of Murder," Harris Poll #41, 17 August, 2001. It is important to note that public support for the death penalty lacks certainty or regularity. The polls show that as people become more informed about the death penalty (e.g., about the execution of the mentally retarded and juvenile murderers), support for it wanes.

65. Gallup, "Support for the Death Penalty Remains High at 74%," 19 May 2003.

66. Walter Berns, *For Capital Punishment: Crime and Morality of the Death Penalty* (New York: Basic Books, 1979).

67. All the following survey results come from the Gallup Institute, which has conducted extensive death penalty surveys since 1936.

68. George H. Gallup, ed., *Gallup International Opinion Polls, Great Britain, 1937–1975* (New York: Random House, 1976), 774.

69. Joshua Micah Marshall, "Death in Venice: Europe's Death-penalty Elitism," *The New Republic* 223, no. 5 (2000): 14. Whether the intensity of U.S. support for capital punishment is different from that in other Western nations is still in question. If pro–death penalty sentiment in the United States is much stronger than that in Europe in its abolition years (i.e., if the depth and intensity rather than the breadth of support for the death penalty is what distinguishes the U.S. pattern from that in other nations), we may speculate that the United States does not necessarily

follow the European scenario, in which public resistance was muted soon after the abolition of capital punishment.

70. Raymond Bonner and Ford Fessenden, "Absence of Executions: States with No Death Penalty Share Lower Homicide Rates," *New York Times*, 22 September 2000.

71. Sara Sun Beale, "Federal Criminal Jurisdiction," in *Encyclopedia of Crime and Justice*, edited by Joshua Dressler (New York: Macmillan, 2002), 775–79.

72. Zimring, *The Contradictions of American Capital Punishment*, 120.

73. Kristi Tumminello Prinzo, "The United States—'Capital' of The World: An Analysis of Why the United States Practices Capital Punishment While the International Trend is Towards Its Abolition," *Brooklyn Journal of International Law* 24 (1999): 878–88.

74. Bohm, *Deathquest*, 187–88.

75. Phoebe C. Ellsworth and Samuel R. Gross, "Hardening of the Attitudes: Americans' Views on the Death Penalty," *Journal of Social Issues* 50, no. 2 (1994): 23.

76. Ibid., 22.

77. Harold Evans, "Candidates Hide Behind Death Penalty," *Times Union*, 22 February 2000.

78. Kristine R. DeMay, "Violent Crime Control and Law Enforcement Act of 1994: The Semi-Automatic 'Assault Weapon'—The Latest Victim in This Country's War against Crime," *Hamline Journal of Public Law and Policy* 16 (1994): 199; Neil A. Lewis, "G.O.P. to Challenge Judicial Nominees Who Oppose Death Penalty," *New York Times*, 15 October 1993.

79. Mark Obmascik, "Death Penalty Politics," *The Denver Post*, 21 September 1997.

80. Lewis, "G.O.P. to Challenge Judicial Nominees Who Oppose Death Penalty."

81. Stuart Taylor Jr., "The Shame of the Ronnie White Vote," *National Journal* 31, no. 42 (1999): 2–5.

82. Eric Horng, "U.S. Bucks International Trend against Capital Punishment," *CNN News*, 31 January 2000.

83. As of January 2006, the total number of death row inmates was 3,373, and among them 40 are on federal death row. NAACP Legal Defense and Educational Fund, "Death Row USA Winter 2006." http://www.naacpldf.org/content/pdf/pubs/drusa/DRUSA_Winter_2006.pdf.

84. Zimring, *The Contradictions of American Capital Punishment*, 127–28.

85. Obmascik, "Death Penalty Politics."

86. Michel Forst, "The Abolition of the Death Penalty in France," in *The Death Penalty: Abolition in Europe* (Strasbourg: Council of Europe Publishing, 1999), 113.

87. National and State Profiles, "Easy Access to the FBI's Supplementary Homicide Reports: 1980–2000." http://ojjdp.ncjrs.org/ojstatbb/ezashr/asp/profile.asp.

88. United States Bureau of Justice Statistics, "Capital Punishment Statistics." http://www.ojp.usdoj.gov/bjs/cp.htm.

CHAPTER 6. CONCLUSION

1. Amnesty International, "Abolitionist and Retentionist Countries."

2. Amnesty International, "Death Sentences and Executions in 1996" (AI index: ACT 51/01/97).

3. Checkel, "Sanctions, Social Learning, and Institutions"; Etheridge, *Can Governments Learn?*; Hall, "Policy Paradigms, Social Learning, and the State"; Levy, "Learning and Foreign Policy": 279–312; John Gerard Ruggie, "What Makes the World Hang Together?: Neo-Utilitarianism and the Social Constructivist Challenge."

4. CCT/3/94; Mihalik, "The Moratorium on Executions": 133.

5. Amnesty International, *When the State Kills*, 204–207.

6. Roger Hood, "The Abandonment of Capital Punishment: Some Reflections on the European Experience," in *Death Penalty: Abolition in Europe* (Strasbourg: Council of Europe Publishing, 1999), 14.

7. Robert F. Drinan, "Even South Africa Drops Death Penalty," *National Catholic Reporter* 31, no. 35 (1995): 20.

8. Frueh, *Political Identity and Social Change.*

9. The terms *the logic of appropriateness* and *the logic of consequences* were coined by James G. March and Johan P. Olsen in *Rediscovering Institutions: The Organizational Basis of Politics* (New York: Free Press, 1989). These terms have been widely used by other scholars of international relations; see, for example, Martha Finnemore, *National Interests in International Society* (Ithaca: Cornell University Press, 1996); Hawkins, *International Human Rights and Authoritarian Rule in Chile*; Ronald B. Mitchell, "Norms as Regulative Rules," paper presented at the Annual Meeting of the International Studies Association, Chicago, IL, February 2001; Moravcsik, "The Origins of Human Rights Regimes": 217–52.

10. Joel Blocker, "France/U.S.: Criticism Tempered on Decision to Seek Death Penalty for Moussaoui," *Middle East News Online*, 2 April 2002; Philip Shenon and Neil A. Lewis, "A Nation Challenged: The Conspiracy Trial; U.S. to Seek Death Penalty For Moussaoui in Terror Case," *New York Times*, 28 March 2002.

11. Hood, "Introduction—The Importance of Abolishing the Death Penalty," 19–20.

12. Koh, "Paying 'Decent Respect' to World Opinion on the Death Penalty": 1085–1131.

13. Klein et al., "The Deterrent Effect of Capital Punishment"; Paternoster, *Capital Punishment in America*; Peterson and Bailey, "Is Capital Punishment an Effective Deterrent for Murder?"

14. Tamara Thiessen, "Secret Executions Going on in Europe," *Straits Times*, Singapore, 12 January 2001.

15. According to the 2001 report of the United Nations Interregional Crime and Justice Research Institute, the violent crime rate in South Africa is twenty times higher than in the United States. See http://www.unicri.it/wwk/documentation/lmsdb.php?kw_=VIOLENT%20CRIME%20STATISTICS.

16. Gerald L. Curtis, "A 'Recipe' for Democratic Development," *Journal of Democracy* 8, no. 3 (1997): 139–49; Fukuyama, "Confucianism and Democracy": 20–33; Pollis, "Cultural Relativism Revisited": 316–44. In some cases, political elites might view adhering to an international norm as compromising the state's sovereignty or their own capacity to rule. For example, ruling elites in many parts of Asia reject international calls for policies reflecting Western conceptions of human rights and political pluralism with appeals to the primacy of "Asian values." Beng Huat Chua, "Asian Values Discourse and the Resurrection of the Social," *Positions: East Asian Culture Critique* 7, no. 2 (1999): 297–316; Michael Freeman, "Human Rights, Democracy, and 'Asian Values,'" *Pacific Review* 9, no. 3 (1996):

355–405; Richard Robinson, "The Politics of Asian Values," *Pacific Review* 9, no. 3 (1996): 309–27.

17. Curtis, "A 'Recipe' for Democratic Development": 144.

18. Ellsworth and Ross, "Public Opinion and Capital Punishment": 116–69; Gross and Kinder, "Ethnocentrism Revisited: Explaining American Opinion on Crime and Punishment"; Mark Warr, "Poll Trends: Public Opinion on Crime and Punishment," *Public Opinion Quarterly* 59, no. 2 (1995): 296–310.

19. Edmund McGarrell and Marla Sandys, "The Misperception of Public Opinion Toward Capital Punishment," *American Behavioral Scientist* 39, no. 4 (1996): 500–14.

20. Haines, *Against Capital Punishment*, 164.

21. Even in the Philippines, for instance, which is a predominantly Catholic country, public opinion has been overwhelmingly in favor of the death penalty.

22. Forst, "The Abolition of the Death Penalty in France," 113.

23. Jacot, "The Death Penalty: Abolition Gains Ground." France was one of the last countries in Western Europe to abolish the death penalty. The last execution took place in 1977, and formal abolition came in 1981. According to Forst, the long reign of the Center-Right parties in national politics delayed abolition. The death penalty was abolished as soon as the Left came to power. Forst, "The Abolition of the Death Penalty in France," 113.

24. Marshall, "Death in Venice": 13.

25. Elisabeth Noelle and Erich Peter Neumann, eds., *The Germans: Public Opinion Polls 1947–1966* (Allensbach, Bonn: Verlag für Demoskopie, 1967); Zimring and Hawkins, *Capital Punishment and the American Agenda*.

26. Marshall, "Death in Venice": 13.

27. Zimring and Hawkins, *Capital Punishment and the American Agenda*, 12.

28. Forst, "The Abolition of the Death Penalty in France," 115.

29. Ellsworth and Gross, "Hardening of the Attitudes"; McGarrell and Sandys, "The Misperception of Public Opinion toward Capital Punishment."

30. For instance, when asked about support for the death penalty and given an alternative punishment of life without parole, respondents' support for it plummets. An ABC/*Washington Post* Poll taken in April 2001 found 63 percent support for the death penalty, but this falls to 46 percent given the alternative of life without parole. See http://pollingreport.com.

31. Gallup, "Gallup Poll Topics: Death Penalty," 2004. http://www.gallup.com/poll/indicators/inddeath_pen.asp.

32. Zimring, *The Contradictions of American Capital Punishment*, 23.

33. Yet this issue should be addressed within the context of domestic political institutions. Even though there exists a "determined political will," it is not always actualized in every political setting. For example, U.S. politicians are frequently accused of being "soft on crime" during a campaign when they take an anti–death penalty stance. They may later change their stance, or, at least, they tend to be extremely cautious in expressing their official position. I discuss this in more detail in the section entitled "Domestic Political Institutions."

34. Marshall, "Death in Venice": 12–14.

35. Richard Buxton, "The Politics of Criminal Law Reform: England," *American Journal of Comparative Law* 21 (1973): 244.

36. CCT/3/94, paragraph 87.

37. Edmund Burke, an eloquent champion of the trustee model, famously argued that democratic representatives are necessarily more than mere agents of the peoples' changing wishes: "Your representative owes you not his industry alone but his judgment; and he betrays, instead of serving you, if he sacrifices it to your opinion." Edmund Burke, "Speech to the Electors of Bristol," in *Edmund Burke on Government Politics and Society*, edited by B. W. Hill (London: Fontana, [1774] 1975), 156.

38. Seymour Martin Lipset, *American Exceptionalism: A Two-Edged Sword* (New York: Norton, 1996), 43.

39. The influence of the U.S. federal government on matters of criminal justice has been minimal. In terms of capital punishment, only forty of more than 3,400 death row prisoners are in federal prisons, as of January 2006. No federal executions took place between 1963 and the recent executions of Timothy McVeigh and Juan Raul Garza in 2001 and Louis Jones in 2003.

40. Notwithstanding, a single state can be the target of international pressure. For instance, the International Court of Justice ordered U.S. courts to review death sentences imposed on Mexican nationals, on whose behalf Mexico brought its lawsuit. Giving special attention to Osvaldo Torres, who was due to be executed in Oklahoma on May 18, 2004, the International Court of Justice found that his rights under the Vienna Convention on Consular Relations (VCCR) had been violated. Under the Convention, authorities must inform detained foreign nationals of their right to contact their consulates. Anthony Deutsch, "Court Orders U.S. to Review Mexican Cases," Associated Press, 31 March 2004.

41. Zimring and Hawkins, *Capital Punishment and the American Agenda*, 155.

42. Moravcsik, "Why Is U.S. Human Rights Policy So Unilateralist?": 345–76.

43. The terms, *motivation*, *capability* and *opportunity* came from a conversation with James McCann. Leigh Raymond offered valuable suggestions for conceptualizing and organizing this model.

44. Bryan D. Jones, *Reconceiving Decision-Making in Democratic Politics* (Chicago: University of Chicago Press, 1994), 87.

45. Hawkins, *International Human Rights and Authoritarian Rule in Chile*, 48.

BIBLIOGRAPHY

Abugre, Charles. "NGOs, Institutional Development, and Sustainable Development in Post-Apartheid South Africa." In *Sustainable Development for a Democratic South Africa*, edited by Ken Cole, 121–48. New York: St. Martin's Press, 1994.

Adler, Emanuel. *The Power of Ideology: The Quest for Technological Autonomy in Argentina and Brazil.* Berkeley: University of California Press, 1987.

Amnesty International. "1,526 executed in 2002." http://web.amnesty.org/library/Index/ENGACT500072003?open&of=ENG-392.

———. "AI Report 2003: China." http:web.amnesty.org/report2003/chn-summary-eng.

———. "China: Execution Is Not a Solution. Amnesty International Condemns 46 Executions in Two Days." http://web.amnesty.org/library/Index/ENGASA17054 2002?open&of=ENG-2AS.

———. "The Death Penalty Worldwide: Developments in 2003." http://web.amnesty.org/library/index/ENGACT500072004.

———. "The Death Penalty Worldwide: Developments in 2004." http://web.amnesty.org/library/Index/ENGACT500012005.

———. "Death Sentences and Executions in 1996." http://web.amnesty.org/library/index/ENGACT510011997.

———. "Republic of Korea (South Korea): Summary of Concerns and Recommendations to Candidates for the Presidential Elections in December 2002." http://web.amnesty.org/library/Index/ENGASA250072002?open&of=ENG-KOR.

———. "Ukraine: Secret Mass Executions in Ukraine Called 'Barbaric.'" http://web.amnesty.org/library/Index/ENGEUR500161996?open&of=ENG-UKR.

———. "USA: Arbitrary, Discriminatory, Cruel, Futile—25 Years of Judicial Killing." http://web.amnesty.org/library/Index/engAMR510072002?Open Document&of=COUNTRIES%5CUSA.

Amnesty International. *When the State Kills . . . The Death Penalty: A Human Rights Issue.* New York: Amnesty International, 1989.

Amsterdam, Anthony G. "Capital Punishment." In *The Death Penalty in America*, edited by Hugo Adam Bedau, 346–58. New York: Oxford University Press, 1982.

Anderson, George. "Organizing Against the Death Penalty." *America* 178 (1998): 10–11.

Arat, Zehra F. Kabasakal. "The Women's Convention and State Reservations: The Lack of Compliance by Muslim States." Paper presented at the Annual Meeting of the International Studies Association, New Orleans, LA, March 2002.

Axelrod, Robert, and Robert O. Keohane. "Achieving Cooperation under Anarchy: Strategies and Institutions." *World Politics* 38, no. 1 (1985): 226–54.

Badinter, Robert. "Preface—Moving Towards Universal Abolition of the Death Penalty." In *The Death Penalty Beyond Abolition*. Strasbourg: Council of Europe Publishing, 2004.

Bae, Sangmin. "Ending State Killing in South Korea: Challenging the Asian Capital Punishment Status Quo." In *The Cultural Lives of Capital Punishment: Comparative Perspectives*, edited by Austin Sarat and Christian Boulanger, 308–27. Stanford: Stanford University Press, 2005.

Bailey, William C., and Ruth D. Peterson. "Police Killings and Capital Punishment: The Post-*Furman* Period." *Criminology* 25, no. 1 (1987): 1–25.

———. "Murder, Capital Punishment, and Deterrence: A Review of the Evidence and an Examination of Police Killings." *Journal of Social Issues* 50, no. 2 (1994): 53–74.

Baldus, David, and George Woodworth. "Race Discrimination and the Death Penalty: An Empirical and Legal Overview." In *America's Experiment with Capital Punishment: Reflections on the Past, Present, and Future of the Ultimate Penal Sanction*, edited by James Acker, Robert Bohm and Charles Lanier, 385–415. Durham: Carolina Academic Press, 1998.

Baldus, David, George Woodworth, David Zuckerman, Neil Alan Weiner, and Barbara Broffitt. "Symposium: Racial Discrimination and the Death Penalty in the Post-*Furman* Era: An Empirical and Legal Overview, With Recent Findings from Philadelphia." *Cornell Law Review* 83 (1998): 1638–1770.

Banner, Stuart. *The Death Penalty: An American History*. Cambridge: Harvard University Press, 2003.

Barkan, Steven E., and Steven F. Cohn. "Racial Prejudice and Support for the Death Penalty by Whites." *Journal of Research in Crime and Delinquency* 31, no. 2 (1994): 202–209.

Barnett, Michael. "Sovereignty, Nationalism, and Regional Order in the Arab States System." *International Organization* 49, no. 3 (1995): 479–510.

Beale, Sara Sun. "Federal Criminal Jurisdiction." In *Encyclopedia of Crime and Justice*, edited by Joshua Dressler, 775–79. New York: Macmillan, 2002.

Beckett, Katherine, and Theodore Sasson. *The Politics of Injustice: Crime and Punishment in America*. Thousands Oaks, CA: Pine Forge Press, 2000.

Bedau, Hugo Adam. *Death Is Different: Studies in the Morality, Law, and Politics of Capital Punishment*. Boston: Northeastern University Punishment. 1987.

———, ed. *The Death Penalty in America: Current Controversies*. New York: Oxford University Press, 1997.

Bell, Daniel A. *East Meets West: Human Rights and Democracy in East Asia*. Princeton: Princeton University Press, 2000.

Berns, Walter. *For Capital Punishment: Crime and the Morality of the Death Penalty*. New York: Basic Books, 1979.

Biersteker, Thomas J. "The 'Triumph' of Neoclassical Economics in the Developing World: Policy Convergence and Bases of Governance in the International Economic Order." In *Governance without Government: Order and Change in World Politics*, edited by James N. Rosenau and Ernst-Otto Czempiel, 102–31. Cambridge: Cambridge University Press, 1997.

Black Sash. "Inside South Africa's Death Factory." Black Sash Unpublished Research Report, 1989. Available upon request from the author.

Bohm, Robert M. *Deathquest: An Introduction to the Theory and Practice of Capital Punishment in the United States.* Cincinnati: Anderson, 1999.

Boulanger, Christian. "Book Review: Mary McAuley, *Russia's Politics of Uncertainty.*" *Comparative Political Studies* 32, no. 2 (1999): 271–78.

Bowers, William. "The Effect of Executions is Brutalization, Not Deterrence." In *Challenging Capital Punishment: Legal and Social Science Approaches*, edited by K. C. Haas and J. A. Inciardi, 49–89. Newbury Park, CA: Sage, 1998.

Bowers, William, Glenn Pierce, and John McDevitt. *Legal Homicide: Death as Punishment in America, 1864–1982.* Boston: Northeastern University Press, 1984.

Bright, Stephen B. "Counsel for the Poor: The Death Penalty Not for the Worst Crime but for the Worst Lawyer." *Yale Law Journal* 103 (1994): 1835–1900.

———. "The Politics of Crime and the Death Penalty: Not 'Soft on Crime,' But Hard on the Bill of Rights." *Saint Louis University Law Journal* 39 (1995): 479–505.

———. "Will the Death Penalty Remain Alive in the Twenty-First Century?: International Norms, Discrimination, Arbitrariness, and the Risk of Executing the Innocent." *Wisconsin Law Review* 2001, no. 1 (2000): 1–33.

Burke Edmund. "Speech to the Electors of Bristol." In *Edmund Burke on Government Politics and Society*, edited by B. W. Hill. London: Fontana, [1774] 1975.

Burnham, Margaret A. "Constitution-Making in South Africa." *Boston Review: A Political and Literary Forum* (December 1997/January 1998).

Buxton, Richard. "The Politics of Criminal Law Reform: England." *American Journal of Comparative Law* 21 (1973): 230–44.

Cahalan, Margaret Werner, and Lee Anne Parsons. *Historical Corrections Statistics in the United States, 1850–1984.* Boston: Northeastern University Press, 1986.

Camus, Albert. "Reflections on the Guillotine." In *Resistance, Rebellion, and Death*, translated by Justin O'Brien. New York: Knopf, 1961.

Carlin, John. "Nelson Mandela: My Life; Fifty Years after the Universal Declaration of Human Rights, the President of South Africa Talks to John Carlin about Reconciliation." *Independent* (6 December 1998).

Checkel, Jeffrey T. "International Norms and Domestic Politics: Bridging the Rationalist-Constructivist Divide." *European Journal of International Relations* 3, no. 4 (1997): 473–95.

———. "Norms, Institutions, and National Identity in Contemporary Europe." *International Studies Quarterly* 43, no. 1 (1999): 83–114.

———. "Sanctions, Social Learning, and Institutions: Explaining State Compliance with the Norms of the European Human Rights Regime." ARENA Working Paper 99/11. Oslo: ARENA/Universitetet i Oslo, 1999.

———. "Compliance and Conditionality." ARENA Working Paper 00/18. Oslo: ARENA/Universitetet i Oslo, 2000.

Chenoweth, Erica, and Jessica Teets. "Constraining U.S. Policy: Adherence to International Norms Post 9/11." Paper presented at the Annual Meeting of the Western Political Science Association, Portland, OR, March 2004.

Chernikov, Andrei. "Incarceration Will Be Different in Ukraine." *Current Digest of the Post Soviet Press* 53, no. 36 (2001): 17.

Choi, Jungwoon. "The Kwangju People's Uprising: Formation of the 'Absolute Community.'" *Korea Journal* 39, no. 2 (1999): 238–82.

Christiansen, Thomas, Knud Erik Jørgensen, and Antje Wiener, eds. *The Social Construction of Europe*. Thousand Oaks, CA: Sage, 2001.

Chua, Beng Huat. "Asian Values Discourse and the Resurrection of the Social." *Positions: East Asian Culture Critique* 7, no. 2 (1999): 297–316.

Chyung, Dai-chul. "Capital Punishment Abolition Campaign in Korea and Its Prospect." Paper presented at a Seminar on "Justice and Human Rights in Council of Europe Observer States: The Abolition of the Death Penalty," Tokyo, Japan, 4–5 May 2002.

Clark, Ann Marie. *Diplomacy of Conscience: Amnesty International and Changing Human Rights Norms*. Princeton: Princeton University Press, 2001.

Cole, David. "Courting Capital Punishment." *Nation* 262, no. 8 (1996): 21–23.

Cook, Kimberley J. *Divided Passions: Public Opinions on Abortion and the Death Penalty*. Boston: Northeastern University Press, 1998.

Cortell, Andrew P., and James W. Davis Jr. "How Do International Institutions Matter? The Domestic Impact of International Rules and Norms." *International Studies Quarterly* 40, no. 4 (1996): 451–78.

———. "Understanding the Democratic Impact of International Norms: A Research Agenda." *International Studies Review* 2, no. 1 (2000): 65–87.

———. "When International and Domestic Norms Collide: Japan and the GATT/WTO." Paper presented at the Annual Meeting of the International Studies Association, Chicago, IL, February 2001.

Council of Europe. "An Assembly Conference on the Death Penalty Opens in Springfield, Illinois." http://assembly.coe.int/Main.asp?link=http%3A%2F%2Fassembly.coe.int%2F%2Fcommunication%2FTemporaryDocs%2FASjur%2Fdeathpenalty.htm.

———. "Capital Punishment: Outline of Basic Issues." Unpublished Report. No. S42A-C. Council of Europe Archives, Strasbourg, 1999.

———. "Compliance with Member States' Commitments." Unpublished Report. AS/Inf (1999) 2. Council of Europe Archives, Strasbourg, 1999.

———. "Honouring of Obligations and Commitments by Ukraine." Doc.8424. http://assembly.coe.int/Documents/WorkingDocs/doc99/EDOC8424.HTM.

———. "Monitoring: Awaiting Significant Progress in Ukraine." *The Europeans*. Electronic Newsletter of the Council of Europe Parliamentary Assembly (June 1999). http://stars.coe.fr/magazine/te0699/session1.htm.

———. "Mr Kuchma, President of the Republic of Ukraine, Made the Following Statement." http://www.cm.coe.int/sessions/97summit2/ukraine.htm.

———. "Protocol No.6 to the Convention for the Protection of Human Rights and Fundamental Freedoms Concerning the Abolition of the Death Penalty CETS No.: 114." http://conventions.coe.int/Treaty/Commun/ChercheSig.asp?NT=114&CM=&DF=&CL=ENG.

———. "Recommendation 1246 on Abolition of Capital Punishment." http://assembly.coe.int/Documents/AdoptedText/TA94/EREC1246.HTM.

———. "Recommendation 1395 (1999): Honouring of Obligations and Commitments by Ukraine." http://assembly.coe.int/Documents/AdoptedText/TA99/erec1395.htm.

———. "Recommendation 1522 (2001): Abolition of the Death Penalty in Council of Europe Observer States." http://assembly.coe.int/documents/AdoptedText/TA01/EREC1522.htm.

———. "Recommendation 1627 (2003): Abolition of the Death Penalty in Council of Europe Observer States." http://assembly.coe.int/documents/AdoptedText/TA03/EREC1627.htm.

———. "Resolution 1112: Honouring of the Commitment Entered Into by Ukraine Upon Accession to the Council of Europe to Put into Place a Moratorium on Executions." http://www.coe.fr/ta/ta97/eres1112.htm.

———. "Resolution 1179 (1999): Honouring of Obligations and Commitments by Ukraine." http://assembly.coe.int/Documents/AdoptedText/TA99/eres1179.htm.

———. "Resolution 1253 (2001): Abolition of the Death Penalty in Council of Europe Observer States." http://assembly.coe.int/documents/AdoptedText/ta01/ERES1253.htm.

———. "Resolution 1349 (2003): Abolition of the Death Penalty in Council of Europe Observer States." http://assembly.coe.int/documents/AdoptedText/ta03/ERES1349.htm.

———. "Statutory Resolution (93) 26 on Observer Status." http://cm.coe.int/ta/res/1993/93x26.htm.

———. *The Death Penalty: Abolition in Europe.* Strasbourg: Council of Europe Publishing. 1999.

———. *The Death Penalty Beyond Abolition.* Strasbourg: Council of Europe Publishing. 2004.

———. "Ukraine: Decision-time for the Assembly." *The Europeans.* Electronic Newsletter of the Council of Europe Parliamentary Assembly (January 1998). http://assembly.coe.int/Magazines/Europeans/1998/te0198/SESSION.HTM.

Crawford, Neta C. *Argument and Change in World Politics: Ethics, Decolonization, and Humanitarian Intervention.* Cambridge: Cambridge University Press, 2002.

Currie, Elliott. "Market, Crime, and Community: Toward a Mid-Range Theory of Post-Industrial Violence." In *The Crime Conundrum: Essay on Criminal Justice*, edited by Lawrence M. Friedman and George Fisher, 17–44. Boulder: Westview, 1997.

Curtis, Gerald L. "A 'Recipe' for Democratic Development." *Journal of Democracy* 8, no. 3 (1997): 139–49.

Dallmayr, Fred. "'Asian Values' and Global Human Rights." *Philosophy East & West* 52, no. 2 (2002): 173–89.

D'Anieri, Paul, Robert Kravchuk, and Taras Kuzio. *Politics and Society in Ukraine.* Boulder: Westview, 1999.

Davis, D. M. "Extenuation—an Unnecessary Halfway House on the Road to a Rational Sentencing Policy." *South African Journal of Criminal Justice* 2 (1989): 205–18.

Davis, Stephen B. "The Death Penalty and Legal Reform in the PRC." *Journal of Chinese Law* 1, no. 3 (1987): 303–34.

Death Penalty Information Center. "Number of Executions by State and Region Since 1976." http://www.deathpenaltyinfo.org/article.php?scid=8&did=186#region.

DeMay, Kristine R. "Violent Crime Control and Law Enforcement Act of 1994: The Semi-Automatic 'Assault Weapon'—The Latest Victim in This Country's War against Crime." *Hamline Journal of Public Law and Policy* 16 (1994):199.

Diamond, Larry, and Byung-Kook Kim. "Introduction: Consolidating Democracy in South Korea." In *Consolidating Democracy in South Korea*, edited by Larry Diamond and Byung-Kook Kim, vii–viii. Boulder: Lynne Rienner, 2000.

Dieter, Richard. *The Death Penalty in Black and White: Who Lives, Who Dies, Who Decides.* Washington, DC: Death Penalty Information Center, 1998.

Drinan, Robert F. "Even South Africa Drops Death Penalty." *National Catholic Reporter* 31, no. 35 (1995): 20.

Dugard, John. *Human Rights and the South African Legal Order.* Princeton: Princeton University Press, 1978.

Dunér, Bertil, and Hanna Geurtsen. "The Death Penalty and War." *The International Journal of Human Rights* 6, no. 4 (2002): 1–28.

Dwyer, Eric. "Teen Life in South Korea." In *Teen Life in Asia,* edited by Judith Slater, 205–22. Westport, CT: Greenwood Press, 2004.

Egeland, Jan. *Impotent Superpower—Potent Small State: Potentials and Limitations of Human Rights Objectives in the Foreign Policies of the United States and Norway.* Oxford: Norwegian University Press, 1988.

Ehrlich, Isaac. "The Deterrent Effect of Capital Punishment: A Question of Life and Death." *American Economic Review* 65 (1975): 397–417.

Elkins, Stanley. *Slavery: A Problem in American Institutional and Intellectual Life.* Chicago: University of Chicago Press, 1968.

Ellison, Christopher G. "Southern Culture and Firearms Ownership." *Social Science Quarterly* 72 (1991): 267–83.

Ellsworth, Phoebe C., and Lee Ross. "Public Opinion and Capital Punishment: A Close Examination of the Views of Abolitionists and Retentionists." *Crime and Delinquency* 29 (1983): 116–69.

Ellsworth, Phoebe C., and Samuel R. Gross. "Hardening of the Attitudes: Americans' Views on the Death Penalty." *Journal of Social Issues* 50, no. 2 (1994): 19–52.

Etheridge, Lloyd S. *Can Governments Learn?* New York: Free Press, 1985.

European Parliament. "Debate on the Abolition of the Death Penalty in Japan, South Korea, and Taiwan." www.radicalparty/org/deathpenalty/pe_speech_depuis_12062002_e.htm.

Fairchild, Erika S., and Harry R. Dammer. *Comparative Criminal Justice Systems.* Belmont, CA: Wadsworth, 1993.

Finnemore, Martha. "International Organizations as Teachers of Norms: The United Nations Educational, Scientific, and Cultural Organization and Science Policy." *International Organization* 47, no. 4 (1993): 565–97.

———. *National Interests in International Society.* Ithaca: Cornell University Press, 1996.

Finnemore, Martha, and Kathryn Sikkink. "International Norm Dynamics and Political Change." *International Organization* 52, no. 4 (1998): 887–917.

Fletcher, Jonathan. *Violence and Civilization: An Introduction to the Work of Norbert Elias.* Malden, MA: Blackwell, 1997.

Florini, Ann. "The Evolution of International Norms." *International Studies Quarterly* 40, no. 3 (1996): 363–89.

Foglesong, Todd S., and Peter H. Solomon Jr. *Crime, Criminal Justice, and Criminology in Post-Soviet Ukraine.* Washington, DC: National Institute of Justice, 2001.

Forst, Michel. "The Abolition of the Death Penalty in France." In *The Death Penalty: Abolition in Europe,* edited by the Council of Europe. Strasbourg: Council of Europe Publishing, 1999.

Frederking, Brian. "Constructing Post–Cold War Collective Security." *American Political Science Review* 97, no. 3 (2003): 363–78.

Freeman, Michael. "Human Rights, Democracy, and 'Asian Values.' " *Pacific Review* 9, no 3 (1996): 355–405.

Fromm, Erich. "The State as Educator: On the Psychology of Criminal Justice." In *Erich Fromm and Critical Criminology: Beyond the Punitive Society*, edited by Kevin Anderson and Richard Quinney. Urbana: University of Illinois Press, [1930] 2000.

Frueh, Jamie. *Political Identity and Social Change: The Remaking of the South African Social Order*. Albany: State University of New York Press, 2003.

Fukuyama, Francis. "Confucianism and Democracy." *Journal of Democracy* 6, no. 2 (1995): 20–33.

———. "The Illusion of Exceptionalism." *Journal of Democracy* 8, no. 3 (1997): 146–49.

Gallup. "Support for the Death Penalty Remains High at 74%." 19 May 2003. http://www.gallup.com/content/login.aspx?ci=8419.

———. "Gallup Poll Topics: Death Penalty, 2004." http://www.gallup.com/poll/indicators/inddeath_pen.asp.

———. "Plurality of Americans Believe Death Penalty Not Imposed Often Enough Basic Support for Death Penalty at 70%." 12 March 2003. http://www.prodeathpenalty.com/articles/gallup.htm.

Gallup, George H., ed. *Gallup International Opinion Polls, Great Britain, 1937–1975*. New York: Random House, 1976.

Gallup Korea. "Gallup Poll: Should the Death Penalty be Abolished?" 27 September 2003. http://panel.gallup.co.kr/svcdb/main.asp.

Garland, David. *Punishment and Welfare: A History of Penal Strategies*. Brookfield, VT: Gower, 1985.

———. *Punishment and Modern Society: A Study in Social Theory*. Chicago: The University of Chicago Press, 1990.

Gibney, Frank. *Korea's Quiet Revolution: From Garrison State to Democracy*. New York: Walker and Company, 1992.

Giliomee, Hermann. "Democratization in South Africa." *Political Science Quarterly* 110, no. 1 (1995): 83–104.

Ginsberg, Anthony. *South Africa's Future: From Crisis to Prosperity*. London: Macmillan, 1998.

Grant, Stefanie. "A Dialogue of the Deaf? New International Attitude and the Death Penalty in America." *Criminal Justice Ethics* 17, no. 2 (1998): 19–33.

Gross, Kimberly, and Donald R. Kinder. "Ethnocentrism Revisited: Explaining American Opinion on Crime and Punishment." Paper presented at the Annual Meeting of the American Political Science Association, Washington, DC, September 2000.

Gurowitz, Amy. "Mobilizing International Norms: Domestic Actors, Immigrants, and Japanese State." *World Politics* 51, no. 3 (1999): 413–45.

Haines, Herbert H. *Against Capital Punishment: The Anti–Death Penalty Movement in America, 1972–1994*. New York: Oxford University Press, 1996.

Hall, Peter A. "Policy Paradigms, Social Learning, and the State." *Comparative Politics* 25, no. 3 (1993): 275–96.

Han, In-sup. "*Yeoksajuk Youmoolroseoui Sahyung* [The Death Penalty as a Historical Artifact]." *Samok*. Seoul: Catholic Bishops' Conference of Korea, 1999.

Han, Sang-jin. "Popular Sovereignty and a Struggle for Recognition from a Perspective of Human Rights." *Korea Journal* 39, no. 2 (1999): 184–204.

Harris Poll. "Support for Death Penalty Still Very Strong in spite of Widespread Belief that Some Innocent People are Convicted of Murder." The Harris Poll #41. 17 August 2001. http://www.harrisinteractive.com/harris_poll/index.asp?PID=252.

Hawkins, Darren. "The Domestic Impact of International Human Rights Norms." Paper presented at the Annual Meeting of the International Studies Association, Chicago, IL, February 2001.

———. *International Human Rights and Authoritarian Rule in Chile.* Lincoln: University of Nebraska Press, 2002.

Heiland, Hans-Gunther, and Louise Shelley. "Civilization, Modernization, and the Development of Crime and Control." In *Crime and Control in Comparative Perspectives,* edited by Hans-Gunther Heiland, Louise Shelley, and Hisao Katoh, 1–19. Berlin: Walter de Gruyter, 1992.

Hoffmann, Joseph L. "Justice Dando and the 'Conservative' Argument for Abolition." *Indiana Law Review* 72 (1996): 21–24.

Holovatiy, Serhiy. "Point of View of an Abolitionist Against Public Opinion." In *The Death Penalty: Abolition in Europe,* edited by the Council of Europe. Strasbourg: Council of Europe Publishing, 1999.

Holt, Nathan V., Jr. "Human Rights and Capital Punishment: The Case of South Africa." *Virginia Journal of International Law* 30, no. 1 (1989): 273–318.

Hood, Roger. *The Death Penalty: A World-Wide Perspective.* Oxford: Oxford University Press, 1996.

———. "The Abandonment of Capital Punishment: Some Reflections on the European Experience." In *Death Penalty: Abolition in Europe,* edited by the Council of Europe. Strasbourg: Council of Europe Publishing, 1999.

———. "Introduction—The Importance of Abolishing the Death Penalty." In *Death Penalty: Beyond Abolition,* edited by the Council of Europe. Strasbourg: Council of Europe Publishing, 2004.

Hopf, Ted. "The Promise of Constructivism in International Relations Theory." *International Security* 23, no. 1 (1998): 171–200.

Howard, Rhoda. "Cultural Absolutism and the Nostalgia for Community." *Human Rights Quarterly* 15, no. 2 (1993): 315–38.

Human Rights Watch. "Beyond Reason: The Death Penalty and Offenders with Mental Retardation." http://www.hrw.org/reports/2001/ustat/.

Im, Hyug Baeg. "South Korean Democratic Consolidation in Comparative Perspective." In *Consolidating Democracy in South Korea,* edited by Larry Diamond and Byung-Kook Kim, 21–52. Boulder: Lynne Rienner, 2000.

Jacobsen, John. "Much Ado about Ideas: The Cognitive Factor in Economic Policy." *World Politics* 47, no. 2 (1995): 283–310.

Jacot, Martine. "The Death Penalty: Abolition Gains Ground." *UNESCO Courier* (October 1999): 37–38.

Jepperson, Ronald L., Alexander Wendt, and Peter J. Katzenstein. "Norms, Identity, and Culture in National Security." In *The Culture of National Security: Norms and Identity in World Politics,* edited by Peter Katzenstein, 33–75. New York: Columbia University Press, 1996.

Johnson, Robert. *Death Work: A Study of the Modern Execution Process.* Belmont, CA: West/Wadsworth, 1998.

Jones, Bryan D. *Reconceiving Decision-Making in Democratic Politics*. Chicago: University of Chicago Press, 1994.

Kahn, Ellison. "The Death Penalty in South Africa." *Tydskrif vir Hedendaagse Romeins-Hollandse Reg* (1970): 12–13.

———. "Remarks at the Symposium on Capital Punishment." In *Proceedings of the Conference on Crime, Law, and the Community* 220/221 (1976): 7–21.

———. "The Relaunch of the Society for the Abolition of the Death Penalty in South Africa" (Speech delivered at the University of the Witwatersrand). *The South African Law Journal* (1989): 39–52.

Kant, Immanuel. *The Metaphysical Elements of Justice*. Translated by John Ladd. New York: Bobbs-Merrill, [1797] 1965.

Katzenstein, Peter, ed. *The Culture of National Security: Norms and Identity in World Politics*. New York: Columbia University Press, 1996.

Keck, Margret E., and Kathryn Sikkink. *Activists Beyond Borders: Advocacy Networks in International Politics*. Ithaca: Cornell University Press, 1998.

Keeler, John T. S. "Opening the Window for Reform: Mandates, Crises, and Extraordinary Policy-making." *Comparative Political Studies* 25, no. 4 (1993): 433–86.

Keohane, Robert O. "The Demand for International Regime." In *International Regimes*, edited by Stephen Krasner. Ithaca: Cornell University Press, 1983.

———. *After Hegemony: Cooperation and Discord in the World Political Economy*. Princeton: Princeton University Press, 1984.

———. "International Institutions: Can Interdependence Work?" *Foreign Policy* 110 (1998): 82–94.

Keohane, Robert O., and Lisa Martin. "The Promise of Institutionalist Theory." *International Security* 20, no. 1 (1995): 39–51.

Keohane, Robert O, Joseph S. Nye, and Stanley Hoffmann, eds. *After the Cold War: International Institutions and State strategies in Europe, 1989–91*. Cambridge: Harvard University Press, 1993.

Kim, Andrew Eungi. "Christianity, Shamanism, and Modernization in South Korea." *Cross Currents* (Spring/Summer 2000).

Kim, Byung-Kook. "Electoral Politics and Economic Crisis, 1997–1998." In *Consolidating Democracy in South Korea*, edited by Larry Diamond and Byung-Kook Kim, 173–202. Boulder: Lynne Rienner, 2000.

Kim, Dae-jung. "Interview: Kim Dae Jung—Democracy and Dissidence in South Korea." *Journal of International Affairs* 38 (1985): 181–91.

———. "A Response to Lee Kuan Yew: Is Culture Destiny? The Myth of Asia's Anti-Democratic Values." *Foreign Affairs* 73 (1994): 189–95.

Kim, Kyong-dong. "Confucianism, Economic Development, and Democracy." *Asian Perspective* 21 (1997): 77–97.

Kim, Sunhyuk. "State and Civil Society in South Korea's Democratic Consolidation: Is the Battle Really Over?" *Asian Survey* 37, no. 12 (1997): 1135–44.

Klein, Lawrence R., Brian Forst, and Victor Filatov. "The Deterrent Effect of Capital Punishment: An Assessment of the Estimate." In *Deterrence and Incapacitation: Estimating the Effects of Criminal Sanctions on Crime Rates*, edited by A. Blumstein, J. Cohen, and D. Nagin. Washington, DC: National Academy of Science, 1978.

Klotz, Audie. *Norms in International Relations: The Struggle against Apartheid*. Ithaca: Cornell University Press, 1995.

Koh, Harold Hongju. "Paying 'Decent Respect' to World Opinion on the Death Penalty." *U.C. Davis Law Review* 35, no. 5 (2002): 1085–1131.

Korea Solidarity for Conscientious Objection. "Recognition of Conscientious Objectors Declaration of 1000 People Urging Alternative Military Services." http://www2.gol.com/users/quakers/korea_solidarity_for_CO.htm.

Kowert, Paul, and Jeffrey Legro. "Norms, Identity, and Their Limits: A Theoretical Reprise." In *The Culture of National Security: Norms and Identity in World Politics*, edited by Peter Katzenstein, 451–97. New York: Columbia University Press, 1996.

Krasner, Stephen D. "Structural Causes and Regime Consequences." *International Organization* 36, no.2 (1982): 185–206.

———. *International Regimes*. Ithaca: Cornell University Press, 1983.

Kroll, Michael. "Florida Day." In *Organizing Against the Death Penalty: A Handbook*, 3rd ed., D4–D9. Washington, DC: National Coalition to Abolish the Death Penalty, 1988.

Kuzmics, Helmut. "The Civilizing Process." In *Civil Society and the State: New European Perspectives*, edited by John Keane, 149–76. London/New York: Verso, 1988.

Kvashis, Victor E. "The Death Penalty and Public Opinion." *Russian Social Science Review* 40, no. 1 (1999): 75–90.

Kwon, Hyuk-chol, and Lee Jae-sung. "*Machimak Ipsenun Thulgo Itnayo* [Are the Last Leaves Trembling?]." *The Hankyoreh 21* 432 (2002): 25–29.

Landsberg, Martin Hart. *Korea: Division, Reunification, and US Foreign Policy*. Berkeley: University of California Press, 1998.

Lane, J. Mark, and Ronald J. Tabak. "The Execution of Injustice: a Cost and Lack-of-Benefit Analysis of the Death Penalty." *Loyola of Los Angeles Law Review* 23 (1989): 59–129.

Legro, Jeffrey W. "Which Norms Matter? Revisiting the 'Failure' of Internationalism." *International Organization* 51, no. 1 (1997): 31–63.

Levy, Jack S. "Learning and Foreign Policy: Sweeping a Conceptual Minefield." *International Organization* 48, no. 2 (1994): 279–312.

Liebman, James, Jeffrey Fagan, and Valerie West. "A Broken System: Error Rates in Capital Cases, 1973–1995." *Texas Law Review* 78 (2002): 1839–67.

Lipset, Seymour Martin, *American Exceptionalism: A Two-Edged Sword*. New York: Norton, 1996.

Lyman, Princeton N. "South Africa's Promise." *Foreign Policy* 102 (1996): 105–20.

March, James G., and Johan P. Olsen. *Rediscovering Institutions: The Organizational Basis of Politics*. New York: Free Press, 1989.

———. "The Institutional Dynamics of International Political Orders." *International Organization* 52, no. 4 (1998): 943–70.

Marquart, James, Sheldon Ekland-Olson, and Jonathan Sorensen. *The Rope, the Chair, and the Needle: Capital Punishment in Texas, 1923–1990*. Austin: University of Texas Press, 1994.

Marshall, Joshua Micah. "Death in Venice: Europe's Death-penalty Elitism." *The New Republic* 223, no. 5 (2000): 12–14.

Masur, Louis P. *Rites of Execution: Capital Punishment and the Transformation of American Culture, 1776–1865*. New York: Oxford University Press, 1989.

Mattern, Janice Bially. "The Power Politics of Identity." *European Journal of International Relations* 7, no. 3 (2001): 349–97.

McGarrell, Edmund, and Marla Sandys. "The Misperception of Public Opinion toward Capital Punishment." *American Behavioral Scientist* 39, no. 4 (1996): 500–14.

Mearsheimer, John J. "The False Promise of International Institutions." *International Security* 19, no. 3 (1994/95): 5–49.

Mendelson, Sarah, and John Glenn. "Democracy Assistance and NGO Strategies in Post-Communist Societies." Democracy and Rule of Law Project, Carnegie Endowment Working Paper (2000): 1–75.

Meyer, John W., David John Frank, Ann Hironaka, Even Schofer, and Nancy Brandon Tuma. "The Structuring of a World Environmental Regime, 1870–1990." *International Organization* 51, no. 4 (1997): 623–51.

Mihalik, Janos. "The Moratorium on Executions: Its Background and Implication." *The South African Law Journal* 108 (1991): 118–42.

Mills, Greg. *War and Peace in Southern Africa: Crime, Drugs, Armies, and Trade.* Cambridge: World Peace Foundation, 1996.

Mitchell, Michael, and Jim Sidanius. "Social Hierarchy and the Death Penalty: A Social Dominance Perspective." *Political Psychology* 16, no. 3 (1995): 591–619.

Mitchell, Ronald B. "Norms as Regulative Rules." Paper presented at the Annual Meeting of the International Studies Association, Chicago, IL, February 2001.

Moravcsik, Andrew. "Explaining International Human Rights Regime: Liberal Theory and Western Europe." *European Journal of International Relations* 1, no. 2 (1995): 157–89.

———. "The Origins of Human Rights Regimes: Democratic Delegation in Postwar Europe." *International Organization* 54, no. 2 (2000): 217–52.

———. "Why Is U.S. Human Rights Policy So Unilateralist?" In *The Cost of Acting Alone: Multilateralism and US Foreign Policy*, edited by Shepard Forman and Patrick Stewart, 345–76. Boulder: Lynne Riener Publishers, 2001.

Müeller, Harald. "The Internalization of Principles, Norms, and Rules by Governments: The Case of Security Regimes." In *Regime Theory and International Relations*, edited by Volker Rittberger, 361–88. Oxford: Oxford University Press, 1993.

Muller, Eric. "The Legal Defense Fund's Capital Punishment Campaign: The Distorting Influence of Death." *Yale Law and Policy Review* 4 (1985): 158–87.

Mureinik, Etienne. "Caring about Capital Punishment." In *Essays in Honour of Ellison Kahn*, edited by Coenraad Visser. Johannesburg: University of the Witwatersrand, 1989.

National and State Profiles. "Easy Access to the FBI's Supplementary Homicide Reports: 1980–2000." http://ojjdp.ncjrs.org/ojstatbb/ezashr/asp/profile.asp.

National Human Rights Commission of Korea. "The Ten Most Serious Human Rights Problems Facing the New Government." (January 28, 2003). www.human rights.go.kr/10agenda.html.

Neary, Ian. *Human Rights in Japan, South Korea, and Taiwan.* New York: Routledge, 2002.

Noelle, Elisabeth, and Erich Peter Neumann, eds. *The Germans: Public Opinion Polls 1947–1966.* Allensbach, Bonn: Verlag für Demoskopie, 1967.

Oh, John Kie-chiang. *Korean Politics: The Quest for Democratization and Economic Development*. Ithaca: Cornell University Press, 1999.

Onuf, Nicholas G. "Constructivism: A User's Manual." In *International Relations in a Constructed World*, edited by Vendulka Kubalkova, Nicolas Onf, and Paul Kowert, 58–78. Armonk, NY: M.E. Sharp, 1998.

Oye, Kenneth A, ed. *Cooperation under Anarchy*. Princeton: Princeton University Press, 1986.

Palley, Howard. "Social Policy and the Elderly in South Korea: Confucianism, Modernization, and Development." *Asian Survey* 32, no. 9 (1992): 787–801.

Parekh, Angina, and Cheryl de la Rey. "Public Attitudes toward the Death Penalty in South Africa: A Life or Death Decision." *Acta Criminology: Southern African Journal of Criminology* 9, no. 1 (1996): 108–13.

Paternoster, Raymond. *Capital Punishment in America*. New York: Lexington Books, 1991.

Patterson, Eric. "Just War on Terror? Reconceptualizing Just War Theory in the 21st Century." Paper presented at the Annual Meeting of the Western Political Science Association, Portland, OR, March 2004.

Peter D. Hart Research Associates. "Study # 6292 Death Penalty Update." March 2001. http:// justice.policy.net/relatives/17760.pdf.

Peterson, Ruth D., and William C. Bailey. "Is Capital Punishment an Effective Deterrent for Murder? An Examination of Social Science Research." In *America's Experiment with Capital Punishment*, edited by James R. Acker, Robert M. Bohm, and Charles S. Lanier, 157–82. Durham: Carolina Academic Press, 1998.

Pierce, Glenn, and Michael Radelet. "The Role and Consequences of the Death Penalty in American Politics." *New York University Review of Law and Social Change* 18 (1990/91): 711–28.

Pollis, Adamantia. "Cultural Relativism Revisited: Through a State Prism." *Human Rights Quarterly* 18, no. 2 (1996): 316–44.

Poveda, Tony. "American Exceptionalism and the Death Penalty." *Social Justice* 27, no. 2 (2000): 252–67.

Price, Richard. "Reversing the Gun Sights: Transnational Civil Society Targets Land Mines." *International Organization* 52, no. 3 (1998): 613–44.

Prinzo, Kristi Tumminello. "The United States—'Capital' of The World: An Analysis of Why the United States Practices Capital Punishment While the International Trend is towards Its Abolition." *Brooklyn Journal of International Law* 24 (1999): 855–89.

Radelet, Michael L., and Margaret Vandiver. "Race and Capital Punishment: An Overview of the Issues." *Crime and Social Justice* 25 (1986): 94–113.

Radelet, Michael L., and Ronald L. Akers. "Deterrence and the Death Penalty: The Views of the Experts." *Journal of Criminal Law and Criminology* 86 (1996): 1–16.

Ravaud, Caroline, and Stefan Trechsel. "The Death Penalty and the Case-law of the Institutions of the European Convention on Human Rights." In *The Death Penalty: Abolition in Europe*, edited by the Council of Europe, 79–90. Strasbourg: Council of Europe Publishing, 1999.

Raymond, Gregory A. "Problems and Prospects in the Study of International Norms." *Mershon International Studies Review* 41, no.2 (1997): 205–45.

Raymond, Leigh S. *Private Rights in Public Resources: Equity and Property Allocation in Market-Based Environmental Policy*. Washington, DC: Resources for the Future, 2003.

Reggio, Michael H. "History of the Death Penalty." In *Society's Final Solution: A History and Discussion of the Death Penalty*, edited by Laura E. Randa, 1–11. Lanham, MD: Rowman and Littlefield, 1997.

Reiman, Jeffrey. "Justice, Civilization, and the Death Penalty: Answering van den Haag." In *Punishment and the Death Penalty: The Current Debate*, edited by Robert Baird and Stuart Rosenbaum, 175–205. Amherst: Prometheus Books, 1995.

Renteln, Alison Dundes. *International Human Rights: Universalism Versus Relativism* Newbury Park, CA: Sage, 1990.

Risse-Kappen, Thomas. "Public Opinion, Domestic Structure, and Foreign Policy in Liberal Democracies." *World Politics* 43, no. 4 (1991): 479–512.

———, ed. *Bringing Transnational Relations Back In: Non-State Actors, Domestic Structures, and International Institution*. Cambridge: Cambridge University Press, 1995.

Risse, Thomas, Stephen C. Ropp, and Kathryn Sikkink, eds. *The Power of Human Rights: International Norms and Domestic Change*. Cambridge: Cambridge University Press, 1999.

Ritter, Khadine L. "The Russian Death Penalty Dilemma: Square Pegs and Round Holes." *Case Western Reserve Journal of International Law* 32, no. 1 (2000): 129–62.

Robinson, Richard. "The Politics of Asian Values." *Pacific Review* 9, no. 3 (1996): 309–27.

Rome Statute of the International Criminal Court. 1998. U.N. Doc A/CONF. 183/ 9. http://www.un.org/law/icc/statute/romefra.htm.

Ron, James. "Changing Methods of Israel State Violence." *International Organization* 51, no. 1 (1997): 275–300.

Ruggie, John Gerard. "What Makes the World Hang Together?: Neo-Utilitarianism and the Social Constructivist Challenge." *International Organization* 52, no. 4 (1998): 855–85.

Russell, Gregory D. *The Death Penalty and Racial Bias: Overturning Supreme Court Assumptions*. Westport: Greenwood Press, 1994.

Rutherford, Kenneth R. "The Evolving Arms Control Agenda: Implications of the Role of NGO's in Banning Antipersonnel Landmines." *World Politics* 53, no. 1 (2000): 74–114.

Sandy, Marla. "Attitudes toward Capital Punishment: Preference for the Penalty or Mere Acceptance?" *Journal of Research in Crime and Delinquency* 32, no. 2 (1995): 191–213.

Sarat, Austin. *When the State Kills: Capital Punishment and the American Condition*. Princeton: Princeton University Press, 2001.

Sarat, Austin, and Christian Boulanger, eds. *The Cultural Lives of Capital Punishment: Comparative Perspectives*. Stanford: Stanford University Press, 2005.

Schabas, William A. "Invalid Reservations to the International Covenant of Civil and Political Rights: Is the United States Still a Party?" *Brooklyn Journal of International Law* 21 (1995): 277–325.

———. "South Africa's New Constitutional Court Abolished the Death Penalty." *Human Rights Law Journal* 16, no. 4 (1995): 133–48.

————. *The Abolition of the Death Penalty in International Law*. Cambridge: Cambridge University Press, 1997.

Schneider, Victoria, and John Ortiz Smykla. "A Summary Analysis of Executions in the United States, 1608–1987: The Espy File." In *The Death Penalty in America: Current Research*, edited by Robert M. Bohm, 1–19. Cincinnati: Anderson, 1991.

Schuler, Corinna. "South Africans Back 'Horrific' Cops." *Christian Science Monitor* 91, no. 111 (1999): 5.

————. "Mob-rule Justice Rises in South Africa." *Christian Science Monitor* 91, no. 176 (1999): 1.

Schwimmer Walter. "Forward." In *The Death Penalty: Beyond Abolition*, edited by the Council of Europe, 1–6. Strasbourg: Council of Europe Publishing, 2004.

Shaw, Mark, 1997. *Policing the Transformation*. Halfway House, South Africa: Institute for Security Studies, 1997.

Shils, Edward. "The Virtue of Civil Society." *Government and Opposition* 26, no. 1 (1991): 3–20.

————. "Reflections on the Civil Society and Civility in the Chinese Intellectual Tradition." In *Confucian Traditions in East Asian Modernity*, edited by Tu Wei-ming, 38–71. Cambridge: Cambridge University Press, 1996.

Shin, Doh Chul. *Mass Politics and Culture in Democratizing Korea*. Cambridge: Cambridge University Press, 1999.

Shin, Doh Chul, and Huoyan Shyu. "Political Ambivalence in South Korea and Taiwan." *Journal of Democracy* 8, no. 3 (1997): 109–24.

Shin, Uiki. "*Siljeongbub Kwanjeomesuh bon Sahyungjeido* [The Death Penalty from a Judicial Perspective]." *Emerge* (2002): 24–41.

Shorrock, Tim. "U.S. Knew of South Korean Crackdown: Ex-Leaders Go on Trial in Seoul." *Journal of Commerce* 27 (1996): 21–47.

Sikkink, Kathryn. "Human Rights and Issue-Networks in Latin America." *International Organization* 47, no. 3 (1993): 411–42.

Simpson, Graeme, and Lloyd Vogelman. "The Death Penalty in South Africa." CSVR Working Paper. Centre for the Study of Violence and Reconciliation. Johannesburg, South Africa, 1989.

Sisk, Timothy D. *Democratization in South Africa: The Elusive Social Contract*. Princeton: Princeton University Press, 1995.

Skocpol, Theda. *Protecting Soldiers and Mothers: The Political Origins of Social Policy in the United States*. Cambridge: Harvard University Press, 1992.

Slaughter, Anne-Marie. "International Law and International Relations Theory: A Dual Agenda." *American Journal of International Law* 87 (1993): 205–39.

Sloth-Nielsen, Julia. "Legal Violence: Corporal and Capital Punishment." In *People and Violence in South Africa*, edited by Brian McKendrick and Wilma Hoffmann, 73–95. Cape Town: Oxford University Press, 1990.

Sloth-Nielsen, Julia, Roelien Theron, and Hugh Corder. *Death by Decree: South Africa and the Death Penalty*. Cape Town: University of Cape Town Press, 1991.

Sohn, Hak-kyu. *Authoritarianism and Opposition in South Korea*. London: Routledge, 1989.

Solchanyk, Roman. *Ukraine and Russia: The Post-Soviet Transition*. Oxford: Rowman and Littlefield, 2001.

Steinberg, David I. "Korea: Triumph Amid Turmoil." *Journal of Democracy* 9, no. 2 (1998): 76–90.

———. "Continuing Democratic Reform: The Unfinished Symphony." In *Consolidating Democracy in South Korea*, edited by Larry Diamond and Byung-Kook Kim, 203–38. Boulder: Lynne Rienner, 2000.

Strange, Susan. "*Cave! hic dragones*: A Critique of Regime Analysis." In *International Regimes*, edited by Stephen D. Krasner, 337–54. Ithaca: Cornell University Press, 1983.

Surette, Ray. *Media, Crime, and Criminal Justice: Images and Realities*, 2nd ed. Belmont: CA, Wadsworth, 1998.

Taiwan Association for Human Rights. "The Taiwan Human Rights Report 2000: The Taiwan Death Penalty Issue in International Perspective." Death Penalty Issue Research Group Annual Report. 2000.

Taylor, Stuart, Jr. "The Shame of the Ronnie White Vote." *National Journal* 31, no. 42 (1999): 2–5.

Technical Committee on Fundamental Rights. "Fifth Report: Death Penalty Agenda." Unpublished Report. Johannesburg: Technical Committee on Fundamental Rights (June 11, 1993).

Thomson, Janice E. "Norms in International Relations: A Conceptual Analysis." *International Journal of Group Tension* 23, no. 1 (1993): 67–83.

Tonry, Michael, and Richard S. Frase, eds. *Sentencing and Sanctions in Western Countries*. New York: Oxford University Press, 2001.

Toscano, Roberto. "The United Nations and the Abolition of the Death Penalty." In *The Death Penalty: Abolition in Europe*, edited by the Council of Europe, 91–104. Strasbourg: Council of Europe Publishing, 1999.

United Nations. "Resolutions and Decisions adopted by the General Assembly." Doc. A/32/45 (1977).

———. "Safeguards Guaranteeing the Protection of the Rights of Those Facing the Death Penalty." E.S.C. Res.1984/50, U.N. Doc. E/1984/84 (1984).

———. "Conference's Committee Continues Adoption of Drafting Committee Texts on International Criminal Court Statute." L/ROM/21(1998).

United Nations Economic and Social Council. "Consideration of Reports Submitted by States Parties under Articles 16 and 17 of the Covenant: Republic of Korea." Reported by the Committee on Economic, Social and Cultural Rights. E/C.12/1/Add.59 (May 2001).

United States Bureau of Justice Statistics, "Capital Punishment Statistics." http://www.ojp.usdoj.gov/bjs/cp.htm.

van Evera, Stephen. *Guide to Methods for Students of Political Science*. Ithaca: Cornell University Press, 1997.

van Niekerk, Barend. ". . . Hanged by the Neck until You are Dead: Some Thought on the Application of the Death Penalty in South Africa." *The South African Law Journal* 86/87 (1969/1970).

van Rooyen, Jan H. "Toward a New South Africa without the Death Penalty—Struggles, Strategies, and Hopes." *Florida State University Law Review* 20 (1993): 737–99.

van Rooyen Jan H., and LC Coetzee. "How Easily Could the Death Sentence be Introduced in South Africa?" *Codicillus* 37, no. 1 (1996): 9–16.

Wapner, Paul. "Politics Beyond the State: Environmental Activism and World Civic Politics." *World Politics* 47, no. 3 (1995): 311–40.

Warr, Mark. "Poll Trends: Public Opinion on Crime and Punishment." *Public Opinion Quarterly* 59, no. 2 (1995): 296–310.

Welch, Claude E., Jr. "The Organization of African Unity and the Promotion of Human Rights." *The Journal of Modern African Studies* 29, no. 4 (1991): 535–55.

Wendt, Alexander. "Constructing International Politics." *International Security* 20, no. 1 (1995): 71–81.

———. *Social Theory of International Politics.* New York: Cambridge University Press, 1999.

Wilkins, Leslie.T. *Punishment, Crime, and Market Forces.* Aldershot, UK: Dartmouth, 1991.

Wilkins, Leslie T., and Ken Pease. "Public Demand for Punishment." *The International Journal of Sociology and Social Policy* 7, no. 3 (1987): 16–29.

Wohlwend, Renate. "The Efforts of the Parliamentary Assembly of the Council of Europe." In *The Death Penalty: Abolition in Europe*, edited by the Council of Europe, Strasbourg: Council of Europe Publishing, 1999.

World Bank. "Ukraine at a Glance." http://www.worldbank.org/data/countrydata/aag/ukr_aag.pdf.

Yi, Sang-don. "*Sahyung Pegi—Songsookhan Bubmoonwhaui Gwajei* [The Death Penalty Abolition—A Task of Maturing Legal Culture]." *Emerge* (2002): 60–69.

Young, Robert L. "Race, Conceptions of Crime and Justice, and Support for the Death Penalty." *Social Psychological Quarterly* 54, no. 1 (1991): 67–75.

Young, Warren, and Mark Brown. "Cross-national Comparisons of Imprisonment." In *Crime and Justice: A Review of Research*, edited by Michael Tonry, 1–49. Chicago: University of Chicago Press, 1993.

Zakaris, Fareed. "A Conversation with Lee Kuan Yew." *Foreign Affairs* 74 (1994): 109–27.

Zawitz, Marianne W., Patsy A. Klaus, Ronet Bachman, Lisa D. Bastian, Marshall M. DeBerry Jr., Michael R. Rand, and Bruce M. Taylor. *Highlights from 20 Years of Surveying Crime Victims: The National Crime Victimization Survey, 1973–1992.* Washington, DC: U.S. Government Printing Office, 1993.

Zimring, Franklin E., and Gordon Hawkins. *Capital Punishment and the American Agenda.* New York: Cambridge University Press, 1986.

Zimring, Franklin E. *The Contradictions of American Capital Punishment.* New York: Oxford University Press, 2003.

LEGAL CASES

Ukraine:

"Decision of the Constitutional Court of Ukraine on the Case Based on Constitutional Appeal of 51 People's Deputies of Ukraine Regarding Conformity with the Constitution of Ukraine (Constitutionality) of the Provisions of Articles 24, 58, 59, 60, 93, 190 of the Criminal Code of Ukraine Which Envisage Death Penalty as a Kind of Punishment." (Case No.1-33/99) (December 29, 1999).

South Africa:

The State v. T Makwanyane and M Mchunu. The Constitutional Court of South
    Africa Case No. CCT/3/94. 1995.

South Korea:

The Constitutional Court of Korea, Case No. 89 *Hunma* 36 (November 25, 1989).
The Constitutional Court of Korea, Case No. 90 *Hunba* 13 (May 1, 1990).
The Constitutional Court of Korea, Case No. 95 *Hunba* 1 (November 28, 1996).

United States:

Furman v. Georgia	1972. 408 U.S. 238.
Gregg v. Georgia	1976. 428 U.S. 153.
McCleskey v. Kemp	1987. 481 U.S. 279.
Callins v. Collins	1994. 510 U.S. 1141.
Atkins v. Virginia	2002. 536 U.S. 304.
Roper v. Simmons	2005. 543 U.S. 551.

INDEX

Korea, South *(continued)*
    ways of norm compliance, 112–13,
      123–24
Korean Central Intelligence Agency
    (KCIA), 66, 68
Korean Christian Counsel for Capital
    Punishment Abolition Campaign,
    75
Kowert, Paul, 11
Krasner, Stephen, 7
Kravchuk, Leonid, 29, 33
Kuchma, Leonid, 29, 31, 35, 36, 39
Kvashis, Victor, 13
Kwangju, Korea, 68, 142n19

Latvia, 27
leadership. *See also under* Ukraine;
    United States
    elite, 15–16
    moral, 117–20
Lee, Man-sup, 74
Legro, Jeffrey, 11
Lithuania, 27
lynching. *See* vigilante activities

Mahommed, Ismael, 53, 54
Makwanyane, Themba, 53, 54
Mandela, Nelson, 49, 50, 53, 57,
    83–84, 111
Mapogo-a-Mathamaga, 52
Marquart, James, 18–19
Marshall, Joshua, 101, 119
Mbeki, Thabo, 58
McCleskey v. Kemp, 95–96
Mchunu, Mavusa, 53–54
Mihalik, Janos, 46, 59
minorities. *See also* racial discrimination
    assimilation into mainstream, 18
Mitterand, François, 105, 117
modernization theory, 66–67
Moldova, 27
Mondale, Walter, 103
Muslims. *See* Islamic countries

National Association for the Advance-
    ment of Colored People
    (NAACP), 98
National Human Rights Commission, 82

National Party (NP), 50, 55
National Security Law (NSL), 65–66, 77
neoliberal institutionalists, 7–9
Nixon, Richard M., 97
nongovernmental organizations
    (NGOs), 16
norm development, 14
norm emergence, 14
norm internalization, 14
norm theory, xiii
norms, 7–8. *See also* international norms
    defined, 7

Ocalan, Abdullah, 134n9
Oh, John Kie-chiang, 72
Onuf, Nicholas, 9
Organization of African Unity (OAU),
    138n30
out-group prejudice, 19

Pan-Africanist Congress (PAC), 43–44,
    49
Park, Chung-hee, 66–68, 80
Parliamentary Assembly of the Council
    of Europe (PACE), 25, 27, 28, 34,
    35, 37
    Committee on Legal Affairs and
      Human Rights, 28
    Resolution 112, 34
penal evolution, 12
Philippines, 18, 64
Poland, 27
policy changes, factors that drive, 126
political elites, 15–16
political institutions. *See also* domestic
    political institutions
    peculiarity of U.S., 101–5
political transformation, radical, 14, 17
politically motivated executions, 43,
    44, 68
politics, electoral, 102
Poveda, Tony, 19, 95, 96
Protestant Church, 75
public opinion, 15, 117–20. *See also*
    specific countries
    abolitionist cause, national con-
      sciousness, and, 56–57
Putin, Vladimir, 27